The Heterodox Theory of Social Costs

T0300381

K. William Kapp's heterodox theory of social costs proposes precautionary planning to preempt social costs and provide social benefits via socio-ecological safety standards that guarantee the gratification of basic human needs.

Based on arguments from Thorstein Veblen, Karl Marx, and Max Weber, social costs are conceptualized as systemic and large-scale damages caused by markets. Kapp refutes neoclassical solutions, such as bargaining, taxation, and tort law, unmasking them as ineffective, inefficient, inconsistent, and too market-obedient.

The chapters of this book present the social costs of markets and neoclassical economics, the social benefits of environmental controls, development planning, and the governance of science and technological standards. This book demonstrates the fruitfulness of the heterodox theory of social costs as a coherent framework to develop effective remedies for today's urgent socio-ecological crises.

This volume is suitable for readers at all levels who are interested in the theory of social costs, heterodox economics, and the history of economic thought.

K. William Kapp (1910–1976) was a German-American economist, one of the founders of Ecological Economics, a leading contributor to the institutional economics movement, and author of *The Social Costs of Business Enterprise*.

Sebastian Berger is a Senior Lecturer of Economics at the University of the West of England, winner of the 2009 Helen Potter Award (Association for Social Economics), and trustee of the Kapp Foundation.

Routledge advances in heterodox economics
Edited by Wolfram Elsner
University of Bremen
and
Peter Kriesler
University of New South Wales

Over the past two decades, the intellectual agendas of heterodox economists have taken a decidedly pluralist turn. Leading thinkers have begun to move beyond the established paradigms of Austrian, feminist, Institutional-evolutionary, Marxian, Post Keynesian, radical, social, and Sraffian econom-ics—opening up new lines of analysis, criticism, and dialogue among dissenting schools of thought. This cross-fertilization of ideas is creating a new generation of scholarship in which novel combinations of heterodox ideas are being brought to bear on important contemporary and historical problems.

Routledge Advances in Heterodox Economics aims to promote this new scholarship by publishing innovative books in heterodox economic theory, policy, philosophy, intellectual history, institutional history, and pedagogy. Syn-theses or critical engagement of two or more heterodox traditions are especially encouraged.

1 **Ontology and Economics**
Tony Lawson and his critics
Edited by Edward Fullbrook

2 **Currencies, Capital Flows and Crises**
A post Keynesian analysis of exchange rate determination
John T. Harvey

3 **Radical Economics and Labor**
Frederic Lee and Jon Bekken

4 **A History of Heterodox Economics**
Challenging the mainstream in the twentieth century
Frederic Lee

5 **Heterodox Macroeconomics**
Edited by Jonathan P. Goldstein and Michael G. Hillard

6 **The Marginal Productivity Theory of Distribution**
A critical history
John Pullen

7 **Informal Work in Developed Nations**
Edited by Enrico A. Marcelli, Colin C. Williams and Pascale Jossart

8 **The Foundations of Non-Equilibrium Economics**
The principle of circular and cumulative causation
Edited by Sebastian Berger

This series was previously published by The University of Michigan Press and the following books are available (please contact UMP for more information):

Economics in Real Time
A theoretical reconstruction
John McDermott

Liberating Economics
Feminist perspectives on families, work, and globalization
Drucilla K. Barker and Susan F. Feiner

Socialism After Hayek
Theodore A. Burczak

Future Directions for Heterodox Economics
Edited by John T. Harvey and Robert F. Garnett, Jr.

Are Worker Rights Human Rights?
Richard P. McIntyre

The Heterodox Theory of Social Costs

K. William Kapp

Edited by Sebastian Berger

Routledge
Taylor & Francis Group

LONDON AND NEW YORK

First published 2016 by Routledge

2 Park Square, Milton Park, Abingdon, Oxon OX14 4RN
711 Third Avenue, New York, NY 10017, USA

Routledge is an imprint of the Taylor & Francis Group, an informa business

First issued in paperback 2017

Copyright © 2016 K. William Kapp; selection and editorial matter,
Sebastian Berger

The right of K. William Kapp to be identified as author of this work has
been asserted by him in accordance with the Copyright, Designs and
Patent Act 1988.

The right of the editor to be identified as the author of the editorial matter,
and of the authors for their individual chapters, has been asserted in
accordance with sections 77 and 78 of the Copyright, Designs and Patents
Act 1988.

All rights reserved. No part of this book may be reprinted or reproduced or
utilised in any form or by any electronic, mechanical, or other means, now
known or hereafter invented, including photocopying and recording, or in
any information storage or retrieval system, without permission in writing
from the publishers.

Notice:
Product or corporate names may be trademarks or registered trademarks,
and are used only for identification and explanation without intent to infringe.

British Library Cataloguing in Publication Data
A catalogue record for this book is available from the British Library

Library of Congress Cataloging in Publication Data
Kapp, K. William (Karl William), 1910–1976.
The heterodox theory of social costs / by K. William Kapp ; edited by
Sebastian Berger.
    pages cm
    1. Externalities (Economics) 2. Economic development–Social aspects.
    3. Economic development–Environmental aspects. 4. Welfare
    economics. I. Berger, Sebastian. II. Title.
    HB846.3.K37 2015
    330.1–dc23   2015005413

ISBN: 978-1-138-77547-3 (hbk)
ISBN: 978-1-138-29935-1 (pbk)

Typeset in Times New Roman
by Wearset Ltd, Boldon, Tyne and Wear

In Memoriam
Frederic S. Lee

Contents

Preface

That the work of Karl William Kapp is more relevant today than ever is actually a sad reflection on our times. In a world that had paid attention to his work, starting more than 60 years ago, humanity might have been able to say "well, what is remarkable about this work?". We might have been living in a society where there was respect for social minima as inviolable standards of conduct for production and consumption and basic interaction on grounds of community, care, social reproduction and distributive justice. Reading Kapp might then have been like reading Ruskin's *Unto This Last* and seeing a lot of what is being said as no longer an issue because society had changed (e.g., in Ruskin's case due to the creation of the liberal welfare state). Yet, this is far from the reality for the social, environmental and economic issues raised by Kapp.

Instead, today the social costs, that Kapp (1950, 1963, 1978b) spent a core part of his life highlighting and explaining, are ever more abundant, intrusive, and damaging. The critique Kapp developed was comprehensive and directed at both the theoretical underpinnings of mainstream economics and the operations of actual economies. In undertaking the construction of this critique he became aware of the interdisciplinary requirements for analyzing what was going on in society.

This led him to explore the basis for knowledge that spans the social and natural sciences (Kapp 1961). His work here would today be criticized for advocating positivism, because the post-modernist perspective has become pervasive and people deride any mention of positivism without even defining what they mean or understand by the term. Kapp appears as a logical positivist referencing the work of the left wing of the Vienna Circle, although he is also critical of this (Kapp 1961: 60–64). Despite his own doubts, the concern for integration via common concepts to create a more comprehensive and consistent human understanding has parallels to Neurath's unity of science project. The work by Kapp on integration, and in other areas, is also a precursor to modern social ecological economics (Spash 2012).

Today there is an even greater necessity to revisit realism. We live in a world where climate deniers funded by multi-national corporations adopt the rhetoric of strong social constructivism to claim environmental problems are a fantasy.

The lack of unity in scientific understanding undermines the possibilities for clear public policy messages. Disunity also prevents agreeing on core concepts and relating these to biophysical and social reality.

In countering this tendency to claim everything is constructed by humans, Kapp's work appears, in modern parlance, more of a critical realist than a 'positivist' position. This claim I think can be further supported by recognizing the role of weak social constructivism in Kapp's theorizing. Kapp was an institutional economist in the critical descriptive tradition (Kapp, Berger, and Steppacher 2011), and as such was fully aware of how social institutions could influence behavior (e.g., Kapp 1978c). He raised the principle of a cumulative sequence of cause and effect viewed as "unending, unteleological, and unconcerned with human wishes" and as processes carried out through social institutions (Kapp 1978a: 23–26). His emphasis on several factors as being causal can also be seen as corresponding to the causal mechanisms of critical realism. This cumulative causation appears as the structure in society which is embedded in its institutions. For example, while the negative impacts of a growth economy and capital accumulation are widely recognized there seems no possibility for modern economies to do anything but conform to the growth imperative. It has become institutionalized and the institutions and social structures of society reinforce the necessity of economic growth.

Still, Kapp was a man of his time and had a strong faith in the role of experts to be able to identify objective social minima (Kapp 1978a: xxvi, 23). Today, there is more suspicion of experts and their role, as well as claims to objectivity, although a needs based approach can be a counter to excessive skepticism. Indeed, Kapp (2011: 252; 1975) himself recognized objective needs as relevant to his concept of social minima and social planning, whilst also discussing, at various points, social and cultural variation in their fulfilment. At the time he died, these ideas were very present in his work, but he had not formed a synthesis. One possibility for doing so is through the framework of Manfred Max-Neef (2009) which combines objective needs and subjective satisfiers. In evaluating such an approach, much of Kapp's discussion remains relevant.

In fact, the problems with which Kapp struggles in trying to determine how social minima could be established and how social evaluation of public policy could be conducted are the same problems that remain today. They concern: How and when should individuals or groups have their positions overridden for the common good? How can democratic societies maintain input from the general population when making important social choices? How should social and value conflicts be addressed and resolved? In answering these question Kapp had great faith in the potential for scientific investigation and public education to aid in determining a desirable future that would be planned and socially just. In his reflections on contemporary China he explored ideas around public participatory planning (Kapp 1974) and this is an advance over his appeal to public opinion polls circa 1971 (see reprint Kapp 1978d). In both cases he is looking for ways in which institutions can be created for democratic process in planning.

While planning has been pushed off the political agenda, by neoliberalism, there is little choice but for it to make a comeback, if there is any hope for addressing the economic, social and ecological crises, and to create a more just future society. The presentation of Kapp's work in this edited volume is both timely and necessary.

What has become self-evident today is the power of vested interest groups, specifically corporations, in lobbying to undermine both democratic process and science, through the creation of doubt and peddling of disinformation for their own ends. The warnings of Galbraith (2007 [1967]) over regulatory capture have not been heeded. The science–policy interface is one of the most contentious exactly because science can reveal the reality of the social, ecological and economic harm required in order to maintain the power and wealth of a global minority under the current political economy. Social action, social choice and social decision making then come to the fore and in opposition to the mainstream economic and neoliberal promotion of the sacrosanct rights of the individual that protect an elite. Understanding the reality of how the current economic system operates requires recognition of the pervasive and endemic practice of creating and shifting costs on to others.

Clive L. Spash
Vienna
November, 2014

References

Galbraith, John Kenneth (2007 [1967]), *The New Industrial State*. Princeton and Oxford: Princeton University Press.

Kapp, K. William (1950), *The Social Costs of Private Enterprise*. New York: Shocken.

Kapp, K. William (1961), *Toward a Science of Man in Society: A Positive Approach to the Integration of Social Knowledge*. The Hague: Martinus Nijhoff.

Kapp, K. William (1963), *The Social Costs of Business Enterprise*. 2nd edn. Bombay/London: Asia Publishing House.

Kapp, K. William (1974), *Environmental Problems and Development Planning in Contemporary China and Others Essays*. The Hague: Mouton & Co.

Kapp, K. William (1975), "Socio-Economic Effects of Low and High Employment." *Annals of the American Academy of Political and Social Science* 418: 60–71.

Kapp, K. William (1978a), "The Nature and Significance of Social Costs," in K. William Kapp (ed.), *The Social Costs of Business Enterprise*, 3rd edn., pp. 13–27. Nottingham: Spokesman.

Kapp, K. William (1978b), *The Social Costs of Business Enterprise*. 3rd edn., Nottingham: Spokesman.

Kapp, K. William (1978c), "The Social Costs of Cutthroat Competition, Planned Obsolescence and Sales Promotion," in K. William Kapp (ed.), *The Social Costs of Business Enterprise*, 3rd edn., pp. 224–247. Nottingham: Spokesman.

Kapp, K. William (1978d), "Towards a New Science of Political Economy," in *The Social Costs of Business Enterprise*, 3rd edn., pp. 281–301. Nottingham: Spokesman.

Kapp, K. William, Berger, Sebastian, and Steppacher, Rolf (2011), *The Foundations of Institutional Economics*. London: Routledge.

xiv   *Preface*

Max-Neef, Manfred (2009), "Development and Human Needs." In Clive L Spash (ed.), *Ecological Economics: Critical Concepts in the Environment*, 4 volumes, pp. 131–149. London: Routledge.

Spash, Clive L. (2012), "Towards the integration of social, economic and ecological knowledge," in Julien-François Gerber and Rolf Steppacher (eds), *Towards an Integrated Paradigm in Heterodox Economics*, pp. 26–46. Basingstoke: Palgrave Macmillan.

1 Introduction

"Social Costs [is] the story of my life"[1]

This book is about K. William Kapp's theory of social costs. Based on unpublished and previously untranslated articles from the Kapp Archive this volume reconstructs this major contribution to heterodox economics. This contribution is important because much is at stake in the struggle to gain hegemony over the interpretation of the social damages arising from the economic system. The accepted boundaries of the discourse on social costs are today the neoclassical works of Pigou and Coase (Aslanbegui and Medema 1998). It is therefore not surprising that the tremendous social costs of recent crises are interpreted mainly through these "market-compatible" lenses. What are the alternatives?

This book contributes to the intellectual project of heterodox economics that seeks to overcome the neoclassical bias of today's conversation on social costs. Kapp's theory of social costs is valuable in this regard precisely because it is the most comprehensive alternative to the above theories, serving as a crucial building block of heterodox economics. More than any other economist, Kapp dedicated a life time worth of intellectual effort to forge a heterodox theory of social costs. In fact, the genealogy of the discourse on "social costs" largely mirrors the genealogy of his intellectual biography. The significant scholarly and policy impact of Kapp's work between the early 1950s and the late 1970s demonstrates its potential for the heterodox economics movement, which seeks to develop and implement effective solutions to social costs. Recovering Kapp's theory of social costs is important for heterodox economics because it proposes solutions to and asks questions about social damages that go far beyond the narrow neoclassical confines of the contemporary conversation. For heterodox economics to change the conversation on social costs it is necessary to make clear why the currently dominating neoclassical theories are a dead end, that there are heterodox alternatives, and their practical value for preventing social costs and for advancing heterodox economics. These tasks were taken up by Kapp and are the subject of this introduction.

Kapp's heterodox theory of social costs

One of the ways to understand the dominating neoclassical narrative on social costs is to ask what lies at its fringe, and beyond its boundaries. Indeed, heterodox economics can be interpreted as the excommunicated "other" of neoclassical economics, (Dow 2011) which serves in the first place to give neoclassical economics a clear identity. Of course, this definition is not accepted by every self-identified heterodox economist (Mearman 2011). Yet, recent research suggests that heterodox economists are not just united in their rejection of neoclassical orthodoxy but are in fact more in agreement on policy and theory than neoclassical economists (Di Maio 2013). This would support Fred Lee's view that a coherent heterodox economic theory is slowly but steadily emerging.

In the first instance this volume showcases that Kapp would have whole-heartedly agreed with Lee's definition of heterodox economics as blasphemy, that is, as a radical critique of neoclassical economics (Lee 2009). This means that Kapp would reject those positions in the contemporary debate that identify heterodoxy with pluralism or an "anything goes" that is inclusive of neoclassical economics (for the pluralism debate in heterodox economics see Mearman 2012; Lee 2010). Quite to the contrary, one of the explicit goals of his theory of social costs was to refute neoclassical economics and its theories of social costs and externalities in their entirety for their faulty logic, ineffective policy proposals, and its hiding normative-apologetic character. Kapp was perhaps the first economist to discuss social costs as an outcome of neoclassical economics itself (see this volume's Chapter 6; Kapp 1950). Such a project is likewise suggested by Lee (2013). Kapp continuously refuted neoclassical economics throughout his work, since his dissertation's critique of Ludwig von Mises' neoliberal[2] impossibility thesis (see this volume's Chapters 2 and 3; for an analysis of Kapp's interactions with neoliberal economists see Berger 2013; 2012). Consequently, proposals to reconcile Kapp's with Coase's neoliberal theory of social costs must be considered groundless (for such an attempt see Niglia and Vatiori 2007).

Second, this volume demonstrates that Kapp's work is a contribution to Lee's project to systematically develop the blasphemous position by crafting heterodox theories that are based on insights from several traditions and can serve as powerful alternatives to neoclassical economic theories. While Kapp was mainly affiliated with the movement of social and institutional economics, his was an approach that integrated insights from a those heterodox traditions that he considered part of the "substantive" or "holistic" school, such as Marx, Veblen, Weber, and List. He neither believed in creating another dogma as a closed system of knowledge that would only repeat the neoclassical plight, nor a postmodern-pluralist cacophony. Rather, he developed an integrated system of social knowledge that remains open because it takes its lead from a given problem situation, as for instance, the socialization of production costs (Kapp 1985). His theory of social costs is thus an ideal building block for an open-system-approach to heterodox economics.

Kapp's open-system-approach (OSA) to social costs and social knowledge (see Chapters 9 and 11 in this volume; Berger and Elsner 2007) is the main reason for the wide acceptance of Kapp's theory of social costs by contemporary heterodox economists from a variety of intellectual backgrounds, such as Marxist environmental sociologists and ecological economists (Foster 2010; Martinez-Alier 2002), as well as institutional economists (Elsner *et al.* 2012). OSA is acknowledged as one of the key concepts of Ecological Economics (Carpintero 2013) and endorsed by economists who propose an integrated heterodox economics as an alternative to neoclassical economics (Spash 2012; Gerber and Steppacher 2012). Even the environmental economist Allen Kneese acknowledged the superiority of Kapp's theory of social costs over that of Pigou and Coase (Ayres and Kneese 1969). Kneese adopted the radical critique of Cost-Benefit-Analysis which had initially been developed by Kapp (see Chapter 12 in this volume) and which is today one of the defining characteristics of heterodox Ecological Economics (Carpintero 2013). Thus, Kapp's theory of social costs serves as a sturdy bridge between various heterodox paradigms. Its flexibility and attractiveness allowed Kapp to move in a variety of intellectual circles, countries, and institutional contexts. While this makes it impossible to fit him into one paradigmatic box the following sections reconstruct the defining aspects of Kapp's heterodox theory of social costs.

Looking back to forge the future of heterodox economics

Despite the above signs of esteem among heterodox economists, Kapp's theory of social costs is largely forgotten, and has so far even failed to attract the attention of historians of economic thought. This contrasts with Kapp's leading role in the discourse on social costs between roughly 1950 and 1980. This contrast can be understood as a result of the demise of the institutional economics movement (Rutherford 2011), the suppression of heterodox economics (Lee 2009), and the great neoliberal transformation of the economics profession (Mirowski 2013). Furthermore, the prohibitively high epistemic costs of trying to reconstruct past theories (Yalcintas 2013) contributes to Kapp's continued eclipse.

The reconstruction of past theories and concepts can be justified on the basis of the notion that ideas or their unrealized potentials are either lost or not fully realized due to incommensurabilities in the evolution of science (Bernstein 1991; Elsner 1986). The goal of a "rational reconstruction" (Rorty 1984) is to recover these losses with a view to influence the contemporary conversation, in this case the conversation on social costs. This follows in the footsteps of Lee's Post Keynesian price theory (Lee 1998), which can be described as "looking back to see the future." The latter has been explicitly proposed with regards to the work of Kapp by the leading socio-ecological economist Clive Spash (2011). The reconstruction is based on unpublished articles from the Kapp Archive and untranslated materials, which were selected so that the reader can follow the genealogy of Kapp's argument on social costs and its application in a variety of contexts.

4 *Introduction*

The socialist calculation debate

Chapters 2 and 3 constitute the first English translation of the core chapters on theory from Kapp's dissertation (Kapp 1936). Kapp considered these chapters to include the nucleus of his theory of social costs (1950, pp. xxvii–xxviii). The latter began as a critique of economic calculation based on market prices in the context of the Socialist Calculation Debate (SCD). This context sheds light on the root of the dispute between Kapp's heterodox and neoclassical/neoliberal theories of social costs. In fact, it shows that the heterodox theory of social costs was born out of an attempt to counter Mises' polarizing and dogmatic impossibility thesis regarding socialist planning and the resurgence of (neo)liberalism in general. This attempt was at the same time a defense of the socialist position on the possibility necessity of using economic planning to prevent social costs and create social benefits. Later, in the 1960s, leading members of the "Neoliberal Thought Collective" (NTC) (Mirowski and Plehwe 2009) criticized Kapp's theory for blaming social costs on markets (see Berger 2012; 2013 for an analysis of these interactions). This neoliberal counter-revolution on social costs may be viewed as a continuation of SCD as its protagonists, such as Mises and Hayek, became leading architects of NTC and the Chicago School (see Mirowski and Plehwe 2009; Van Horn *et al.* 2011)

In Chapter 2, Kapp argues that instead of trying to refute Mises' thesis regarding the impossibility of rational allocation under socialism, a "countervailing thesis" regarding the market economy should be developed and empirically validated. This thesis holds in essence that economic calculation based on market prices cannot be rational from the perspective of society because it systematically socializes costs and ignores the substantive (material) nature of the economic process. Chapter 8 evidences that Kapp understood the genealogy of his theory of social costs as part of the debate between Weber and Mises on the rationality of the price system. Chapter 7 corroborates this interpretation as it juxtaposes Weber's substantive rationality and Mises' formal rationality.

However, instead of Weber's concept of substantive rationality, the dissertation relies only on the substantive and socio-economic arguments developed by Menger, Wieser, Schäffle, List, and Polanyi,[3] evidencing the large influence of Austrian economics discourse on the formation of Kapp's initial argument. In addition, Kapp references Pigou on the numerous social damages of markets which systemically undermine the gratification of social needs: the disruption of national health, employment related illnesses and accidents, inadequate protection of motherhood, excessive smoke concentrations, noise pollution, unhealthy construction work, retardation of scientific progress due to patents, advertisement, and premature resource depletion. Based on these socio-economic and substantive arguments, Mises' "rationality" of the price system is exposed as a merely *formal* rationality. The latter is not rational from a societal perspective because markets socialize costs and disregard the needs of the poor, both of which work against the gratification of social needs. Substantive rationality inverts the perspective and thereby exposes the hidden normative sources of

Mises' formal rationality. The rationality of markets now appears as a system that ignores and even represses social knowledge because it is not of interest from the point of view of private ownership. Market rationality thus leads to a violation and disregard of social needs and values. This reveals a veritable will to ignorance inherent in Mises' formal rationality (see Mirowski 2013 for a different interpretation of the neoliberal will to ignorance as an epistemological challenge).

The myopic rationality of markets necessitates, according Kapp, economic planning based on the precautionary principle to prevent social costs and guarantee the satisfaction of social needs. In defending the necessity and possibility of substantively rational planning, Kapp predominantly drew on the works of socialist economists, such as Friedrich Pollock, Emil Lederer, and Otto von Neurath. While social policies in liberal-capitalist economies compensate retroactively for social damages, precautionary planning can prevent social costs and thus guarantee the gratification of social needs. Planning thus yields important social benefits, which Kapp described in his subsequent (unpublished) book project (see below, Chapter 5).

The social costs of markets and the social benefits of planning

Chapter 3 shows that, by the early 1940s, Kapp had developed his SCD argument into a full scale book project with the working title *Social Costs and Social Returns—A Critical Analysis of the Social Performance of the Unplanned Market Economy*. Because the term social returns was later dropped for "social benefits" (see Chapter 7) this project is here referred to as "Social Costs/Social Benefits" (SC/SB).

The first goal of this project was to provide an empirically grounded critique of "19th century liberalism" (with explicitly reference to the works of Hayek and Mises), the "unplanned market economy," "capitalism," as well as "equilibrium economics" and "conventional economic theory." The second goal was to develop a theory of the social benefits of planning that would be "derived from the gratification of collective needs […] and the maintenance of a social minimum with respect to essential foodstuffs, medical care, housing, and education." This theory would require the development of valid criteria "for […] economic policy, and perhaps to prepare the way for the elaboration of a positive theory of social value" (Chapter 3). This part is directed at and strongly disagrees with the tenets of the "prophets of gloom"—especially Hayek—that economic planning implies an inevitable road to serfdom (Chapter 3).

The SB portion of SC/SB remained unfinished and unpublished for a number of reasons. One of them may be that John M. Clark had criticized Kapp for failing to provide any detailed formulation and evaluation of the potentials and limitations of a collectivist alternative (Berger 2013). Further reasons are given by Kapp himself in Chapter 4 which states that providing solutions to each instance of social costs via the social benefits of planning would have unduly enlarged the manuscript, destroyed the continuity of the text, and raised the important issue of liberty, which required a separate treatment. Chapter 8[4] reveals that only three chapters were finished by the mid-1940s and that completing the entire manuscript on social benefits would have taken too long. It also evidences that Kapp viewed *Hindu Culture, Economic Development and Economic Planning in India* (Kapp 1963b) as the completion of this work on SB. Therefore, this book's key chapter on "Social Costs and Social Benefits: Their Relevance for Public Policy and Economic Planning" is reprinted in the present volume (Chapter 7).

Since the 1940s, Kapp perceived the theory of social costs merely as a stepping stone towards a social economics that includes theories of social valuation (social accounting), social needs, social knowledge, social minima, social benefits, and social controls. Kapp explicitly pursued the project of social economics outlined by John M. Clark (Berger 2013) under the working title *The Foundations of Social Economics*, which was posthumously published (Kapp 2011). This work elucidates how Kapp sought to integrate the basic insights of European and American socio-economic traditions, namely, the works of Karl Marx, Max Weber, Thorstein Veblen, and their mid-twentieth century followers (Kapp 2011). Kapp's publications *Readings in Economics* (1949) and *History of Economic Thought* (1956) narrate a development of the history of economic ideas that culminates in social economics as the pinnacle of economic thought.

The social costs of markets

The above SC/SB project resulted in the publication of Kapp's main work on social costs, published as *The Social Costs of Private Enterprise* (SCPE) in 1950. The second enlarged and revised edition was entitled *The Social Costs of Business Enterprise* (1963a) (SCBE). Chapter 4 evidences that the title "The Social Costs of Free Enterprise" was also given consideration. As Chapter 8 evidences the term "business enterprise" was eventually chosen because large scale government involvement in the economy had already rendered the terms "private" and "free" enterprise inappropriate for analytical purposes. Additionally, the preface of SCBE declares that the theory of social costs was in the tradition of Veblen's *Theory of Business Enterprise* (1904) as "Veblen [...] called for an investigation [...] 'of the various kinds and lines of waste that are necessarily involved in the present businesslike control of industry.'" (Kapp 1963a, p. xxvii). In this view the system's organizing principle of investment for profits acts as a systemic incentive to socialize costs of production by shifting them to society, third parties and future generations. Chapter 4 defines social costs:

> the term "social costs" refers to all those harmful consequences and damages which third persons or the community sustains as a result of productive processes, and for which private entrepreneurs are not held accountable. These social losses may be reflected in damages to human health; they may find their expression in the destruction or deterioration of property values and the premature depletion of natural wealth; or they may be evidenced in an impairment of less tangible values.

This definition of social costs is consistent with John M. Clark's notion of "cost shifting" (Berger 2013) and adopts the view held by American institutionalists that social costs are systemic and large-scale problems inherent in the business-like control of industry, that is, Veblen's "principle of investment for profits" (Rutherford 2011). Consequently, only systemic solutions in the form of institutional reforms and social controls can effectively remedy social costs.

In conclusion, SCPE integrates Kapp's earlier Weberian argument from the SCD (see above) with Veblen's argument. Chapter 7 demonstrates that Kapp understood these two arguments as essentially the same for his analytical purposes. However, SCPE and SCBE also abound with references to Karl Marx's *Capital* volumes I–III, and one of Kapp's last articles on social costs highlights Marx's prescient insight:

> No matter how economical capitalist production may be in other respects, it is utterly prodigal to human life [...]. Capitalism looses on one side for society what it gains on another for the individual capitalist.
> (Marx, *Capital*, vol. III, 1909, p. 104 in Kapp 1970: 844)

In fact, the editorial preface of the Polish translation of SCPE extols Kapp's work and deems it to be consistent with Marxism (Unpublished Manuscript 1: Kapp Archive). Additionally, SCPE includes a chapter on the conceptual history of social costs, which traces its development from classical economists, the socialists, Marx, the German Historical School, and Veblen to the social economists. Consequently, Kapp provides an integrative basis for a heterodox theory of social costs.

Kapp's understanding of social costs leads him to various insights. For instance, in the same vein as Karl Polanyi's "double movement" Kapp states that the "political history of the last 150 years [...] [is] a revolt of large masses of people (including business) against the shifting of part of the social costs of production to third persons or to society" (Kapp 1950, p. 16). This makes clear that Kapp's theory of social costs is a social conflict theory, that is, the extent of the victims' ability to leverage countervailing power determines the extent of social costs. In this view, the relative success and positions of companies and industries reflect their power to socialize costs (for this view see also Chapter 7).

Social benefits of planning

We recall that Kapp's dissertation (Chapter 2) had already hinted at his intention to develop a theory of social benefits that accrue from planning the prevention of social costs and the gratification of social needs. As already mentioned this idea became part of the above SC/SB project (Chapter 3) but was abandoned by the mid-1940s and largely forgotten since. In order to reconstruct this aspect of Kapp's theory, the three completed yet unpublished chapters on social benefits from the initial SC/SB manuscript are presented in Chapter 5. This reconstruction of the "lost" SB portion is important because it evidences that Kapp did not just develop a theory of the social costs as a critique of markets and an argument for precautionary planning. Importantly, he also developed a theory of the social benefits of planning, which is a vital complement to the theory of social costs. The main reason for this is the fact that social benefits arise from the gratification of social needs by means of economic planning. The prevention of social costs contributes to the gratification of social needs and thus provides social benefits. Social costs and social benefit are thus interrelated. These chapters take inspiration from Friedrich List (see also Kapp 1962) whose argument on the social benefits of balanced economic development planning still resonate in the contemporary Neo-Listian and circular-cumulative-causation literature (Berger 2009; Selwyn 2009).

Chapter 8 evidences that Kapp considered only three chapters on social benefits to be completed. From their stage of development it follows with considerable certainty that these are the chapters on international policies (Chapter 5.3), transportation (Chapter 5.4), and multi-purpose projects (Chapter 5.5). The chapters on collective needs, social minima and science that are part of the table of contents (Chapter 5.1) remained as torsos and do not constitute publishable material. The torso on social minima is fully developed and published in Kapp 2011. The torso on science became part of SCPE, later work on science and technology (Kapp 2011), and Chapter 12 on the organization of science along environmental goals. The torso on collective needs (Chapter 5.2) is published here as an exception because it illustrates Kapp's understanding of collective needs, as an early version of his concept of social needs.

Chapter 5.2 develops the dynamic understanding of collective needs in the light of their historical emergence. Public health measures to prevent epidemics, education, social security, and national self-sufficiency are examples of the generally accepted set of common interests; that is, "the object of a genuine collective need." Kapp recognizes that it is the trans-boundary character of problems, such as epidemics, and the complexity of modern production processes that give rise to *Wagner's Law* of increasing public activity and the collectivization of ends observable in all advanced countries. Thus, collective needs result from life in complex communities, they are dynamic and grow due to growing complexities. Another factor is the increase of influence of the working class thanks to democracy, which has led to the recognition of a common responsibility for the weak members of society. Kapp argues that the gratification of collective needs and the protection of the weak against socially harmful effects of competition yield social benefits. In addition, there are common interests of a less tangible kind, such as the ethical and humanitarian aspirations of a community, which are collective needs and which have economic implications. In the end, collective needs are a matter of political practice.

Chapter 5.3 highlights the social benefits of protectionism, and the inseparability of the political-economic sphere that includes concerns over security, sovereignty, and the dangers of dependency. Kapp argues that the social benefits of protectionism include the development of genuine productive capabilities and powers that are the true source of wealth because they produce general prosperity.

Further social benefits of protectionism are independence, a balanced economy, and the prevention of economic vicious cycles that result from foreign competition, price wars, dependency and migration.

Chapter 5.4 emphasizes the social benefits of social provisioning of transportation in the form of lower transportation costs, new settlements, national unity, national wealth, enhanced land values, and increased rewards to general industry. The definition of social benefits is advanced as "[effects that] are largely inappropriable to private producers and consumers" or "cannot be easily appropriated by private producers, but rather accrue to society as a whole." These social benefits of transportation ultimately have positive effects on private balance sheets as they are "intrinsically connected." The main arguments advanced for the social benefits of a well-planned and integrated transportation system are the large fix costs of projects, large overhead costs, higher efficiency and economies of scale.

Chapter 5.5 discusses the social benefits of multi-purpose projects, such as soil conservation, stream and water projects, and flood controls. Their social benefits include: the reduction of run-off of rainfall, maintenance of groundwater stores, equalization of stream flows, protection of wildlife, prevention of sedimentation of rivers and reservoirs, reduction of floods, positive health effects, conservation of land values, irrigation, and pollution abatement. These multiple purposes are of a "social character" and their "beneficial effects accrue to other people, or to the community as a whole." Kapp adopts the complexity perspective regarding the interrelatedness of regional or national ecosystems, which was developed by the National Resource Committee and Richard T. Ely.

Substantive rationality and social knowledge: bases for planning

Chapter 7 bases the theory of the social benefits of planning on Weber's notion of substantive rationality (see also Berger 2008 for this aspect of Kapp's theory):

> Substantive rationality [...] measures the extent to which a given group of persons is or could be adequately provided with goods by means of an economically oriented course of social action.
>
> (Kapp, Chapter 7)

In dealing with the phenomena of social costs and social benefits scientifically, Kapp heeded Weber's caveat of the ethics of conviction and his banning of social values from science. Weber's notion of substantive rationality and favorable remarks on Otto Neurath's planning in real physical terms of resources became the basis for Kapp's quest to render the phenomena of social costs and social benefits accessible to scientific, meaning, quantitative and objective treatment. This evidences once more Kapp's continued association with the very theoretical position that had triggered Mises' response and had thereby initiated the SCD (see above). Kapp's idea was to investigate social costs and social benefits in terms of the satisfaction of scientifically derived minima of adequate living conditions. In this view social costs are a violation of social minima and social-environmental safety standards that reflect social needs rooted in human needs. The project of a scientific theory of social costs and social benefits was thus tied up with the substantive investigation of human needs and behavior. The latter was explicitly launched against Mises' purely formal theory of behavior, that is, praxeology (Kapp 1985; 2011), and against the neoclassical theory of behavior, namely, hedonism (Kapp 1985; 2011). Hence, Kapp translates Weber's substantive rationality into a "rational humanism" that considers the gratification of substantive human needs as the goal of an explicitly normative economics (Kapp 1985), and a step towards a democratic theory of consumption (Chapter 7). Both consist of a process of deliberation that relates ends to means, that is, Kapp's adaptation of John Dewey's version of American pragmatism. The latter's insistence on pragmatic revisions in the light of empirical tests, realist theory, empirical relevance, and the rejection of universal validity and absolute certainty became programmatic for Kapp's approach (Kapp 1985, 2011)

Investigating the relationship between human needs and the quality of the natural and social environment necessitated, according to Kapp, the integration and humanization of social knowledge and social science (Kapp 1961). This meant bringing to bear all relevant insights from philosophical anthropology, social psychology, and existential philosophy on the unique bio-cultural openness of the human being and the existential needs that result therefrom. This integrated view of biological and cultural/social aspects of existential human needs was part of the quest to scientifically establish social minima and safety standards that guarantee the gratification of basic human needs. If fully enforced, these standards and minima would yield social benefits and preempt social costs. Kapp traced this differentiation between basic and higher needs back to the works of Veblen, Menger, and Maslow.

The proposal to integrate social knowledge on basic bio-cultural needs, however, must be seen in the light of Otto von Neurath's positivist project of the unification of knowledge (Spash 2011). The influence of positivism on Kapp's theory of social costs and social benefits is also evident in Chapter 7, which develops a detailed defense of the use of theoretical terms in scientific inquiry and its relation to observable phenomena. The concept of social costs captures a variety of tangible and less tangible phenomena that have in common that they are causally related to the principle of investment for profits and formal rationality. It follows the "conceptual turn" in positivism in the 1950s which was based on Carnap's insight that concepts cannot be reduced to the sense data of observable properties of physical systems. Therefore, the ontological status of theoretical terms is a real entity because it refers to implicit structures as underlying unitary causes that are linked to explicit and empirical phenomena, also referred to as a depth-realist position (Steinmetz 2005)

This nuanced understanding of the problem of social costs and social benefits as a systemic problem that demands institutional reform, substantive rationality, and social knowledge avoids the simplistic dualisms of capitalism vs. socialism, or state vs. market. Kapp's work primarily dealt with the social benefits of economic development planning in socialist countries such as Soviet Russia (Kapp 1936), India (Kapp 1963), and China (Kapp 1974) but also investigated the social costs that emerge due to ineffective public administration (1960).

The open system approach and circular cumulative causation

Chapters 9 and 10 develop and apply the concept of open systems for purposes of the sustainable development debate. Chapter 9 argues that the normative goal of the development process is the protection and improvement of the environment, as well as the prevention of its deterioration in the form of social costs. The means are an inventory of ecological conditions and comprehensive public planning; that is, "eco-development." This chapter develops the connection between normative economics of long term ecological development planning and the fundamental vision of the open systems character of the economy. Kapp argues that the open-system-approach (OSA) correctly conceptualizes the substantive and interrelated character of economic problems. OSA constitutes Kapp's fundamental vision for economics that requires a transdisciplinary and integrated approach, the long term determination of normative goals, deliberation, and action oriented research.

Chapter 10 was presented at the Bellagio Center in 1967, which was sponsored by the Rockefeller Foundation and hosted a number of high profile meetings,[5] underscoring the significance that was attributed to Kapp's work. It showcases that Kapp perceived economic development to be a system of circular cumulative causation between various elements of the socio-economic system. In this system perspective, rapid economic growth can actually be abortive to the development process if it is accompanied with high social costs and not supported by viable institutional arrangements that guarantee the satisfaction of existential needs. An "open system" perspective is necessary to identify tensions in the development process and to adapt strategies to guarantee the fulfillment of "survival needs." Kapp applies Ludwig von Bertalanffy's definition of a system to the economic development process, adding valuable insights beyond the seminal *The Open System Character of the Economy* that earned Kapp his status as an open system thinker (Berger and Elsner 2007). Namely, it demonstrates how Kapp blended his systems thinking, which he developed since the early 1950s in the wake of the general systems theory movement (Kapp 1985) with the "circular cumulative causation" (CCC) theory of the economic development process. The blend of OSA and CCC is unique to Kapp and based on his own work on complex and interrelated problems and systems since the 1940s. The significance of CCC is underlined by the fact that Gunnar Myrdal received the 1972 Bank of Sweden Prize in Memory of Alfred Nobel partly for its application in *Asian Drama* (Myrdal 1968), which he had sent Kapp for review prior to its publication (for the collaboration between Kapp and Myrdal see Berger and Steppacher 2011; see Berger 2009 for the similarities between Kapp's and Myrdal's development theory and CCC).

Social costs and the critique of neoclassical economics

Chapter 6 constitutes Kapp's pioneering attempt to formulate an argument on the social costs of neoclassical economics. As we recall this chapter was partly published in SCPE, which was intended as a critique of neoclassical economics (see Chapter 3). Its current form presents novel material on Kapp's critique of neoclassical economics. Chapter 13 is one of Kapp's latest formulations of the critique of neoclassical economics as a form of ideology, taking its central inspiration from Veblen. Both critiques have gained momentum in the wake of the Great Financial Crisis of 2008 in movements such as "rethinking economics," "new economic thinking," and "reteaching economics." They are also reflected by various recent heterodox book publications, such as *The Social Costs of Markets and Economics* (Lee 2013) and *The Crimes of the Economy—A Criminological Analysis of Economic Thought* (Ruggiero 2013).

Chapter 11 develops the critique of neoclassical theories of social costs; that is, its market-based and closed-system approach, its polluter-pays principle and cost-benefit-analysis. This article was partly used for a keynote address at the meeting of UNESCO's International Social Science Council in Kyoto in 1975. As a standing member of this organization Kapp participated in these meetings at least since 1970 where he met with other economists, such as Ignacy Sachs and Allen Kneese who pioneered the analysis of environmental disruption as a consequence of interactions between the socio-economic and ecological system (Tsuru 1970).

In this chapter, Kapp critiques of the solutions to social costs that rely on taxation, tort law and bargaining, all of which are based on the neoclassical "Polluter-Pays Principle" (PPP). We recall that Kapp relied on Pigou's treatment of social damages in his dissertation's argument on social costs (see above). Likewise SCBE (Kapp 1963a) acknowledges Pigou's call for the socialization of the means of production in the face of increasing social costs. This reflects Kapp's ambiguous attitude towards Pigou's work. While acknowledging the latter's increasingly radical political-economic conclusions and initially relying on his assessment of social damages, SCPE (Kapp 1950) and several later articles roundly reject Pigou's taxation solution and his concept of externalities. The tort law solution was likewise consistently rejected by Kapp (Kapp 1950; Berger 2013). Chapter 11 shows that Kapp also objected to the "bilateral market" solution since the early 1970s. This is remarkable since the latter only slowly made its way into the mainstream (for a history of the "Coase Theorem" see Medema 2011) and evidences Kapp's astute awareness of new developments in neoclassical theories of social costs. In the context of this critique Kapp, however, does not refer to Coase or Stigler, but to Buchanan's dogmatic insistence that "individual decision making" delimits the scope of economics. Buchanan had previously rejected Kapp's theory of social costs and gone on to develop his own approach to externalities (Buchanan 1962). In turn, Kapp criticizes Buchanan's methodologically individualist approach to social costs as ineffective because treating each case of social costs in isolation inhibits the recognition of the problem's systemic scope and its complex causation.

In this context Kapp reiterates his argument from SCD on the flaws in the rationality of the price system and the distortions to which it gives rise. Thus, market solutions to social costs are arbitrary because they rely on the ability to pay, which relies on the arbitrary distribution of income. Kapp attacks the anti-scientific, dehumanizing, and anti-democratic animus of the PPP. He also considers the PPP to be ineffective due to the slow legislative process, high implementation costs, and the lack of a prevention strategy. Moreover, the PPP is highly vulnerable to the influence of (neo)"liberal" lobby groups:

> An additional problem endemic to regulatory agencies is that their decisions may be influenced by liberally financed interest and pressure groups, which may engage in selective research and release of information, counter-information, denials, and counter-denials which render the search for correct and impartial decisions difficult or impossible.
>
> (Chapter 11)

The PPP is also deemed unjust because it does not guarantee improvements. Yet, Kapp admits that the PPP would be "important" if the alternative is to not do anything at all about social costs, which would be even worse. Addressing the issue of the determination of the level of the charges under the PPP, Kapp identifies the vast requirements of data gathering as a major problem; that is, the knowledge requirements for the estimation of the damages and the costs of the measures of public action. The PPP faces the problem of determining a fixed level of charges in relation to uncertain variables. Kapp concludes that this is the principle reason why direct measures are advantageous because they can actually guarantee the prevention and reduction of social costs and do not merely shift the costs to consumers. They also avoid the issue of avoidance strategies, such as shifting pollution from water to air. With regard to the option to compensate social costs via liability law, Kapp notes several inadequacies. The latter are due to the complexities involved in social cost cases that make the burden of proof and the costs involved in it prohibitive and inefficient. Inconsistent rulings across similar cases of social costs are also a major problem with the legal solution (for the similarities between Kapp and the legal realist position on social costs see Gaskins 2007; 2010). Instead of legal solutions Kapp refers to the possibility of radical changes to the socio-legal structure that would require precautionary technological assessment and impact studies that guarantee safety standards and social minima. Yet, Kapp is aware that the latter faces stiff opposition from producers (Chapter 11).

As Kapp points out in Chapter 9, the PPP reflects a faulty understanding of the substantive and interrelated character of the problem of social costs. This faulty understanding is the closed system approach. What is required instead is the recognition of the open system character of the economy, with its circular and cumulative causation, which requires a multi-disciplinary and integrated scientific approach that has as its goal the protection, prevention and improvement of the human environment. In assessing 20 years of discussions on SCPE with neoclassical economists, Kapp was able to identify the root of the disagreement:

> the institutionalized system of decision-making in a system of business enterprise has a built-in tendency to disregard those negative effects on the environment. [...] Predictably, this critical view, which runs counter to the presuppositions and biases of conventional economic analysis, has not *met* with general approval. Thus, various alternative explanations for *the* occurrence of social costs have been advanced. These have one thing in common: to exonerate the principle of investment for profits from any causal connection with environmental disruption.
>
> (Kapp 1971, pp. xiii–xiv)

The brave new world of social costs

Kapp's critique of the PPP notwithstanding, it has become today's predominant approach to social costs, which are increasingly deferred to the legal and the market system, especially in the United States. The theoretical foundation for the legal approach to social costs is Mises' praxeology, which is viewed as a pure logic that can be applied without regard to ethical predispositions (rule utilitarianism) (Gunning 2000, pp. 6, 8). It is worth recalling Kapp's topical objection to Mises' praxeology as a point of departure for his version of substantive rationality and the integration and humanization of social knowledge in continuation of his dissertation's anti-Misean argument during the SCD (see above). Mises adopts Pigou's terminology of "external costs" but places it under the rubric of "limits of property rights" and defines them as "consequences of action that the agent is not held accountable [for]." Further, he admits that the agent "will not bother in his planning about all the effects of his action. He will disregard [...] those costs which do not burden him." (Mises in Gunning 2000, p. 10). Yet in his research Mises does not devote any considerable attention to the theme that "the property system is a system of rights to control actions that have external effects" (Gunning p. 11).

Based on these foundations, social costs are deferred to judges and tort law to determine "which rights to control actions that have external effects should be defined and enforced" (Gunning, p. 14). In this, PPP is interpreted as the applicability of tort law that makes the victims of externalities whole in a way that fully addresses the grievance, eliminates the emissions, and confines them to the polluters own property (Cordato 2004, p. 12). When in doubt about property rights, the advice is that courts ought to enact the "first come, first serve principle" to reduce the uncertainty of plans of first users by enhancing the amount and quality of information. The usefulness of Coase's market-rule for establishing initial rights "to the person or persons they believe would end up with the rights after a hypothetical zero-transactions costs exchange" is acknowledged (Gunning, pp. 15–16). To be sure, even these authors state that "nothing [...] warrants the view [of an] active and interventionist government [...] the assignment of initial legal rights is a function of government in the light of the goal of maintaining a property system in the entrepreneur economy" (ibid., p. 17). Some authors in this tradition, however, reject Coase's outcome as utilitarian, which is perceived to be at odds with Mises rule utilitarianism (praxeology). Their goal is to avoid any possibility that "politicians determine what is and isn't pollution and what the appropriate emissions targets are" (Cordato 2004; p. 15).

The discussion on the merits of Coasian bargaining notwithstanding, the core tenet of the legal solution is that all damages are conceived as human interpersonal conflicts. Environmental disruption, for example, is thus viewed as a "human problem[s] of mutual plan formulation and the achievement of goals" (Cordato 2004, p. 7). The tenet that human conflict should be minimized via the assignment of property rights is deduced from Menger's Principles (1st edn.), and inserts the notion of "legal failure" for "market failure" (ibid., p. 8). The logical yet quixotic conclusion is that social costs do "not exist[ing] either as measurable or even theoretical concept[s]" because they are purely subjective (Cordato 2004, p. 5). This perspective guides the legal approach to environmental policy, in which "externalities are a pseudo problem" (Dawson 2013, p. 184). This approach is adamant that science is too uncertain to provide definitive solutions for governmental rules that reduce or prevent social costs (Dawson 2013).

What these approaches fail to mention is that courts and tort law cannot escape the necessity of establishing causality, which requires scientific proof about causality between the polluter and polluted. Consequently, the strategy of proponents of the legal solution to social costs has been to frame the legal use of science in such a way that it can never become dangerous to corporations (see Mirowski 2011 for an analysis of this strategy). In this scheme, the so-called "sound science" movement engineers the use of science in court to banish what neoliberals declare as "junk science," meaning social cost science speaking in favor of the victims of corporate cost shifting. For instance, Federal Rules of Evidence in the US apply criteria for the admissibility of scientific experts and evidence, and impose prior conditions of testability and whether the science has been generally accepted. Judges are turned into arbiters who block "junk science" and ensure "sound science." The litigants with the biggest financial resources can now

> issue seemingly endless pre-trial challenges to the quality of the science of the opponent [...] [placing] the burden on the plaintiff to validate each and every study referenced in the case [...] "sound science" [...] restores the asymmetric bias toward corporate science [in the courtroom].
>
> (Ibid., p. 302)

Additionally, the Shelby Amendment to the freedom of information act is used by business organizations to harass and challenge publicly funded scientists whom they dislike, using legal challenges to turn science with policy implications into an ordeal of legal maneuvers and threats. Since there is no freedom of information act for corporate funded research it is immune to subpoena and reinforces the asymmetry in favor of corporate research. The net result of the "sound science" argument is in fact a degradation of the quality of the entire scientific research base in cases on social costs. "Sound litigation science" is viewed as responding to the market demand and as superior to slow academic science, which brings science home to the market (Mirowski 2011).

The above account demonstrates that the PPP is an ex post strategy of dealing with social costs via tort law and the ex post assignment of property rights based on "first-come-first-serve" or the "Coase-rule." In practice this approach turns the problem of social costs into an issue of the market for science (see Mirowski 2013 for this paragraph's analysis). This essentially means that the market is the only entity holding sufficient knowledge to deal with social costs; that is, an epistemological challenge of the publicly funded system of science and the democratic governmental process. The challenge consists in willfully accepting human ignorance because humans as either scientific experts or democratically elected representatives cannot be trusted to understand social costs because they are too complex. Essentially, this view holds that social costs are solved by markets in the fullness of time and spreads doubt and confusion about science and intellectuals. Markets know better and market solutions have to be developed and implemented. This step buys important time as these schemes take many years to be designed and implemented before it becomes evident that they do not work to resolve the social cost problem (see e.g., Cap & Trade and Geoengineering). The net result is that private property rights that had to be assigned in the process have commodified further realms of the social and natural environment.

A parallel development is that the increasing pressures caused by the social cost of ecological or financial crises create moments of emergency, in which standard rules are suspended and PPP-based solutions can be imposed without democratic accountability: social costs crises thus impose a road to delimiting democratic controls and imposing a kind of "liberal dictatorship" (see Farrant, McPhail and Berger 2012). The term used by German Chancellor Angela Merkel is the "market-compatible" democracy, which refers to imposing solutions for social costs that would never stand the test of a democratic referendum. Democratic and scientific solutions to social costs are kept impotent (for a theory of the neoliberal state see Mirowski 2013; pp. 335–350).

Conclusion

The reconstruction of Kapp's theory of social costs provides an important contribution to the project of building an integrated heterodox economics as an alternative to neoclassical economics and the neoliberal economic system. Kapp's theory serves this purpose particularly well since it integrates key insights on social costs from several important heterodox economic traditions—Marx, Weber, Veblen—to counter not only neoclassical and neoliberal theories of social costs, but also to critique the rationality of the market system. Kapp's contribution is important today as social costs are dramatically increasing and neoclassical theories have proven their ineffectiveness in reducing, preventing or mitigating social costs. In fact, they have become instrumental in usurping further realms of society into the market by enforcing the PPP. If Kapp is right about the PPP's fatal flaws, this regime will lead to higher levels of social costs. The great value of Kapp's theory is that it provides a sophisticated articulation of an alternative approach of effective precautionary social controls of the economic system to prevent social costs. The key elements of Kapp's theory of social costs may be summarized in brief:

1 Markets socialize costs to third parties, future generations, and society as a whole.
2 Social costs are large-scale and systemic problems requiring precautionary, systemic and comprehensive remedies at the macro and societal level. Social costs are not minor temporary failures of an otherwise functioning and harmonious system, and can thus not be effectively remedied via ad hoc and ex post measures.
3 Social costs happen behind the back of the victims and are one-sidedly forced upon them in situations characterized by power asymmetries. Social costs are not voluntary exchange relationships between equals.
4 Social costs are subject to circular and cumulative causation between the open economic system and its social and natural environment, which makes them non-linear, unevenly spread out along the time axis, hidden for considerable periods of time, and often irreversible. Social costs are not linear and direct causal relationships, which makes it often impossible to determine their exact causality or value ex post.
5 Social costs do not have exchange value, because human life and health are not exchangeable commodities. Human life and health have an absolute value and are of a substantive kind.
6 Social cost prevention and reduction are matters of institutional reform and their extent depends upon the level of countervailing power that can be leveraged via social controls of corporations.
7 Instituting precautionary safety standards and social minima can protect human life and health, guarantee the gratification of basic human needs, and thereby effectively prevent social costs, and create social benefits. Protective measures reflective of existential human needs are a matter of the integration and humanization of social knowledge.

Kapp's theory may be differentiated from PPP-based theories by way of the typology in Table 1.1.

Table 1.1 Typology of social costs

	Neoclassical (Pigou)	Neoliberal (Coase)	Libertarian (Mises)	Heterodox (Kapp)
Social costs	Accidental, minor disturbance of an otherwise harmonious and rational system	Accidental "legal failure" of specify property rights	Systemic socialization of costs due to profit principle; major ecological-social incompatibility of markets
Ontology of the economic system	Closed system, market exchanges, mechanistic, reversibility, perfect knowledge, risk individualist, micro, formal rationality	Formal rationality, market exchanges	Open system, entropy law (substantive), irreversibility, complexity, uncertainty, ignorance, social-ecological, systemic, macro-level
Solution	Taxes, ad hoc, ex post	Bargaining, Individual private insurance markets, ad hoc, ex post	Legal system, tort law, ad hoc, ex post	Precautionary principle, social controls of technology and investment decisions, safety limits, social minima, ex ante
Political Economy	Slightly interventionist: does not call into question the market as a mechanism of allocation	Strongly interventionist: constructs markets that shift power to the wealthy ("the poor sell cheap")	Strongly anti-interventionist: power is with the large property owners	Strong social-ecological control of the mechanism of allocation: planning, prevention, controls of eco-social safety limits, countervailing power to protect the disadvantaged
Ethics	Outcome utilitarianism (although Coase may also be viewed as a rule utilitarian)		Rule utilitarianism	Humanist ethics

Notes

1 Kapp, interview by *The Economist* (Chapter 8 of present volume).
2 Neoliberalism is defined here as the set of principles established by Mirowski (2009; 2013).
3 For the influence of Polanyi on Kapp see Berger 2008. It remains an open question why Kapp does not cite or reference Polanyi's work in his dissertation.
4 This chapter is an interview conducted in 1962, most likely as part of a survey on the Japanese economy by the magazine *The Economist*. It shows how Kapp perceived the genealogy of his SC/SB project.
5 Bellagio conferences included Hayek's renowned analogy symposium in 1966 (Caldwell 2004, p. 308) and Machlup's Bellagio group for world monetary reform between 1964–1977 (Connell 2012).

References

Aslanbeigui, Nahid and Medema, Steven G. (1998), "Beyond the Dark Clouds: Pigou and Coase on Social Costs," *History of Political Economy*, 30, 4: 601–625.
Ayres, Robert and Kneese, Allen (1969), "Production, Consumption and Externalities," *The American Economic Review* 59, 3: 282–297.
Berger, Sebastian (2008), "Karl Polanyi's and Karl William Kapp's Substantive Economics: Important Insights from the Kapp–Polanyi Correspondence," *Review of Social Economy*, 66, 3: 381–396.
Berger, Sebastian (ed.) (2009), *The Foundations of Non-Equilibrium Economics: The Principle of Circular and Cumulative Causation*. London: Routledge.
Berger, Sebastian (2012), "The Discourse on Social Costs—Kapp's Impossibility Thesis vs. Neoliberalism," in Wolfram Elsner, Pietro Frigato, and Paolo Ramazzotti (eds), *Social Costs Today—Institutional Analyses of the Present Crisis*. London: Routledge.
Berger, Sebastian (2013) "The Making of the Institutional Theory of Social Costs: Discovering the K.W. Kapp and J.M. Clark Correspondence." *The American Journal of Economics and Sociology*, 72, 5: 1106–1130.
Berger, Sebastian and Elsner, Wolfram (2007), "European Contributions to Evolutionary Institutional Economics: The Cases 'Open Systems Approach' (OSA) and 'Cumulative Circular Causation' (CCC). Some Methodological and Policy Implications," *Journal of Economic Issues*, 41: 529–537.
Berger, Sebastian and Steppacher, Rolf (eds.) (2011), "Introduction," in *The Foundations of Institutional Economics – K. William Kapp*. London: Routledge.
Bernstein, Richard J. (1991), *Beyond Objectivism and Relativism*. Pennsylvania, PA: University of Pennsylvania Press.
Buchanan, James M. (1962), "Politics, Policy and the Pigovian Margins," *Economica*, 29, 113: 17–28.
Carpintero, Óscar (2013), "When Heterodoxy becomes Orthodoxy: Ecological Economics in the New Pelgrave Dictionary of Economics," in Frederic S. Lee (ed.), *Social Costs of Markets and Economic Theory*. Chichester: Wiley.
Caldwell, Bruce (2004), *Hayek's Challenge*. Chicago, IL: The University of Chicago Press.
Connell, Carol M. (2012), *Reforming the World Monetary System: Fritz Machlup and the Bellagio Group*. London: Pickering & Chatto Publishers Ltd.
Cordato, Roy (2004), "Towards and Austrian Theory of Environmental Economics", *The Quarterly Journal of Austrian Economics*, 7, 1: 3–16.
Dawson, Graham (2013), "Austrian Economics and Climate Change," *The Review of Austrian Economics*, 26, 2: 183–206.
Di Maio, Michele (2013), "Are Mainstream and Heterodox Economists Different? An

Empirical Analysis," in Frederic S. Lee (ed.), *Social Costs of Markets and Economic Theory*. Chichester: Wiley.

Dow, Sheila C. (2011), "Heterodox Economics: History and Prospects," *Cambridge Journal of Economics*, 35: 1151–1165.

Elsner, Wolfram (1986), *Economic Institutions Analysis—The Paradigmatic Development of Economics and the Relevance of a Recourse to the Economic Classics. (German: Ökonomische Institutionenanalyse)*. Berlin: Duncker & Humblot.

Elsner, Wolfram, Frigato, Pietro, and Ramazzotti, Paolo (eds) (2012), *Social Costs Today—Institutional Analyses of the Present Crisis*. London: Routledge.

Farrant, Andrew, McPhail, Edward and Berger, Sebastian (2012), "Preventing the 'Abuses' of Democracy: Hayek, the 'Military Usurper' and Transitional Dictatorship in Chile?" *American Journal of Economic Issues*, 71, 3: 513–538.

Foster, John B. (2010), *The Ecological Rift: Capitalism's War on Earth*. New York: Monthly Review Press.

Gaskins, Richard (2007), "Social Insurance and Unpaid Costs of Personal Injury: A Second Look at K. William Kapp" (Conference Paper European Society for Ecological Economics).

Gaskins, Richard (2010), "Accounting for Accidents: Social Costs of Personal Injury," *Victoria University of Wellington Law Review*, 41: 37–50.

Gerber, Julien-François and Steppacher, Rolf (2012), *Towards an Integrated Paradigm in Heterodox Economics—Alternative Approaches to the Current Eco-Social Crises*. Basingstoke: Palgrave Macmillan.

Gunning, J. Patrick (2000), "The Property System in Austrian Economics," *Review of Austrian Economics*, 13, 2: 209–220.

Kapp, K. William (2011), *The Foundations of Institutional Economics*, S. Berger and R. Steppacher (eds). London and New York: Routledge.

Kapp, K. William (1985) *The Humanization of the Social Sciences*, J. E. Ullmann and R. Preiswerk (eds). Lanham, NY and London: University Press of America.

Kapp, K. William (1971) *The Social Costs of Private Enterprise*. New York: Schocken Books.

Kapp, K. William (1970), "Environmental Disruption and Social Costs: A Challenge to Economics," *Kyklos*, 23, 4: 833–848.

Kapp, K. William (1963a), *The Social Costs of Business Enterprise*. Bombay: Asia Publishing House.

Kapp, K. William (1963b) *Hindu Culture, Economic Development and Economic Planning in India*. Bombay and London: Asia Publishing House.

Kapp, K. William (1962), "Friedrich List's Contribution to the Theory of Economic Development," *The Political Science Review* 1, 1: 17–22.

Kapp, K. William (1961), *Toward a Science of Man in Society—A Positive Approach to the Integration of Social Knowledge*. The Hague: Martinus Nijhoff.

Kapp, K. William (1960), "Economic Development, National Planning, and Public Administration," in *Kyklos*, 13, 2: 172–204.

Kapp. K. William (1956), *History of Economic Thought—A Book of Readings*. New York: Barnes & Noble.

Kapp, K. William (1950), *The Social Costs of Private Enterprise*. Cambridge, MA: Harvard University Press.

Kapp, K. William (1949), *Readings in Economics*. New York: Barnes and Nobles.

Kapp, K. William (1936), *Planwirtschaft und Aussenhandel*. Genève: Georg & Cie.

Kapp, K. William, "Unpublished Manuscript 1—French translation of Polish Preface of *The Social Costs of Private Enterprise*."

Lee, Frederic S (1998), *Post Keynesian Price Theory*. Cambridge: Cambridge University Press.

Lee, Frederic S. (2009), *A History of Heterodox Economics—Challenging the Mainstream in the Twentieth Century*. London: Routledge.

Lee, Frederic S. (2010), "Pluralism in Heterodox Economics," in R.F. Garnett, E.K. Olson, and M. Starr (eds), *Economic Pluralism*, pp. 19–35. London: Routledge.

Lee, Frederic S. (ed.) (2013), *Social Costs of Markets and Economic Theory*. Chichester: Wiley.

Martinez-Alier, Joan (2002), *Environmentalism of the Poor—A Study of Ecological Conflicts and Valuation*. Cheltenham: Edward Elgar.

Mearman, Andrew (2011), "Who Do Heterodox Economists Think They Are?" *The American Journal of Economics and Sociology*, 70, 2: 480–510.

Mearman, Andrew (2012), "Heterodox Economics and the Problem of Classification," *Journal of Economic Methodology*, 19, 4: 407–424.

Medema, Steven G. (2011), "A Case of Mistaken Identity: George Stigler, 'The Problem of Social Costs,' and the Coase Theorem," *European Journal of Law and Economics*, 31, 1, 11–38.

Mirowski, Philip (2011), *Science-Mart—The Commercialization of American Science*. Cambridge, MA: Harvard University Press.

Mirowski, Philip (2013), *Never Let a Serious Crisis Go to Waste*. Verso.

Mirowski, Philip and Plehwe, Dieter (eds) (2009), *The Road from Mont Pèlerin—The Making of the Neoliberal Thought Collective*. Cambridge, MA and London: Harvard University Press.

Myrdal, Gunnar (1968), *Asian Drama: An Inquiry into the Poverty of Nations*. New York: Random House.

Niglia, Guiseppe and Vatori, Massimiliano (2007), "K. William Kapp e Ronald H. Coase— un tentative di riconciliazione", in *Studi e Note di Economia*, Anno XII, n3, pp. 369–383.

Rorty, Richard (1984), "The Historiography of Philosophy: Four Genres," in Richard Rorty, J.B. Schneewind, and Quentin Skinner (eds), *Philosophy in History*. Cambridge: Cambridge University Press.

Ruggiero, Vincenzo (2013), *The Crimes of the Economy—A Criminological Analysis of Economic Thought*. London: Routledge.

Rutherford, Malcolm (2011), *The Institutionalist Movement in American Economics, 1918–1947*. Cambridge: Cambridge University Press.

Selwyn, Ben (2009), "An Historical Materialist Appraisal of Friedrich List and his Modern-Day Followers," *New Political Economy*, 14, 2: 157–180.

Spash, Clive (2011), "Social Ecological Economics: Understanding the Past to See the Future," *American Journal of Economics and Sociology*, 70, 2: 340–375.

Spash, Clive (2012), "Towards the integration of social, ecological and economic knowledge," in Julien-Francois Gerber and Rolf Steppacher (eds), *Towards an Integrated Paradigm in Heterodox Economics*, pp. 26–46. Basingstoke: Palgrave Macmillan.

Steinmetz, George (ed.) (2005), "Introduction: Positivism and Its Others in the Social Sciences," in *The Politics of Method in the Human Sciences*, pp. 1–58. Durham, NC: Duke University Press.

Tsuru, Shigeto (ed.) (1970). *Environmental Disruption—Proceedings of International Symposium* (The International Social Science Council). Tokyo: Asahi Evening News.

Van Horn, Rob, Mirowski, Philip, and Stapleford, Thomas (eds) (2011), *Building Chicago Economics—New Perspectives on the History of America's Most Powerful Economics Program*. Cambridge: Cambridge University Press.

Yalcintas, Altug (2013), "The Problem of Epistemic Cost: Why Do Economists Not Change Their Mind (About the "Coase Theorem")?" in Frederic S. Lee (ed.), *Social Costs of Markets and Economic Theory*. Chichester: Wiley.

2 The planned economy and international trade[1]

The problem of economic calculation

If we now turn to the problem of economic calculation, we recognize that a full treatment of this problem would far exceed the scope of this chapter, since it would require an examination of almost all of the problems of theoretical economics. Therefore, we will limit ourselves to an indicative presentation, and only after a critique of economic calculation based on market values will we attempt to hint at the possibility of a theoretical solution that thus far seems to have received inadequate attention.

The problem of economic calculation in a liberal-capitalist and planned organization of the economy has already occupied earlier economic theory. Schäffle discussed the difficulties that must arise for the maintaining of the economic principle under the central administration of the means of production.[2] Pareto also pays attention to the problem of economic value in a centrally administrated economy, and concludes that, to achieve a maximum of ophelimity, the economic center must make the same decisions that would occur under free competition absent any planned guidance.[3] And Pierson was the first to systematically deal with *The Problem of Economic Value in the Socialist Society*.[4]

In conjunction with the scientific discussion on socialization in the post-war period, it was Mises who then postulated that a rational economy cannot exist under conditions of a centrally organized community, because the exclusion of the means of production from market exchange would make their exact valuation in the decisions of the central economic administration impossible.[5] Today, the discussion of the problem of economic calculation essentially still takes Mises' formulation as a starting point.

The economic principle

The essence of the economy—the so-called economic principle—cannot be grasped more clearly than by juxtaposing it with the essence of technology.

It is part of the principle of technology that individual success is achieved with as little effort as possible. The task of the technician is, for example, to extract from a machine a maximum of service with a minimum use of fuels (coal, oil, etc.). His goal in every individual activity is to keep the loss of energy at a minimum. Every technology-oriented behavior, just like any reasonable behavior, is thus governed by the premise: Act always in such a way that success is achieved with a minimum of effort. In this form, the principle of technology is doubtlessly universal.

The implementation of the technological principle in an individual process of production, however, does not yet say anything about the economic status of this process. The production of atmospheric air can—to use an example from Max Weber—completely correspond to technological principles; yet whether the production of air can be deemed economical is thereby not decided.[6] Thus, the economic principle has to differ from the technological principle.

The economy regularly seeks the satisfaction of several needs, i.e., the attainment of several aims. Any utilization of economic means for the production of a good necessarily means that these means are withdrawn from other production processes, and that other needs must remain unsatisfied. The use of means in one location means, in general, that other goods cannot be produced. An *economic* utilization of goods only exists when the available economic means being used in one production process are not withdrawn from other processes and products which are deemed more important. The economic principle is not adhered to as long as the commitment of available means to one branch of production does not require foregoing a more valuable good for the sake of a less valuable one.[7]

The technician will regularly succeed in increasing the productivity of a machine, according to the latest insights of scientific research. Whether the respective production process can be deemed economic in the context of the whole economic activity depends on factors that exceed the scope of the individual production process. This requires determining the meaning of the available means for the satisfaction of needs. The technician who, in the production of a good, does not know the meaning of alternative raw materials that are available for utilization, is in danger of utilizing raw materials that could be used for the satisfaction of more important needs.

In order to realize the meaning of individual products and the economic means necessary for their production with respect to the satisfaction of needs, it is necessary to compare all available economic means. This comparison between goods of different material character, (copper, coal, oil, etc.) can only occur with the aid of a standard of comparison.

Economic calculation in the liberal-capitalist economy

The free-market economy solves this problem in the following manner. Most persons participating in economic exchange value all goods in a certain way. In the money using economy, all available goods appear as certain price magnitudes. Prices, in a way, constitute an objective form of the subjective valuations of the individuals participating in exchange, such that they effectively express the valuation of goods with respect to the satisfaction of needs associated with these goods. While price as a standard of measurement provides the technical precondition for a valuation of goods in the context of the whole economy, there remains one question: How do the conditions of the liberal-capitalist economy guarantee that every individual production process meets the requirements of the economic principle? The success of every capitalist enterprise apparently depends on how much the sum of prices of the produced goods surpasses the sum of prices of the expanded goods and services. Naturally, it occurs under the circumstances of the capitalist economy that the expenditures of an enterprise exceed its return (calculated in prices). But if this condition continues, and if this enterprise is not continually provided with means from other sources, it will eventually be forced to discontinue production. The capitalist enterprise must, therefore, strive to select the means available on the market in such a way as to minimize the magnitudes of expenditure relative to the prices of produced goods. In other words, the enterprise will always utilize only those means which receive the comparatively lowest valuation from the economic units participating in economic exchange, and which can be procured at the lowest relative cost.

Since the capitalist enterprise normally only continues production as long as the prices of the goods exceed the sum of prices of the expanded goods, it will regularly only allocate the means of production to those production processes that yield products of higher value than the economic means utilized in production. If, due to the individual valuations, the price of certain goods declines so far that it no longer covers the magnitudes of expenditure of the enterprise, the expected shutdown of production will make economic means available that will, in turn, be allocated to other production processes in which the relationship between magnitudes of expenditure and prices of goods is the relatively most advantageous. In this way, the economic principle, which was initially developed abstractly as the basis of economic behavior, manifests itself in the context of the individual enterprise, namely with the aid (and as a consequence) of individual valuations which are expressed in market prices.

Mises' objection to the planned economy and its treatment in the literature

In the planned economy, the regulating function of the market is replaced by the conscious coordination of production processes and their adaptation to the needs of consumption, with the aid of the unified economic plan. Now, can such a plan be developed according to the economic principle? Mises answers this question negatively. In the planned economy, it would, above all, be impossible to compare the different available economic means with one another; the standardized measure for the exact valuation of goods would be lacking. Mere estimates of the means of production in the modern and complicated methods of production would, sooner or later, lead to production processes that contradict the economic principle. The existence of the following conditions would have to be considered as a precondition for every exact economic calculation:

1   "To begin with, not only the goods of first order, but also the goods of higher order, have to be subject to economic exchange. If they were not

subject to economic exchange, the formation of exchange ratios would not take place."

2 "The second condition is that a generally accepted means of exchange, that is money, is in use, and plays its role of mediation in the exchange of productive goods. If this were not the case, it would be impossible to find a common denominator for all exchange relations."[8]

Neither of these two conditions would be fulfilled in the planned economy. Not only would the means of production not be subject to economic exchange (they are subject to the state's central planning authority), but a generally accepted means of exchange (that is, money) would not exist either. However, with respect to the latter, Mises makes the following qualification: "While the socialist economy does not necessarily have to abandon money completely, it makes the expression of the prices of the means of production (including labor) in terms of money impossible, such that money can play no role in economic calculation."[9] Without the capability of exactly valuing goods, an economy cannot exist at all. "There would not be any means to recognize what is rational, and thus production could not effectively be adjusted to being economical."[10]

The problem of economic calculation in the planned economy has received very different kinds of treatment in the literature. One group of authors proposes that calculation in natural units suffices for the planned economy, instead of the economic calculus with magnitudes of prices in the liberal-capitalist economy. This view is held, above all, by Neurath[11] and Tschajanow,[12] and also in outlines by Weil.[13]

Contrary to Tschajanow, Strumilin and Varga considered it evident, based on the objective theory of value, to propose a certain expenditure of labor as a unit for the calculation of value.[14] In 1920, before the introduction of the New Economic Plan, a governmental commission in Russia even dealt with these questions. Iurowsky, the former head of the foreign currency administration at the treasury, reports, however, that "these enquiries did not yield any results whatsoever, neither in theory nor in practice."[15] In the collectivized Russian agriculture today, however, the expenditure of human labor is once again the basis for calculating the individual peasant's and worker's share of the total yield of the collective economy. Thus, §15 para. 9 of the sample statute of an agricultural production cooperative, which was approved by the Council of the People's Commissars of the USSR on February 17, 1935 states the following: "The distribution of the incomes of the productive cooperative amongst its members is solely based on the amount of a day's productive effort of every member."[16]

Generally accepted is Mises' objection to a centrally administered economy, in which the goods that are produced according to the plan are distributed via direct allocation to consumers. Under these conditions, the subjective valuations of consumers cannot find expression. A direct allocation of goods to consumers is, however, according to general perception, neither intended in the planned economy nor necessarily related to the planned organization of the economy.

Incidentally, one can differentiate the following types of approaches to the problem: According to one orientation, the valuation of the means of production in the planned economy should be feasible on the basis of general cost accounting. To this orientation belong, for example, the works of Schiff[17] and Leichter[18]; likewise, Lederer[19] talks about a valuation of the means of production based on costs. A calculation of the value of goods in the planned economy is also included in the works of Cläre Tisch, who seeks to make price formation in the realm of consumer goods the starting point for the valuation of the means of production, following Wieser's solution to the assignment problem.[20]

Another group categorically proposes, with reference to the problems which conflict with any calculation, to maintain a market in modified form for the means of production in the planned economy as well. This view seems recently to have spread, especially among English economists. Herein belong also the attempts to find a solution via a syndicalist, or rather guild-socialist, organization of the economy. In such an economic system, the individual guilds or syndicates would maintain exchange relations, so that price formation in the area of the means of production could occur.

Clarification of the theoretical starting points

From the point of view of classical economics and the objective theory of value, the Misean problem of economic calculation in the planned economy, does not exist. According to the objective theory of value, the value of all goods, and thus their valuation in the different production processes, is determined by the socially necessary average labor time. The common measure for the valuation of all goods would have to be found, according to this theory, in labor time—calculated in units of time.

Only those economists who derived the value of all goods from the subjective valuations of individuals in their exchange relationships could develop the thesis that the elimination of exchange relationships would also dispense with the basis for the determination of the economic value of the goods. It was thus no coincidence that the difficulties that would be faced by economic calculation in the planned economy were first brought forward by representatives of the subjective theory of value. Viewed in this way, however, the intellectual effort to refute Mises' thesis of the impossibility of economic calculation in the planned economy does not seem to be commensurate with the results that could potentially be achieved on this basis. That is to say, if one is of the opinion that the value of all goods is solely determined by the valuation of individuals in exchange relationships and only derivable from the individual, it is nothing but the repetition of this assertion in negative form to say that economic value in an economic system without exchange relationships between individuals cannot be determined. But if the value of economic goods cannot be determined, their economic utilization is in fact not possible. The correctness of Mises' argument cannot be logically refuted on this basis.

The question is, however, what kind of results are at all obtainable by an economic calculus that is based on the valuations of single individuals? The further question then arises whether the aggregation of the economic units into a planned economy would yield unique principles of valuation, which would in turn necessitate new methods for the determination of value of the available economic means. The answer to the first question leads to a critique of the economic calculation based on the market prices of goods.

The critique of the economic calculus based on market prices

It would be relatively easy to provide proof that the economic situation of today already fails to meet the expectations one could have for a rational economy from the standpoint of the individual. An economic order in which the free for-mation of prices is inhibited by the existence of monopolistic organizations and the interventions of the state, means that—even in the view of Mises—the less, rather than the more, valuable goods are produced.[21]

A critique of the economic calculation based on market prices must, there-fore, initially take its departure from the conditions of the liberal-capitalist ideal type. To these conditions belongs primarily the free competition of a multitude of producers and consumers. Only under these conditions can the necessary price movements emerge on the market, which provide business owners with the cues for their behavior. But what about the economic calculation based on market prices under *these* conditions? In general, Schiff has pointed out that, in many cases, it would be impossible to arrive at an exact expression of the price for certain goods:

> Also here (that is, in the capitalist economy), many positions can only be inferred by approximate estimates. How uncertain is often the valuation of inventories and receivables. How arbitrary are the write-offs, how arbitrary the allocation of total costs to individual products. In addition, the future of the business cycle and the price level play a big role for the calculation.[22]

Moreover, a whole series of conditions—apart from social and political counter-forces—conflicts with the "automatic" adjustment to changing circumstances, and an expedient exploitation of the respective economic potentials. To these belong, among others, the familiar habituality and inertia of consumers, the con-tractual commitment of businesses for long periods of time,[23] and the economic subjects' lack of overview over different markets. Nevertheless, is it possible to say that the individual households in the capitalist economy are, time and time again, forced anew, by the necessity to observe the profit principle, to devote their attention to the detection of advantageous opportunities.

Fundamental objections to the economic calculation based on market prices can only be raised from another side.

The disregard for the needs of those members of society who are excluded from exchange

The market price can always express only the valuations of the persons *partici-pating* in market exchange; However, the ability of individuals to participate in market exchange depends not on their needs, but solely on whether they are endowed with the income. For example, if the price of a good is between 115 and 120, those contenders who are incapable of offering more than 100 have no influence on the formation of the exchange value. Yet, this still does not say anything about the needs of these contenders. The intensity of their needs can rise, the number of persons excluded from exchange can even increase; but as long as the intensity of their valuations does not increase *such* that they stop being excluded, their needs are not a factor in the formation of price.[24] Thus Menger maintained that, in business, even the most compelling and urgent needs of the destitute have no weight at all, even among financially comfortable people who are the most sympathetic. "In our amiable organizational life, it is not the genuine human needs of the population, but only the needs of those who are able and willing to pay that are the object of passionate convictions in the business world."[25]

An economic order that time and time again produces income differentials anew, and in which a planned equalization of incomes would be a first violation of its foundational principles, can, with the aid of an economic calculation based on market prices, always reach only a very relative efficiency. While on the one hand the most basic needs of that part of the population endowed with a relatively low income remain unsatisfied, the method of valuation based on market prices allows and enforces the production of goods which serve the satisfaction of less important, luxury needs of the part of the population endowed with a relatively high income.

In their recently published book, S. and B. Webb also emphasize this shortcoming of the economic calculation based on the prices of the free market.[26]

The sources of error in the formation of individual wants

The valuations which the individuals reveal about goods depend, on the one hand, to a great extent on the awareness of needs, and, on the other hand, on the individual views of the usefulness of the different goods for the satisfaction of needs.

The awareness of needs is, however, influenced in varying degrees by unawareness, error, and passion. Menger speaks in these cases of illusionary, undeveloped, and pathological needs. "The more inadequate a person's available means, the less incentive she has to mull over her less-important needs with practical deliberation and cognitive interests."[27] In other words, these persons do not get beyond a certain degree of awareness of needs. An economic calculation that is solely based on individual valuations, however, acts more or less implicitly on the assumption that the consciousness of the individuals completely suffices for the awareness of needs.

Also, the individual awareness of the usefulness of the different goods for the satisfaction of needs is often not only limited, but subject to the most diverse external factors. To begin with, there are numerous cases in which certain goods are granted a relatively large relevance for the satisfaction of needs based on the awareness of the consumers, but which in reality are either of relatively low relevance, or even harmful when consumed.

In an economic calculation based on the prices of goods, it suffices that the individual valuations for these goods rise for the means of production to be withdrawn from their current employment, and to then be used for the production of the mentioned goods. The relevance which the goods have in reality for the satisfaction of needs (or whether their consumption is not downright harmful) cannot find consideration in an economic calculation based on market prices. Only the subjective view of the individuals, not the objective usefulness, is the deciding factor. It is at the very least questionable whether, on this basis, the highest possible welfare of the individuals is really achievable. But if one bears in mind, especially in this context, that the degree of success of every capitalist enterprise depends on the magnitude of the earned sales prices, one can grasp how much every entrepreneur must depend upon increasing consumer demand, especially for the good produced by himself. That the potentials of psychological manipulation of the views of consumers about the relative usefulness of different goods are exceptionally great can hardly be questioned, but such means are not even necessary. In the entire entrepreneurial activity, the psychological manipulation of consumers rather regularly plays a large and absolutely legitimate role. Modern sales and advertisement methods are to be named first. Fashion and its deliberate promotion are also of great significance in this context. It is not essential here to enumerate the different possibilities and methods of psychological manipulation of consumers in detail. The result is in all cases the same: One arouses in consumers the view that certain goods possess a relatively high usefulness for them. The demand for such goods therefore rises, and the immediate consequences are increases in the market prices of these goods. Subsequently, means of production are withdrawn from other applications and allocated to those production processes of which the products have become subject to consumer demand due to psychological manipulation. In these cases, one can be of the opinion that the different methods of psychological manipulation of consumers awaken *new* needs in them, and that the newly-awakened needs find their highest satisfaction provided by the availability of means on the basis of an economic calculation based on market prices. To speak of "economical" in this sense would mean, however, that one would consider every production as economical, for which one merely awakens in some manner the "needs" of individuals.[28]

It seems to us, however, that an economic calculation based on individual valuations which result from psychological manipulation by means of modern advertisement and sales techniques, fulfills the economic principle only formally. Because parts of the income are spent on the purchase of goods which the consumers would not have demanded without the psychological manipulation by the producers, individuals must forego the enjoyment of other goods. Thus, less important needs are satisfied at the cost of more important ones.

The impossibility of achieving society's economic principle based on the economic calculus of market prices

A third objection to the economic calculation based on market prices arises when one is ready to view the economy from the standpoint of society.

The disregard for the social and political disadvantages of economic decisions

The economic calculation based on market prices very often fails to capture or consider the social disadvantages and damages of an economic decision. The economic measures of a private enterprise can, according to the requirements of the foregoing calculations on the basis of prices, be completely consistent with the economic principle, and thus secure the profitability of the enterprise. Whether the respective decision about an expansion or limitation of production can be viewed as economical from the standpoint of society cannot yet be said.

In fact, the cases in which the economic decisions of private enterprises (which meet the requirements of the economic principle calculated on the basis of market prices) yield disadvantages and damages for society are numerous, as has been shown above all by the works of Pigou.[29] For instance, production processes can yield disadvantages for society in a double respect: On the one hand, the produced good can cause social damages that need not be limited to disruption of national health, but are expressed generally by an increase in crime, accidents, etc. On the other hand, damages of the persons employed in production can occur (employment related illnesses, accidents, etc.); in this context, women's labor ought also to be mentioned in certain circumstances, because it can be related to disadvantages for society caused by the direct damages due to an inadequate protection of motherhood. Under an economic calculation based on market prices, furthermore, such disadvantages remain unaccounted for, and accrue to society due to the penetration of private economic activity on the environment. To this belong the excessive smoke concentrations in industrial centers, disruptions due to noise, unhealthy construction work, etc. For losses, which arise for society today due, for example, to excessive smoke concentration in big industrial cities, Pigou cites damages of homes and crop plants, increased costs for the cleaning of clothes, and expenditures for additional lights. Pigou reports in this context the results of an expert commission which estimated in 1912 the costs of smoke damages in Pittsburg to be 4 English pounds per capita of the population every year.[30] Next to a series of other examples, Pigou cites the case in which investments in foreign countries lead to diplomatic and war-like complications. Also in this case, the damages which are inflicted upon society due to war do not find entry into the economic calculation of those enterprises which undertake investments abroad.[31]

From the standpoint of society, patent protection and the protection of business secrets are direct losses, because they make impossible the utilization of the means of production according to the latest technological developments. Also, the advertisement costs of individual enterprises must in this sense count as losses from the standpoint of society.[32] The expenditures for advertising in the US were estimated to be $1.5 billion in the year 1927.[33] Of special significance in this context are also the exploitation of sources of energy and raw materials by private enterprises (coal, ore, and oil deposits, forests, etc.). On the basis of an economic calculation based on market prices, this exploitation can be quite profitable; however, whether the unlimited exploitation of these sources is economical from the standpoint of society, given their stocks' limited availability, is a different question, one which absolutely cannot be answered by an economic calculation based on market prices.[34]

How can it be explained that, in the valuation of goods according to market prices, *societal* needs and interests do not find consideration? The reason for this is, evidently, that societal needs and interests frequently cannot find *any value expression* in the market exchange between isolated individuals, and accordingly also do not find entry into the economic calculation. This means that, achieving economic viability from the standpoint of society based on an economic calculation of market prices is out of the question entirely. It is known that, under today's conditions, it is the task of social policy to more or less compensate for this non-consideration of disadvantages and damages to society, via a series of corrections. Especially in this area, therefore, an essential difference would arise between the liberal-capitalist and the planned economy. While the capitalist economy can only apply retroactive corrections to social damages via laws, social policies, and charitable measures, these damages could be calculated from the start in a centrally planned economy and taken into account in economic decisions.

The disregard for social goals and needs

Theoretical economics, in recent years, usually views the single individual is the center of economic life. This method is supported by the assertion that the task of every economy is primarily the satisfaction of human needs. However, it makes a difference whether one views the human being as an isolated individual being withdrawn into himself and his individual interests, or as a social being in relation to other humans in his surroundings. He who views society as an organization that constrains the "natural" individuality of humans will tend to view the task of the economy *first of all* to be the satisfaction of the needs of *individuals*. In contrast, he who views humans first of all as *social beings* will, if anything, be ready to place the totality and development of society in the center of the economy. This difference in point of view, which may initially be purely a matter of worldviews, has a very concrete relevance for all statements concerning human needs. As an isolated individual, the human being has a series of needs which result from the sustenance of his individual existence (food, clothing, shelter, etc.). As a social being, it is a need of the human being to defend against dangers which threaten the existence of society: epidemics, illnesses, enemy attacks, etc. As a member of society, the human being has an additional interest in such agencies that serve not only the maintenance, but also the improvement, of general welfare and public health, as well as the elevation of the cultural level of the whole. Thus, this is not about construing a difference between the needs of the individual and those of society. On the contrary: Only if one conceptualizes the individual not as an isolated, but as a social, being is it possible to recognize, in an objective sense, that the needs of society are the needs of all individuals.

Another question, however, is whether individuals also recognize social needs as subjectively their own, and whether they tolerate their satisfaction. It is even to be expected that the human being—as long as he does not become, directly and primarily, conscious of his characteristics as a social being—lets himself be guided and acts according to his individual needs and private interests as an isolated individual being.

Therefore, in economic exchange relations, humans will demand the satisfaction of their individual needs *before* the satisfaction of societal needs, and express this in the valuations of goods. Thus, an economic calculation guided by consumer valuations, which even in their objective form as exchange values cannot be anything other than the valuations expressed by isolated individuals according to their interests, can indeed satisfy the respective needs of (solvent) individuals; social needs and goals will, however, find no realization.

One does not only have to refer to the case of war, in which the goal of society is the highest material readiness for conflict, and to which all utilizations of means of production are subservient, to illustrate what kind of dangers can be associated with an organization of production according to the expressed value judgments of isolated individuals. The realization of this danger is also the reason that the liberal-capitalist society, whenever societal interests are at risk before all *others* (as in periods of war and crisis), must create organizational forms that provide a relatively better guarantee for the attainment of the societal goal (the "war economy").

In normal times, societal needs also exist, and the interests of society are always at risk. A neglected economy would thus necessarily be associated with the gravest dangers for societal development. In the free-market economy, the state tries to do justice to these societal interests and problems with the aid of governmental economic policies. If, in this case, theoretical economics regularly brings up the question: "Which are the economic sacrifices of this or that measure of the state's economic policy?", then it seems to us just as legitimate to ask: "Which are the social and societal sacrifices if the government were actually to leave the economy to itself?"

A centrally-administered planned economy would be able to derive all economic decisions from the concrete societal situation. Societal valuations, not the valuations of individuals, would determine the utilization of goods. The "individualistic definition of the economic principle"[35] would be replaced by a societal definition.

The previous treatment of the problem of economic calculation in the literature followed without protest the critique of the planned economy by leaving outside of its purview the capturing of the economic principle from the stand-point of society.[36]

It would be much more important, and more in keeping with the character of the planned economy, to establish principles for the valuation of goods based on the needs and goals of society. The problem of "social value," which played a certain role in the economics of List, Schäffle, and Wieser, may thus have not lost its relevance in the context of the question of an economic calculation in the planned economy.[37]

Notes

1 This section is the first English translation of Chapters 3 and 4 of Kapp's dissertation "Planning and International Trade" (1936).
2 A.E.F. Schäffle, *Bau und Leben des Sozialen Körpers*, 3 Bd., pp. 278 and 332.
3 V. Pareto, *Cours d'économie politique*, II Bd., pp. 364 §§1012–1023, Théories des organizations socialistes.
4 N.G. Pierson, "Das Wertproblem in der sozialistischen Gesellschaft", in *Zeitschrift für Volkswirtschaft und Sozialpolitik*, Neue Folge, IV Bd., p. 607, 1925. Initially published in Dutch in the 41st year of *De Economist* (1902). Newly reprinted in English translation in Hayek, F.A., *Collectivist Economic Planning*, pp. 41–85.
5 L. Mises, "Die Wirtschaftsrechnung im Sozialistischen Gemeinwesen", in *Archiv für Sozialwissenschaften und Sozialpolitik*, 1920/21 pp. 86–121 (47 Bd.). This article is reproduced in Mises' book *Die Gemeinwirtschaft*, the 2nd edn. (1932) of which is being cited.
6 M. Weber, "Wirtschaft und Gesellschaft," in *Grundrisse der Sozialökonomik*, Abt. III, p. 33.
7 C. Tisch, *Wirtschaftsrechnung und Verteilung im zentralistisch organisierten sozialistischen Gemeinwesen*, p. 14.
8 L. Mises, *Die Gemeinwirtschaft*, p. 96.
9 L. Mises, ibid., p. 100.
10 L. Mises, ibid., p. 98.
11 O. Neurath, *Wirtschaftsplan und Naturalrechnung*. Berlin 1925.
12 Tschajanow, cit. by B. Brutzkus, *Die Lehren des Marxismus im Lichte der russischen Revolution*, p. 19.
13 F. Weil, "Gildensozialistische Rechnungslegung," *Archiv für Sozialwissenschaft und Sozialpolitik*, 1924 (52 Bd.), pp. 196.
14 These proposals are reported in detail by K. Elster, *Vom Rubel zum Tscherwonjez*, pp. 128ff., and B. Brutzkus, op. cit., p. 20.
15 N. Iurowsky, *Die Währungsprobleme Sowjetrusslands*, p. 27.
16 *Rundschau über Politik, Wirtschaft und Arbeiterbewegung*, 1935, p. 660. Article 15 of the sample statute also contains further details about the methods of the calculation and accounting of a day's work effort.
17 W. Schiff, *Die Planwirtschaft und ihre ökonomischen Hauptprobleme*.
18 O. Leichter, *Die Wirtschaftsrechnung in der sozialistischen Gesellschaft*.
19 E. Lederer, *Planwirtschaft*, p. 47.
20 C. Tisch, *Wirtschaftsrechnung und Verteilung im zentralistisch organisierten sozialistischen Gemeinwesen*. Compare to this work also H. Zassenhausen, "Über die ökonomische Theorie der Planwirtschaft" in *Zeitschrift für Nationalökonomie*, 1934, pp. 507.
21 L. Mises, op. cit., pp. 354. If one agrees with F. Wieser (*Theorie der gesellschaftlichen Wirtschaft*, p. 110) that "power is not always being carried into the economy from the outside but that it is being produced to a large extent from within" then the

compliance with the economic principle in this sense would generally be impossible in the capitalist economy in the long run.

22 W. Schiff, op. cit., p. 81.
23 E. Wagemann, op. cit., p. 49.
24 E. Böhm-Bawerk, "Kapital und Kapitalzins", Abtl. 2. Bd. 1. *Positive Theorie des Kapitals*, p. 281 and 284.
25 C. Menger, *Grundsätze der Volkswirtschaftslehre* (2nd edn.), p. 49.
26 S. and B. Webb, *Soviet Communism, A New Civilization?* II Bd. pp. 674–675.
27 C. Menger, op. cit., p. 88.
28 This case in particular, in which production occurs first and needs are awakened afterwards with a corresponding advertisement effort, may practically play no small role today.
29 A.C. Pigou, *The Economics of Welfare*.
30 A.C. Pigou, op. cit., pp. 186.
31 A.C. Pigou, op. cit., p. 188.
32 A.C. Pigou, op. cit., pp. 197.
33 Compare recent economic changes in the US *Report of the Committee on Recent Economic Changes of the Presidents Conference on Unemployment*. H. Hoover, Chairman, Vol. I, p. 402.
34 It would be an interesting task for statistics to develop correct methods for the capturing of disadvantages and damages which accrue to society in a free market economy due to the activity of independent entrepreneurs that is solely based on the principle of highest profitability.
35 F. Wieser, "Theorie der gesellschaftlichen Wirtschaft" in *Grundriss der Sozialökonomik*, I Abt. II. Teil, p. 116.
36 With the exception of S. and B. Webb, who have recently emphasized the possibility of the consideration of societal goals and problems via a unified economic plan in a planned economy. S. and B. Webb, op. cit., pp. 677–678.
37 Because this question would exceed the frame of this work, a systematic treatment of the system of economic calculation on the basis of "social value" should be reserved for a later treatment.

3 Social costs and social returns—a critical analysis of the social performance of the unplanned market economy[1]

Project outline

In harmony with the faith of nineteenth century liberalism, traditional equilibrium economics states that the unregulated forces of supply and demand in an unplanned market economy tend to lead to an optimum allocation of scarce resources among competing ends and objectives. This doctrine continues to be regarded by many as an apparently scientific foundation for all arguments against positive intervention with the economic process in the capitalist economy; its strength is attested by the current success of the books by Hayek and Mises. Economic planning is still on the defensive, and in many minds the presumption seems to be against purposive action in economic affairs, despite all experiences of depressions and other inefficiencies in the operation of the capitalist economy.

This study offers a critique of the basic premises of nineteenth century economic liberalism by examining the social performance of the unplanned market economy in the light of several facts which are usually omitted and neglected in economic theory. After a brief analysis of various obstacles to rational behavior in modern industrial society, Part II of the study traces a wide variety of social costs which individual producers are able to shift to third persons or to society at large, and which consequently fail to be taken into consideration in the cost calculations of private enterprise. An attempt is made to reveal the nature of these social costs by tracing the causal relationship between private production and such phenomena as air and water pollution, the impairment of the human factor of production, the premature exhaustion and destruction of natural resources, soil erosion, deforestation, etc. Attention is also paid to the social losses associated with technological improvements, economic fluctuations, and the existence of monopolistic elements in modern economic life. The general examination of these social costs is followed in each case by a brief summary of various quantitative estimates of their relative magnitude. These estimates support the final conclusion that the social costs of production that are not reflected in outlays of entrepreneurs reach substantial proportions in modern industrial society.

Part III undertakes to show that, in many cases, goods and services are capable of yielding social returns (i.e., utilities) which diffuse themselves among all members of society; these utilities are, to a large extent, inappropriable by individual producers, and cannot always be appraised in monetary terms. As a result, the creation of these utilities is unprofitable (in terms of monetary outlays and returns), and tends to be neglected in an economy in which the relative worthwhileness of producing different goods and services is measured only in terms of the expected surplus of private returns over costs. Among the more important social returns discussed are the social benefits derived from the gratification of collective needs; from international economic policies designed to achieve a balanced economy and maintain economic stability despite depressions abroad; and from the improvement of transportation facilities. Other social returns discussed are those resulting from scientific research, multiple purpose projects (such as TVA), and the maintenance of a social minimum with respect to essential foodstuffs, medical care, housing, and education.

As an analysis of the social inefficiency of the unplanned market economy, the study inevitably assumes the character of a critique, not only of capitalism, but also of traditional equilibrium economics. The concluding part of the study outlines its general results, as well as its implications for the scope of economic science. In the first place, it attempts to indicate the limitations of all economic calculations in terms of private costs and private returns. To allocate economic resources merely in accordance with private costs and private returns defeats any endeavor to find a rational solution to the economic problem. As far as the implications for economic science are concerned, the main thesis of the concluding part is that economic science has to broaden its scope so as to consider social costs and social returns as typical economic phenomena, and not merely as exceptional cases or minor disturbances. By including social costs and social returns within the scope of economic analysis, economic science will finally be able to close the gap which exists between economic theory and practice.

Preface 1

It is the thesis of this book that there are important social costs of production which private enterprise in a market economy fails to consider in its economic calculations. Our study attempts to demonstrate both the nature and significance of these social costs, which tend to be shifted to, and borne by, third persons or the community at large. The analysis is thus a critique of the market economy and traditional economic theory, which, in its devotion to the interpretation of the price system, has so far excluded from the range of its investigations many of the less harmonious (though not less important) aspects of economic reality which no responsible government can afford to overlook in the formulation of economic policies.

The result has been an almost continuous intensification of the traditional tension between economic theory and practice.

Our study reflects the conviction that, in order to close the present gap between economic theory and practice, it is necessary to widen the scope of economic science and to incorporate into its general philosophy some of the broader aspects of economic life, which until now have been regarded as "non-economic" and outside the scope of economics proper. As pointed out in the introductory chapter, the present analysis represents merely a first step towards this goal.

At the same time, however, it is believed that a study of social costs may be of immediate practical significance, in so far as it emphasizes the need for active governmental regulation of the economic process in various fields. In the light of the conclusions of traditional economic theory, such regulation appears to be not only unjustified, but harmful. The realization and recognition of social costs as a typical phenomenon in modern industrial society makes public regulation and control of the economic-process not only necessary, but imperative in the interest of achieving the optimum utilization of scarce resources.

Although our conclusions deviate substantially from those of traditional economic theory, they are neither revolutionary nor original, in the sense of being derived from entirely new insights. Quite the contrary, the basic ideas and principles which underlie these conclusions have found widespread acceptance outside of economic science, and especially in economic practice. It is only that sacred sphere of economic science, the theory of value and distribution, which has not yet felt the impact of these ideas and principles.

Preface 2

The present study is an attempt to show that the social efficiency of the capitalist exchange economy is impaired considerably by various obstacles to rational conduct in modern industrial society, as well as by social costs of private enterprise, and by the neglect of certain important social returns of productive activities. As a result of these three factors, the capitalist economy is unable to maximize the want-satisfying power of available resources.

By thus calling attention once again to the inherent limitations of the competitive calculus, our analysis is bound to assume the character of a critique of classical and neo-classical equilibrium economics. For more than 150 years, orthodox economic science has lent seemingly objective support to the claim that, by directing available resources into the relatively most profitable channels, private enterprise serves not only its own interest, but also those of the community as a whole, and thus tends to achieve the optimum solution to the economic problem. Our analysis attempts to subject these claims to a constructive criticism—constructive in the sense of opening the way for a better appraisal of the over-all efficiency of the productive process under any form of economic organization. With this end in view, the study concludes with an appeal for a re-orientation of economic science. Such a re-orientation may finally enable economists to include within the range of their investigations those omitted aspects of reality which today are classified as non-economic, and whose relevance in connection with the allocation of scarce means for the attainment of competing ends can no longer be denied. To indicate a possible approach to such a re-orientation of economics; to explore the possibilities for the establishment of valid criteria for economic planning and the formulation of economic policy; and perhaps to prepare the way for the elaboration of a positive theory of social value are, ultimately, the chief purposes of this inquiry. The author is fully aware of the fact that the re-orientation of an established system of knowledge can never be the work of one individual student; it depends rather upon the collaboration of many minds—a collaboration which can be secured only by convincing other students of the limitations of the established system of knowledge. The present study will have served its purpose if it succeeds in carrying this conviction to other economists and social scientists.

The author wishes to make it clear that his criticism of economic science is directed primarily against the scope of traditional equilibrium economics. He is well aware of the fact that many individual economists have criticized the limitations of economic science and have attempted to broaden its scope. As far as he is conscious of the influence which earlier critics have had upon his own line of thought, he has endeavored to acknowledge it.

The basic idea of the present study was first advanced, in a highly tentative manner, in the author's attempt to deal with the problem of economic calculation in connection with his analysis of the economic relations between a foreign trade monopoly and private exporters and importers.[2] His interest in the problems of social costs and social returns was further stimulated by J.M. Clark's contributions to "Social Economics," as well as by the results of the unique and still largely neglected research carried out under the auspices of the National Resources Planning Board.

I also wish to acknowledge gratefully the many helpful comments which friends and former colleagues at New York University made, especially during the earlier stages of the preparation of the manuscript. Furthermore, I should like to record my gratitude for the critical suggestions offered by J.M. Clark, Emile Gruenberg, M.F.W. Joseph, Vernon Mund, Frederick Pollock, Walter Schiffer, Eugene Staley, and Paul Studenski.

The contributions which my wife has made to this book are too comprehensive to be explained fully. She has rendered indispensable aid in connection with the research work; she prepared preliminary drafts for certain sections; and she has borne many of the numerous burdens involved in the final completion of the study. I also wish to mention with warmest thanks that Dr. Joseph Finnegan has helped with the editorial revision of the manuscript.

The untiring cooperation of Mr. Mulford Martin, librarian of the Library of the School of Commerce, Accounts and Finance of New York University, and his staff greatly facilitated the collection of material. I am further indebted for detailed information and material dealing with specific phases of the study to the following agencies and institutions: The Mellon Institute of Industrial Research at the University of Pittsburgh, the US Public Health Service, The US Department of Agriculture, the National Resources Planning Board, the Independent Petroleum Association of America, the Bureau of Mines of the US Department of the Interior, and the Library of the League of Nations in Geneva.

Finally, I wish to acknowledge gratefully the grant-in-aid which I received from the Institute of Social Research at Columbia University for the completion of the manuscript.

Preface addendum

As its title indicates, the book is a critique of the unplanned market economy; it is concerned primarily with the diagnosis of the defects of capitalism, and not with proposals of economic reform. Two reasons have militated against the inclusion of any practical suggestions of economic reform. First, the further the study advanced, the clearer it became that, apart from a general presumption in favor of government planning and national ownership of essential facilities and resources, the particular techniques of planning in different segments of the economy are likely to vary considerably. A detailed presentation of practical proposals of reform after each chapter would not only have unduly enlarged the scope of the study, but would have destroyed the continuity of the argument. Second, any suggestion of economic reform raises the question of liberty and the relationship of the individual to society, which no adequate discussion of economic planning can overlook. Since an analysis of the role of the individual under conditions of economic planning would have exceeded the scope of the present study, and because it is my intention to deal with this question in a special study at a later date, the idea of advancing specific proposals of reform was abandoned altogether. To recognize that economic planning once more raises the problem of the relationship between the individual and society does not mean that we share the fears of the prophets of gloom who hold that planning is incompatible with democracy and is of necessity the road to serfdom. It is significant to note that similar fears were also expressed by the early opponents of democracy who were convinced, as Tocqueville put it, that equality was "the road which seems to lead to inevitable servitude."[3] What these opponents of economic change forget is the fact that eighteenth and nineteenth century notions of economic liberty have already lost much of their meaning under monopoly capitalism, and that their insistence upon unlimited economic freedom (as for example in wartime) may be carried to a point where it becomes destructive to society itself.

Chapter 1: the inadequacy of modern economic analysis

Ever since Adam Smith's work established economics as a separate and distinct discipline, many economists have fought the limited nature of most economic analysis, and have tried to broaden the scope of economic investigation. The vague economic romanticism of Adam Muller and his modern followers; Friedrich List's doctrine of "productive forces"; the writings of both the "utopian" and "scientific" socialists; the early historical school in Germany; the "organic" and socio-ethical approaches to economics of such writers as A.E.F. Schäffle, John Ruskin, J.A. Hobson, and H.G. Hawtrey; to a certain extent even the "welfare economics" of the Cambridge school and its forerunner Henry Sidgewick; more recently, the institutional approach in the United States; and, above all, J.M. Clark's contribution to "social economics" are all attempts to carry the scope of economic investigations beyond the traditional analysis of economic phenomena solely in terms of market prices.

The great majority of economists, however, continue to approach the study of the economic process in essentially the same "classical" way which provoked the development of the various dissident types of thought mentioned above. Instead of interpreting critically and impartially the functioning of the present economic system, modern economic theory has been mostly satisfied, as J.M. Clark pointed out more than 20 years ago, with a "search for levels of equilibrium," and "hardly dares press beyond those processes that can be shown to tend toward equilibrium [...] of the exchange value sort."[4] This characterization of modern economic theory holds true even today, after we have seen the development of a theory of monopolistic competition which likewise runs essentially in terms of the traditional equilibrium approach in terms of market prices. In particular, economists have continued to recognize as truly economic ends only those which are recorded in the market, and to measure the relative importance of both ends and means solely in terms of exchange values.

In order to better set forth the criticism that is to be advanced against this widely accepted method of theoretical economic analysis, it will be useful to summarize briefly its most essential characteristics.

Starting with the analysis of market demand, economic theory first explains how the individual consumer reaches a position of individual equilibrium by spending his money in such a way as to satisfy his wants in the order of their relative intensity. In other words, by purchasing goods and services which have the comparatively greatest want-satisfying power, the consumer is supposed to maximize the satisfaction obtainable from his limited money resources at prevailing market prices. He achieves the optimum distribution of his disposable means at the point where no unit of his income would yield a higher utility if used for the purchase of another commodity; i.e., the individual equilibrium is defined as the position where the marginal utility of all goods and services bought reaches equality.

Proceeding further in its analysis of the functioning of our economy, modern economic theory explains how the productive process adapts itself to the effective demand of the individual consumer. In their search for maximum profits, producers, it is said, tend to devote their energies and capital resources to the production of those goods and services which are expected to yield the relatively highest returns. While thus endeavoring to make the best possible use of our limited resources, each producer will tend to expand production to the point beyond which any further increase ceases to be profitable. This equilibrium and optimum position of the individual firm is reached when marginal costs equal marginal returns.

Furthermore, in combining different factors of production, entrepreneurs are supposed to substitute factors yielding relatively higher returns for factors of production which, in proportion to their cost, yield smaller ones. In other words, as long as units of our resources yield relatively higher (monetary) returns in one line of production than in another, producers tend to transfer them to the more "productive" use. A general equilibrium (and optimum) position for the whole economy is reached at the point where the marginal productivity of all factors of production is equal.

The foregoing analysis of the productive process contains already the elements of the modern theory of distribution. Indeed, the same forces which were said to account for the transfer of productive factors to those uses in which they yield the highest relative returns are held responsible for the fact that each factor tends to receive a remuneration measured by its marginal productivity, in terms of market prices. For as long as it receives less, excessive profits would be made, and the subsequent increase in demand for the factor would raise its prices. This rise in price, however, could not go substantially beyond an amount measured by the marginal productivity of the factor, because the resulting losses would cause the demand, and concomitantly the price, of the factor of production to go down.

It cannot be emphasized too strongly that the foregoing analysis and interpretation of the economic process is based largely on the assumption of the "economic man" and the rationality of his conduct. As consumers, we are assumed to desire and be able to make the best possible use of our disposable income; as producers, economic theory likewise assumes us to be motivated by the desire to maximize profits, and to achieve the "optimum" allocation of available resources. It is, therefore, not astonishing to find that this assumption has always been, and still is, the object of suspicion and objections on the part of all critics of classical and modern economics. Most of these objections are, however, based upon a misconception of the general nature of all theoretical analysis. In particular, it is frequently overlooked that the analysis of a complex reality would be impossible without artificially reducing it to greater simplicity through the use of simplifying assumptions, and by studying different aspects of a given problem in isolation from one another. In other words, "general economics [...] must simplify in order to interpret; otherwise its description will be just as unwieldy and baffling as the world itself."[5]

However, this is not to say that all objections to the assumption of rational human conduct can be dismissed as misconceptions of the simplifying nature of general economic analysis. There are a number of arguments, especially those directed against the assumed rationality of the individual consumer, which deserve a careful reexamination, especially in view of the evidence advanced by recent studies on consumption, nutrition, and choice manipulation (advertising, etc.). To undertake such a reconsideration of the assumption of rational human conduct will be the first step in our approach to social economics.

As regards the traditional interpretation of the entrepreneurs' response to effective market demand, it has been pointed out, among other objections, that entrepreneurs often are unaware of the profitability prevailing in various branches of the economy; that their shifting of capital and human resources from enterprises with relatively lower returns to more profitable industries is seriously impeded by the costs of change, inertia, tradition, and other considerations foreign to a strictly economic conduct. However, these objections against the traditional equilibrium analysis again overlook the simplifying nature of all theoretical reasoning. It is undoubtedly true that numerous obstacles prevent a competitively organized economy from ever reaching that position where the marginal productivity of every unit of our resources could not be increased further. But does this fact invalidate the general thesis that entrepreneurs, in their search for maximum profits, tend to devote their capital and energies to those productive processes which yield relatively the highest return? Certainly not, if we realize that, in this instance, economic theory points to general tendencies only, and seeks to explain the mechanism through which the productive process adapts itself to changes of individual preferences, as expressed in market demand.

There are, however, much more serious objections to the traditional analysis of the productive process, and its adjustment to changing conditions. We think first of all those cases in which supply (and production) respond only slowly, if at all, to falling prices. For instance, declining wages often not only fail to cause a reduction, but actually lead to an increase, in the supply of labor in all those cases where laborers seek to maintain their total wage income while wage rates are declining.[6] Similar conditions characterize the supply of farm products, as well as production in all those industries in which fixed costs form a substantial part of the total costs of production. Still more important is the case of loanable funds, the supply of which seems to be determined much more by other factors than the price that has to be paid for their use. As a result, declining interest rates often fail to show the equilibrating effects on the supply of, and demand for, loanable funds that economic theory attributes to all prices. It is perhaps no accident that these cases have not been thoroughly explored by an economic theory which, in its "search for levels of equilibrium," tends to neglect the analysis of those aspects of economic life which fail to exhibit equilibriating tendencies.

However, the most fundamental objection to modern economic theory must be raised against its interpretation of general equilibrium conditions (in terms of market prices) as the optimum solution to the economic problem for the community as a whole. This identification of the equilibrium position with the "social optimum"—a theoretical conclusion which permeates both classical and modern economics—would be correct only if, on the one hand, market prices expressed in any significant way the total social returns of economic activities, and, on the other, if private costs actually measured the total social costs of production. Under such conditions, private returns might indeed be accepted as a significant measure of the "worthwhileness" of production, and the entrepreneur who varied production according to the profitability thereof would not only maximize his private income but, at the same time, make for the optimum use of the available factors of production. In other words, he would direct the society's limited resources into those productive channels where they had the relatively greatest want satisfying power.

Actually, however, there is no basis for the economists' acceptance of product prices as a measure of the total social returns of economic activities, and their identification of private costs with the total social costs of production. First of all, it should be clear that private costs fail to measure the total social costs of production whenever productive processes cause social damages and economic losses which are not fully reflected in the cost reductions of private business enterprise. In order to illustrate this point, we need only refer to such conditions as soil erosion, soil depletion, floods, deforestation, the exhaustion of irreplaceable resources, water and air pollution, occupational diseases, and damages to persons in general. Other social losses of a similar nature are those resulting from economic fluctuations, technological unemployment, unused productive capacities, and all those wasteful effects which follow from the existence of monopolistic elements in the economy (namely, the restriction of output, high prices, price rigidities, commercial manipulation of choice, non-exploitation of patent rights, etc.). The economic and social losses resulting from these harmful consequences of private economic activities and business practices are costs of production in fundamentally the same sense as the many outlays recorded in the cost accounts of business enterprise. To the extent to which these losses are not charged against, and are not fully borne, by those industries which are responsible for their emergence (i.e., in so far as these losses are shifted to other persons or the community) private outlays fall short of the total social costs of producing the goods and services we consume. Part II of our investigation undertakes to reveal the extent of these social losses, and analyzes their broader economic implications. The second reason why it is misleading, and indeed wrong, to interpret general equilibrium conditions in terms of market prices as conducive to the optimum solution of the economic problem for the community as a whole is to be found in the fact that product prices fail to measure the total social returns of production, because they reflect neither certain "inappropriable" (i.e., non-exchangeable) utilities, nor certain "concealed disutilities" of goods and services produced. As a result, private returns measured in terms of market prices often exceed, and sometimes fall short of, the total social returns of economic activities. To demonstrate the significance of such divergences between private and social returns, and to reveal both the possibility and extent of "inappropriable utilities" on the one hand, and the existence of "concealed disutilities" on the other, is the object of the third part of our study.

If the foregoing objections against the traditional interpretation of the economic process can be proved correct, the theory of distribution based thereon is in need of revision as well. For, if consumers are unable to make the best possible use of their income resources, some goods will command higher and some goods lower prices than they would if consumers were less arbitrary in their choices. Consequently, some factors of production (namely those used in producing goods for which the demand is lower than it would be if consumers made better use of their income) receive a greater remuneration than they would under conditions where consumers made the best use of their resources. Likewise, if market prices are no measure of the total social returns of productive activities, then, obviously a distribution of the total product in accordance with marginal productivity (in terms of market prices) is bound to result in a highly arbitrary remuneration of the owners of the various factors of production. In other words, while some factors receive less than they contribute to the total social returns, other factors are likely to receive more than they add to the social product.

In short then, our main objections to modern economic theory may be summarized by the following four propositions:

1   The assumption of the economic man and the rationality of his conduct is untenable, at least as far as the individual consumer is concerned.
2   Private costs do not measure the total social costs of production.
3   Private returns do not reflect the total social returns of productive activities.
4   Prices of the factors of production, and consequently the monetary incomes of their owners, are no measure of their actual contribution to the social product.

If these propositions are typically correct—that is, if they are not merely based upon generalizations deduced from exceptional cases—the whole system of theoretical conclusions as to the basic rationality of the market economy is, at the very least, seriously undermined. For, if consumers are unable to make the best use of their monetary incomes; if private costs do not measure the total social costs of production; and, finally, if product prices fail to measure the total social returns of productive activities, the utilization of limited resources orientated by market prices will obviously be anything but conducive to the optimum solution of the economic problem. The next logical step in our analysis would be to show that, in order to make the best use of limited resources, man must go beyond the stage of competitive production guided by profitability in terms of market prices, and organize the economic process in such a way as to assure a more rational utilization of scarce means for the gratification of competing human wants.

The present investigation, however, is confined to the examination of the first three propositions listed above, reserving the examination of the problem of "social distribution" raised in the fourth proposition to a study at a later date, when all aspects of "social returns" and "social costs" have been sufficiently explored. The concluding section of our analysis presents the practical inferences which are necessarily drawn from our deductions, and discusses finally their implications for the economics of government and public finance.

Notes

1 This is the title of the project outline (3.1) which along with the various versions of the prefaces (3.2 and 3.3.) is estimated to have been written between 1939–1944.
2 *Planwirtschaft und Aussenhandel*, Librarie de l'Université, Geneva, 1936.
3 The reference for this quotation is missing and the exact quote by Tocqueville reads "the road that seems to lead men to inevitable servitude." Cf. Alexis de Tocqueville, *Democracy in America*, Book 4, Chapter 7, available online at www.marxists.org/reference/archive/de-tocqueville/democracy-america/ch43.htm1831 (accessed August 30, 2014).
4 J.M. Clark, *Economics and Modern Psychology*, reprinted from the *Journal of Political Economy*, Vol. 26 (1918) in "Preface to Social Economics," p. 93.
5 J.M. Clark, *Socializing Economics*, in "Preface to Social Economics," p. 10.
6 For a stimulating discussion of this and other cases in which the equilibrating effects of market prices do not necessarily materialize, at least not in the short run, see L.D. Fraser, *Economic Thought and Language*, 1937, Ch. X ("Supply and Demand").

4 Social costs of free enterprise[1]

Social costs are anything but new phenomena. They have plagued our economic system ever since its inception, and individual economists have from time to time called attention to their occurrence and their magnitude. Nor is it altogether certain that other economic systems will do away automatically with social costs, although there is a presumption that economic planning can minimize the social costs of production more easily than a system of unregulated competition—provided that the planners are disposed to do so. In any event, the present article deals with the social costs which are likely to arise under conditions of free and unregulated private enterprise.

Before entering upon a detailed discussion of the most significant cases of social costs, it is important to point out that an increasing proportion of public policy in liberal democratic societies is designed to prevent and repair various social losses, which seem to be implicit in the competitive structure of our economic life. In fact, the need for such remedial action, and the adoption of preventive measures, can be considered the most convincing evidence of the occurrence of social costs in the competitive market economy. However, the fact remains that many of the preventive measures adopted so far have remained highly inadequate, and have neither prevented nor eliminated the shifting of substantial costs by producers to other or persons, or to the community as a whole.

Social costs may arise in different ways. Some clearly have their origin in individual industries, and can be traced to specific productive processes and business practices. Other social costs arise in the operation of the competitive system, within a given framework of generally-accepted institutions and government policies. In some cases, the social costs of production are felt immediately; in other instances, the ill effects of private production remain hidden for considerable periods of time, so that the injured persons do not become immediately aware of their losses. Furthermore, certain social losses affect only a limited group, whereas others may be felt by all members of society. Indeed, the actual damages caused by private productive activities may be distributed over so many persons that any one of them may individually sustain only a relatively small loss. Although aware of his losses, the individual may not consider it worthwhile to take defensive action against the particular industrial concern responsible for his losses. In short, the term "social costs" refers to all those harmful consequences and damages which third persons or the community sustains as a result of productive processes, and for which private entrepreneurs are not held accountable. These social losses may be reflected in damages to human health; they may find their expression in the destruction or deterioration of property values and the premature depletion of natural wealth; or they may be evidenced in an impairment of less tangible values.

The most generally recognized, but certainly not the only, cause of social costs is the impairment of the physical and mental health of workers in the course of private production. Such impairment may take the form of work injuries, occupational diseases, and the manifold negative effects of woman and child labor. In its economic implications, such impairment of physical and mental health does not differ from the deterioration of non-human durable factors such as machines, buildings, etc. And yet, whereas the depreciation of the latter tends to be translated into monetary costs by means of depreciation charges, the impairment of the human factor remains largely unaccounted for in private costs under conditions of free enterprise.

The total number of work injuries exceeded two million in 1947, of which approximately 20,000 were fatalities and total disabilities, and 100,000 were permanently partially disabled. It may be argued that workmen's compensation laws tend to translate the monetary losses (loss of wages, medical expenses, etc.) incident upon work injuries into private costs by way of insurance premiums paid by the entrepreneur, and hence that there is no point in speaking of social costs. Such reasoning, however, overlooks first that only slightly more than 50 percent of the nation's working force is covered by workmen's compensation acts; second, that 44 percent of all temporary injuries are barred from any compensation because of waiting periods; and third, that all compensation acts place far-reaching limitations on compensation payments, and hence tend to provide only a highly inadequate indemnification for the impaired worker or his dependents. Taking these facts into consideration, a recent sample study for the state of Massachusetts (which has a relatively progressive Workmen's Compensation Act) shows that considerably more than half of the total wage loss caused by work injuries was borne by the injured worker and his family. To the extent, therefore, that the impairment of the health of workers fails to be compensated fully, it may be said that private enterprise is being subsidized by the men and women who make up the labor force. While depreciation charges help to keep intact the value of the original capital equipment, the capital value of the human factor of production is not being adequately accounted for in modern industrial society, despite the extension of protective labor legislation.

If we accept the thesis that the human factor of production is subject to depreciation by work injuries and occupational diseases, it is not difficult to see that labor also entails certain fixed costs for its maintenance and "production." Workers and their families must eat, they must be clothed and sheltered, and new employees must be provided with the necessary training. Whether the laborer is employed or not, these costs must be met. Otherwise, not only the individual but also our productive system would suffer losses, in the form of a deterioration of our working power. These costs, then, are overhead costs, in an even more definite sense than the fixed charges on financial debts and capital equipment. And yet, in the absence of an annual wage or salary system, the overhead costs of labor are translated into variable costs which will be paid only as long as the laborer is employed. Consequently, it becomes possible for the entrepreneur to disregard the fixed costs of labor completely as soon as a decline of business sets in. In fact, such a decline will be met most easily by a dismissal of workers—a procedure which, in view of the legally fixed charges on most capital outlays, is not only the easiest, but practically the only, method of reducing costs. Hence, in times of depression, the fixed costs of labor tend to be disregarded and shifted to the laborers or the community. Unemployment insurance may cover these costs partially, and only for a limited time. Nor is this disregard of the fixed costs of labor confined to periods of contracting business activity. It is present whenever the entrepreneur decides on the introduction of new machines replacing labor and rendering obsolete the capital equipment of competitors. The fixed costs of others are not considered, and yet it stands to reason that these fixed charges are no less real simply because they tend to be borne by others.

The social costs of unemployment and idle plants can best he expressed in terms of the potential real income lost as a result of the decline in output and employment. In 1939, the National Resources Committee estimated that the loss of national income caused by the depression years of 1929 to 1937 amounted to over 200 billion dollars.

> The significance of this figure [...] is hard to grasp, but some idea can be obtained by considering what 200 billion dollars would mean in terms of concrete goods. If all the idle men and machines could have been employed in making houses, the extra income would have been enough to provide a new $6,000 house [1939] for every family in the country. If, instead, the lost income had been used to build railroads, the entire railroad system of the country could have been scrapped and rebuilt at least five times over. Of such is the magnitude of the depression loss in income through failure to use available resources. It means a lower standard of living for practically every group in the community.

Social costs also arise in the competitive utilization and exploitation of natural resources; they may find their expression either in the gradual destruction of soil fertility, forests, wildlife, etc., or in the premature depletion of exhaustible energy and mineral resources. The destruction of natural wealth is most easily understood in the case of wildlife. Here the resource is not privately owned and, therefore, tends to become a matter of indifference for each producer drawing upon it. Even if the individual hunter or fisherman should desire to maintain the common capital asset intact, he cannot be expected to do so if cost-price conditions make it profitable for his competitors to intensify production to the point where their more efficient method of hunting and fishing interferes with the normal reproduction of the resources.

A close analogy to this destruction of various types of wildlife is found in the premature depletion of oil resources in a competitive economy. The analogy between the two cases is due primarily to the "migratory" character of wildlife and oil, and the fact that private property rights are not established prior to their capture. Just as the game belongs to the hunter who killed it, the oil belongs to the owner of the oil well from which it is produced, regardless of whether or not it migrated from a neighbor's land. Consequently, whenever a new pool is discovered under conditions where the surface land is scattered among several owners, each operator tends to drain the field before the oil migrates and is produced through a neighboring well. Even if an individual owner might prefer to postpone production in anticipation of higher prices in the future, he is unlikely to do so, because any postponement of production benefits only the competitor and may mean, as far as he is concerned, the loss of the resource altogether.

It need not be emphasized that an industry producing under such conditions is likely to suffer periodically from over-production. The general race to drain newly discovered oil fields as rapidly as possible will tend to cause oil prices to be lower than they would be if a more orderly program of production were followed. Low prices, instead of causing production from existing wells to contract, in turn accelerate the premature depletion of oil resources. Not only do they force the individual producer to make use of inferior and less efficient equipment, as a result of which a greater proportion of the reserves will ultimately remain underground, but even more important, they induce the use of exhaustible and relatively scarce resources for purposes for which other non-exhaustible materials would have been used if the price of oil had been higher. In other words, the tendency toward depletion generated by the competitive process becomes cumulative and self-sustaining.

The fact that the social losses resulting from the premature exhaustion of valuable resources are borne partly by future generations does not make them less real and less important. The fact of the matter is that, so far, all potential new sources of energy and substitutes can be produced only at considerably higher costs. It is true, then, that the extent of the social losses resulting from the premature exhaustion of resources cannot be determined with any reasonable degree of accuracy.

Above all, it is impossible to say definitely how long present reserves of various natural resources will last. For, obviously, their life expectancy is dependent upon such unpredictable factors as new discoveries of reserves, improvements in their recovery and use, the development of substitutes, and future demand. Furthermore, it is impossible to estimate the economic value which future generations may attribute to the resources which are lost as a result of the premature depletion of reserves by the present generation. Nevertheless, this impossibility to predict when the point of complete exhaustion of irreplaceable resources will be reached, and the difficulty to estimate the magnitude of the economic losses sustained by future generations, should not becloud the fundamental fact that losses do arise from the premature depletion of natural wealth. For, even before we reach the point of complete exhaustion of resources, their recovery will become increasingly costly. Drilling and mining will have to shift to deposits with leaner and leaner contents, and will have to be undertaken at greater depth and in more and more inaccessible regions As a result, future generations will be able to secure these resources only at increasing costs. In other words, they will be able to produce their goods and services only at higher prices—at least if their industrial civilization should be based upon essentially the same resources and raw materials as those upon which our present one rests.

In short, the competitive desire to maximize profits defeats the social objective of making the most economical use of these exhaustible resources. It is true that what constitutes "the most economical use" of irreplaceable resources always implies a difficult comparison of the potential future utilities to be derived from such resources, and the sacrifices involved in forgoing their present use. But the difficulty involved in such a comparison is no satisfactory excuse for the fact that the competitive process tends to exploit the capital assets represented by natural wealth at an accelerated rate, and with almost complete disregard for their depletion.

Still another case of social costs arising in the course of private exploitation of natural wealth is found in soil erosion and depletion, as well as in the destruction of forest resources. Unlike wildlife and petroleum, land and forest resources are neither "migratory" in character, nor is there any difficulty in establishing clear-cut ownership rights with respect to any particular acre of farm or forest land. What is more, the farm is usually not merely a factor of production —i.e., a capital asset— it is the home of the farmer. In addition, the fertility of the farmer's land is the basis of his prosperity. The question, therefore, is whether or not it is likely that the farmer (or the owner of forest land) will do everything in his power to maintain the soil's fertility (and the forest's productivity). Will he not, in his own interest, avoid all destructive methods of cultivation which would not only depreciate the value of his land, but also disrupt the basis of his existence? The answer is—not necessarily. For instance, as long as returns exceed costs, it might simply be profitable to continue soil-depleting methods of cultivation. In other cases, the diminishing physical productivity of the land (resulting from its intensive utilization) might be obscured by constant, or even increasing, monetary returns, under conditions of rising prices of farm products in times of increasing demand of a rapidly growing population. And even if the farmer realizes that he is gradually destroying the soil, he is not likely to apply soil-conserving methods of cultivation as long as worn-out land can be abandoned for virgin soils. Under these conditions—which prevailed in America until recently—the utilization of the land, though profitable for the individual farmer, tends to be accompanied by a gradual deterioration of soil fertility. Other factors making for over-intensive and destructive methods of land utilization are excessively high valuations of land and high property taxes. In both cases, the farmer may be forced to use the land so intensively as to gradually deplete its fertility. Likewise, farm prices may be so low as to prohibit the application of soil-conserving methods of cultivation.

Private forestry and lumber operations provide another case in point. The desire of private owners of forest land to realize a maximum income from their initial investment makes for keen competition between different timber-producing regions, and low prices which not only stimulate the demand for lumber, but may, at the same time, induce the cutting of the better trees only. Or with declining returns, it may become too costly for the private operator to apply such minimal conservational practices as selective logging and tree renewal, without which forest resources deteriorate and may, under certain conditions, become fire hazards.

The most characteristic feature of the social costs that arise in the course of agricultural production and forestry is, however, the fact that they go far beyond the loss of the capital value of the individual site. Whereas the social losses involved in the destruction of wildlife and the premature depletion of energy resources are limited to, and in a sense measured by, the value of the capital asset which they represent, soil-depleting methods of cultivation and forest depletion may have consequences which exceed in importance those involved in the loss of soil fertility and forest resources. We refer in particular to such damages as erosion, floods, the silting of streams and reservoirs, the diminution of ground water stores, the pollution of rivers, the destruction of irrigation schemes, the harmful effects of dust storms, and the disappearance of wildlife.

It would carry us too far afield to trace the social costs of air and water pollution within the context of this article. Suffice it to say that the harmful consequences of the pollution of the atmosphere and the contamination of water by various kinds of untreated industrial waste materials are reflected in the destruction of property values, the impairment of human health, destruction of plant and animal life, and a decrease in crop production. Available estimates place the losses caused by smoke pollution alone at $500,000 (in pre-war dollars) for the country as a whole.

Turning to the social costs in the field of distribution, we cannot do more than raise the following questions: (1) What price, in terms of higher costs, does the community pay for the "luxury" of 100,000 retail outlets with sales of less than $30 per day? (2) What are the social costs of an annual rate of business failures of from 9.4 to 35.9 percent for different retail trade groups? (3) Granted that advertising not only manipulates demand but also increases the consumer's knowledge of existing alternatives, the question remains whether the increasing volume of advertising is not mainly of a manipulative kind, reflecting a steady increase of monopolistic elements (such as product differentiation) in modern industrial society. (4) To what extent have the high and increasing costs of advertising, and the high costs of distribution in general, had the effect of merely offsetting the increasing productivity of manufacturing? (5) Is it socially desirable that the costs of advertising should reach 35 percent of the costs of distribution and 14 percent of the net value of sales for particular commodities?

There are other social costs, such as certain negative effects of monopolistic practices; the diseconomies of the present system of transportation; the duplication of research facilities, each surrounded by secrecy; the retardation of some lines of scientific research conducted with a one-sided emphasis on the immediate prospects of profitable application; and the neglect of social benefits in the utilization of urban land and the location of industrial production. While the significance of these losses cannot be overestimated, a detailed discussion of these diseconomies would require too many qualifications which cannot be presented within the scope of the present article.

Of course, we may refuse to recognize the existence of social costs. We may act as if entrepreneurial outlays are accurate measures of the total actual costs of production. But we cannot hope to avoid paying for these costs in one form or another, as long as we do not establish a more comprehensive system of social-cost accounting. In many instances, the systematic application and extension of the principle of social insurance could be used to translate the social costs of production into insurance premiums, and thus into monetary entrepreneurial costs. If properly set up and administered, this method would have the further advantage of providing an incentive for the private producer to prevent the occurrence of social losses, and thus to reduce their magnitude. If, as a result, it should become evident that some enterprises cannot absorb their total cost of production, it would be clear that they are deficit enterprises which owe their past existence and prosperity to their subsidization by society. It can then be decided whether such subsidies are worthwhile, and hence should be continued out of public funds. In other instances, more specific social controls and prohibitions may be required to prevent and minimize social costs. In still other cases, it may turn out that a complete reorganization of the industry along the lines of public ownership may be the only way of taking into account the social costs of production.

Whatever practical solution we may wish to adopt, however, the phenomena of social costs ultimately call for a comprehensive system of social economic accounting which takes into consideration not only the social costs, but also the social returns, of productive activities—namely those costs and utilities which so far have remained outside the competitive cost-price calculus. Only by weighing *total* costs and *total* returns can we hope to appraise in a meaningful manner the actual performance and efficiency of our economy. Economic analysis seems to be of limited aid in such an undertaking because of its traditional preoccupation with the analysis of exchange value. However, with the growth of the public economy and the increasing importance of public expenditures and investments, it has already become evident that economics must supplement its study of market price with a study of social value (in the sense of value-to-society), in order to arrive at a full and objective understanding of modern economic life. Indeed, by including social costs, social returns, and social value within the range of its analysis, economic science would finally become "political economy" in a deeper and broader sense than even the classical economists conceived of the term. In fact, economic science could then truly be said to deal with the problem of social economy, and would thus at last prove its status as a system of knowledge concerned with the study of the nature and causes of the wealth of nations.

Note

1 A handwritten note on the manuscript indicates that this article was either prepared for, submitted to or published by Labor and Nation in 1950.

5 Social returns

A critical analysis of the social performance of the unplanned market economy[1]

Table of Content[2]

Collective needs and social returns

The growth of collective needs and the nature of social goals

Like individual wants, collective needs are shaped by a complex combination of
rational and emotional factors. New experiences tend to create the conditions for
the development of new collective needs; for example, the devastating effects of
certain contagious diseases during the Middle Ages, and the realization that the
spread of these diseases could be averted only by sustained and compulsory
action, made protection against epidemics a matter of public responsibility.
Therefore, certain elementary measures of public health became part of the
generally-accepted set of common interests—in other words, the object of a
genuine collective need.[3]

The nineteenth and twentieth centuries have seen a further extension of
common responsibilities and collective needs. This was especially evident in
Soviet Russia, where the collectivization of the means of production was accompanied by an equally far-reaching collectivization of "ends" and "objectives."
There can be no doubt, for example, that education, social security, and the
maintenance of a degree of economic independence and national self-sufficiency
were genuine collective needs and common responsibilities in Soviet Russia, but
they are by no means confined to the type of socialist civilization found in the

USSR; in fact, a similar collectivization of ends and objectives can be observed in practically all advanced countries. Such collectivization is seen primarily in the steady expansion of the public economy at the expense of private economic activity. This tendency, which Adolf Wagner has designated a "law," of increasing public and state activities,[4] is due to the increasing complexity of modern production processes, the growing division of labor, depressions, and international security, among other factors. The expansion of the public economy also reflects the increase in political influence of a great number of relatively poor people in democratic societies, especially in the past 50 years. Even without a more thorough analysis of this development, it is obvious that the increase in political influence and consciousness of the working classes in modern capitalist societies has been accompanied by a growing recognition of common responsibility to the weaker members of society, as well as to a fuller realization of the social returns resulting from the protection of all members of society against the socially harmful effects of competition. It is thus clear that the number of collective needs is not an eternally fixed one. Just as individual wants are unlimited and subject to change and expansion, the number of collective needs is also indefinite. Whether or not a particular end is regarded as a collective need at any given time is, in the last analysis, a matter of political practice. Generally speaking, it may be said that a particular objective has become a genuine collective need if public authorities consistently assume responsibility for it, and if its gratification is accepted as a first charge on the resources of the public economy.

In addition to these collective needs, there exist in every advanced society a number of common interests of a less tangible and material nature. Indeed,

> in any society, there is not only a clash of various interests but also a wide sphere of common interests, and there are many achievements benefiting an overwhelming majority of the people which will be contested only by small groups representing social interests.[5]

Foremost among these common interests are those of a political-national character. "In every society sufficiently well integrated to deserve the name of a nation, there is a common conception ill-defined and partly irrational, but deeply felt of what constitutes the 'vital interests' of the nation."[6] In addition to the common conceptions of vital interests, there is also considerable area of agreement on certain ethical and humanitarian ideals. These ideals, although rarely based on a consensus of opinion, nevertheless give expression to the honest aspirations of large segments of the community, and as such, reflect some degree of basic agreement on ultimate values. These are the common political-national or ethical-humanitarian interests we refer to as social or common goals.

In assessing the economic implications of these common goals, it is important to realize the difficulties inherent in such a discussion. Social goals are easily exploited by both ruling *and* minority groups for the promotion of their political aims and personal interests. In recent years, the art of identifying sectional interests with alleged national objectives has been greatly refined through the development of new methods of manipulating mass emotion, until it appears as if "the whole world has become a gigantic fancy-dress ball of masquerading ideologies which leaves to the economist and sociologist the unpleasant task of [...] exposing the usually disappointing reality behind it."[7] Even greater difficulties arise from the "ethical relativity" characteristic of most modern discussions of social and ethical goals. Indeed, as F.D. Graham puts it, "much has been written of good and evil and much has been disputed until, in a hopeless mental fog, we wander in the wilderness of ethical relativity where there is no light, no hope, no standard."[8] In practice, social goals are also contradictory, inconsistent, and incompatible with each other; and yet it cannot be denied that there is a "disquieting logical possibility that the simultaneous collective pursuit of incompatible 'ends' may be actually better, on the whole (from the standpoint of those who do possess some concrete conception of the 'given end') than no collective action at all."[9] For this reason, and because of the role social goals have played and are likely to continue to play in the formulation of economic policy, they must be included in economic investigations, no matter how great the difficulties to be encountered and how unpleasant their discussion may be to the economist. In the following chapter, it will be shown that collective needs and social goals have played an important role in the formulation of past international economic policies, and are bound to play one as well in the future.

In summary, it must be recognized that the most typical social returns arise in connection with the gratification of collective needs. These needs come into existence whenever people begin to live together in larger communities, and are common exigencies which transcend the sphere of the individual. Collective needs, like individual wants, are not fixed; they are shaped by new experience, and their range is likely to grow with the advance and steadily growing complexity of civilization. The gratification of collective needs yields inappropriable social utilities, which tend to diffuse themselves throughout society, and which cannot be separated into advantages and benefits to individuals or groups. The general recognition of this fact makes it necessary, at least in political and economic practice, to discuss social returns in greater detail.

The importance of social returns in the formulation of international policies

Nowhere has the gap between economic theory and practice been more pronounced than in the field of international economic relations. While professional economists preached the doctrine of free trade and experts at international economic conferences unanimously endorsed the abolition of all trade and exchange controls, statesmen placed one obstacle after another in the path of the free flow of commodities and capital between their countries and the rest of the world. This seemingly paradoxical situation has done more than anything else to discredit economic science in the eyes of the public. How are we to account for such an open break between economic theory and practice? The fundamental answer appears to be that, in advocating a policy of free trade, traditional economic theory fails to account sufficiently for the social returns responsible governments cannot afford to neglect when formulating their international economic policies. The nature of these social returns will be better understood in the context of a brief analysis of the origins and basic suppositions of the classical argument for free trade.

The origins and basic presuppositions of the doctrine of free trade

The doctrine of free trade is best understood by first understanding its origins. Its early purpose was eminently practical and political: namely to disprove the validity of mercantilist arguments in favor of import and export policies designed to secure a favorable balance of trade. In opposition to this mercantilist doctrine, and in accordance with their general belief in a natural orderliness in economic affairs, the physiocrats and classical economists tried to demonstrate that the principles of a free division of labor were fully applicable to the field of international trade. Just as a policy of *laissez-faire* within the domestic economy could be relied upon to bring about the most efficient specialization, so would free international trade lead to an optimal division of labor and yield a maximum of output value with a minimum of input costs. The maintenance of a balance between total payments to and from foreign countries did not depend on the adoption of government controls, but could be left entirely to the operation of the monetary mechanism that has come to be known as the international gold standard.

Classical economists could thus cite seemingly reliable self-equilibriating tendencies in the balance of payments; an excess of payments made to foreigners over those received from abroad (as a result, for example, of an excess of imports over exports) would tend to increase the price of foreign currency. As soon as the rise in the foreign exchange rate exceeded the cost of transferring gold to the creditor country, the country with the unfavorable balance of payments would begin to ship gold, which would set into motion the self-equilibriating tendencies referred to above. By raising its bank rate, the debtor country would not only be able to attract short-term funds from abroad, but would also produce a contraction of long-term bank credit, thereby contributing to lower price levels at home. In the creditor country, the inflow of gold would have the opposite effects: a lower bank rate would make possible an increase in gold reserves, which in turn would lead to the transfer of short-term funds on the one hand, and to an expansion of bank credit on the other. The resulting higher price levels in the creditor country, and the decline of prices in the debtor country, are precisely the adjustments which would correct the imbalance of trade: importers in the country with an excess of imports over exports would find it less attractive to buy abroad in view of the higher prices there and the lower ones at home, while the country with the favorable balance of trade and the higher price levels caused by the inflow of gold would tend to import more and see its exports decline.

Considering that this international adjustment mechanism depends on policies favoring far-reaching variations in price levels, incomes, production, and perhaps employment, it may be wondered how it was possible to advocate and rely upon such a system. Did it not occur to the classical economists that governments might refuse to carry out the domestic policies required to make the gold standard effective? The answer is simply that the theories of free trade and the gold standard were formulated in the same manner as is usual in social and economic theory: what had developed over a period of many years was translated into an apparently coherent system of thought, in accordance with the prevailing social and political aspirations of its author. It was as if an inventor had built his invention *before* drawing up a plan for its construction.

> Observing how the relative values of different currencies became established over a period of time, observing how gold movements between countries were brought about and the effects of such movements, observing changes in interest rates, in purchasing power in prices and in costs—that occurred in different countries as they dealt with each other—analytical minds discovered in these matters what they considered basic and reliable tendencies. These they offered as an explanation of the conclusion to which they gave support—that without the intervention of governments the payments of each country to all others tended to be brought into balance with the payments received by that country.[10]

In endeavoring to disprove the validity of the doctrine of the favorable balance of trade, Hume, Smith, and Ricardo simply assumed that certain basic presuppositions of their theoretical reasoning would be vindicated by practice, which seemingly made it unnecessary even to raise the question of whether responsible governments would carry out the domestic policies required for the successful operation of the international monetary mechanism.

In addition to such explicit assumptions as a high degree of mobility of capital and labor, it would appear that the classical doctrine of free trade is based upon three additional and implicit assumptions; namely:

1   that the nations of the world have reached a more or less perfect union and that, in the absence of war, there is nothing to be gained by the efforts of less economically-advanced countries to achieve a more balanced economy than that which the system of international free trade seems to doom them;
2   that all productive resources, including labor, are used so fully that their utilization is not subject to pronounced fluctuations; and
3   that individual countries can be expected to endure in common whatever degree of economic instability occurs in some part of the world economic system.

None of these assumptions were ever stated explicitly, and indeed it took almost a century before it was fully realized that the apparently impressive system of theoretical arguments against any kind of restriction on foreign trade rested upon these tacit presuppositions.

The rest of this chapter attempts to demonstrate that, by tacitly basing their conclusions on these three presuppositions, the advocates of the doctrine of free trade ignored important features of socio-political reality. It will be seen that it is this fact that explains why governments have rejected the doctrine of free trade as a guiding principle for the formulation of international economic policies. In the course of this discussion, the objectives of various policies of economic protectionism will become clear, and with them the nature of social returns usually neglected by free trade.

Free trade and the neglect of the social returns of a balanced economy

The essence of the doctrine of free trade may be summarized as follows: Each nation serves its own interests, as well as those of the rest of the world, if it devotes its resources to the production of those commodities which it can produce at the lowest relative costs, and then employs those commodities as means for the acquisition of those goods which can be purchased more cheaply from other countries. In other words,

> just as individuals by purposing their own good, unconsciously compass the good of the whole community, so nations in serving themselves serve humanity. Universal free trade was justified on the ground that the maximum economic interest of each nation was identified with the maximum economic interest of the whole world.[11]

If a nation finds it cheaper to obtain its manufactured goods by making wine and exchanging it against British textiles than to produce its own cloth, it should continue to do so, regardless of any desire to develop its own industries and to reduce the degree of its dependence upon British manufactured goods in times of international conflict. Or to put it differently,

> if Russia or Italy, for example, were not strong enough to build up industries without the intervention of tariffs, then—the *laissez-faire* liberal would have argued—they should be content to import British and German manufactures and supply wheat and oranges to the British and German markets. If anyone had thereupon objected that this policy would condemn Russia and Italy to remain second-rate powers economically and militarily dependent on their neighbors, the *laissez-faire* liberal would have had to answer that this was the will of providence and that this was what the general harmony of interest demanded.[12]

It is significant that the anti-mercantilist doctrine of free trade was first challenged systematically not in England but in the United States and Germany—the two countries which were destined to become England's closest rivals in industrial development during the nineteenth and twentieth centuries. In the US, Alexander Hamilton hinted at some of the weaknesses of the free-trade doctrine in terms which indicate his awareness of the broader social returns usually neglected by free traders. Rejecting the ideas of those who believed that the people of the United States should continue to devote their energies to agriculture as in the past, Hamilton, as early as 1791, outlined the great advantages in wealth and productivity which the development of manufacturing in America would provide.

> Not only wealth but the independence and security of a country appear to be materially connected with the prosperity of manufacture. Every nation, with a view to these great objects, ought to endeavor to possess within itself all the essentials of national supply. These comprise the means of subsistence, habitation, clothing and defense. The possession of these is necessary to the perfection of the body politic; to the safety as well as to the welfare of society. The want of either is the want of an important organ of political life and motion; and in the various crises which await a state, it must severely feel the effects of any such deficiency. The extreme embarrassments of the United States during the late war from an incapacity of supplying themselves, are still matter of keen recollection; a future war might be expected again to exemplify the mischiefs and dangers of a situation to which that incapacity is still, in too great a degree, applicable, unless changed by timely and vigorous exertion.[13]

In Germany, it was Friedrich List who, strongly influenced by his experiences in America and his knowledge of industrial conditions in England, produced the first systematic refutation of what he called the cosmopolitan doctrine of free trade. List's argument in favor of protective tariffs, particularly his elaboration of the mercantilistic doctrine of "productive forces," is based upon a definite concept of social returns; that is, of utilities which tend to accrue to society as a whole. The social returns List had in mind in advocating protective tariffs for countries which had not yet reached the same degree of industrial development as early-nineteenth-century England are those which a nation derives from greater security and political independence, as well as the attainment of a higher level of civilization. The fundamental difference between List and the classical school is that the former was willing to include in his speculations the broader political implications of economic policy, which the followers of Adam Smith were inclined to ignore as "non-economic." This key difference must be kept in mind when evaluating List's contribution to the doctrine of social returns.

The cornerstone of List's system of political economy, then, is his political realism, specifically his realization that the existence of sovereign nations is little more than a precarious and temporary solution to the problem of maintaining peace. This is not to say that List rejects the pacifist aspirations of the liberal economist; on the contrary, all nations would attain their ends to a much greater extent if they were united by the rule of law, perpetual peace and free intercourse [...]. But at present the union of nations [...] is still very imperfect since it can be shattered, or at least weakened, by way, or by the selfish action of individual nations. By war a nation can be robbed of its independence, property, freedom, laws and constitution, its national character, and, still worse, of the culture and well-being to which it has attained. It can, in a word, be reduced to a state of servitude.[14]

According to List, it is precisely these facts which classical economic theory ignores when it bases its theoretical arguments in favor of free trade on the "cosmopolitical dream" that the perfect union among nations has already been realized.

It does not understand the needs of the present and the meaning of nationality— in fact, it ignores national existence, and with it the principle of national independence. In its exclusive cosmopolitanism, it considers mankind only as a whole, and the welfare of the whole race; not caring for the nation or national welfare, it shudders at the teachings of politics, and condemns theory and practice as mere worthless routine.[15]

The practical implications of these considerations are not the same for all countries. For England, which reached the most advanced stage of industrial development in the early and middle nineteenth century, it was not only economically advantageous but politically expedient to pursue a policy of free trade, since it enabled England to enjoy all the benefits of the international division of labor while also perpetuating its industrial and economic supremacy in the world. The situation is different, however, for countries which, for political and historical reasons, have not been able to develop their wealth-producing powers. These so-called "productive forces" are the real causes of wealth.

A person may possess wealth, i.e., exchangeable value; if, however, he does not possess the power of producing objects of more value than he consumes, he will become poorer. A person may be poor; if he, however, possesses the power of producing a larger amount of valuable articles than he consumes, he becomes rich. The power of producing wealth is therefore infinitely more important than wealth itself; it insures not only the possession and the increase of what has been gained, but also the replacement of what has been lost. This is still more the case with entire nations [...] than with private individuals.[16]

These powers to produce, especially the "manufacturing powers," are thus a prerequisite not merely of general prosperity but also of all higher levels of civilization. For

in a purely agricultural nation, even when it enjoys free trade with manufacturing and commercial nations, a great part of its productive powers and

natural resources lie idle and unused. Its intellectual and political development and its powers of defense are hampered. [...] All its prosperity, so
far as it results from international trade, can be interrupted, injured, or
ruined by foreign regulations or by war. Manufacturing power, on the contrary, promotes science, art and political development, increases the well-
being of the people, the population, national revenue and national power.
[...] Through it alone can home agriculture be raised to a high pitch of
development.[17]

For predominantly agricultural or industrially less-advanced countries, free trade
prevents or delays the development of the manufacturing power. Only temporary
protection of domestic industry can offset this handicap. List acknowledges that
protective tariffs imply higher prices for manufactured goods, and thus a lower
standard of living, but argues that this is the price which must be paid to develop
a nation's productive power.[18]

The significance of List's doctrine of limited and temporary protectionism is
not confined to industrial production; it applies as well to agriculture, despite the
fact that List did not believe that the protection of the latter could produce any
advantages either for the individual or society.[19] In making these conclusions,
however, he assumed that agricultural production in Europe, and in particular in
Germany, could not be menaced by foreign competition. The self-sufficiency of
most of the continental countries in agricultural produce, and the relatively high
costs of transportation in the first half of the nineteenth century, seemed to preclude such a possibility—yet this is precisely what happened. Improvements in
transportation and the subsequent reduction of freight rates exposed Europe's
agricultural system to competition from overseas and from Russia. This new
competition caused not only a disastrous reduction in prices, but at the same time
led to a decline in European agricultural production—a decline manifested both
by the fact that some European countries became dependent for an ever-
increasing proportion of their needed bread grains and other foodstuffs from
abroad, and in a decrease in the farm population through their migration into
cities and their immigration overseas. These developments illustrated that List's
fundamental refutation of free trade as a universal rule of international economic
policy was even more valid than he himself had realized.

A manufacturing country which, under the influence of foreign competition,
becomes dependent on foreign sources of supply for essential foodstuffs, is
exposed to similar if not more far-reaching economic and political hazards than
a predominantly agricultural country that has failed to develop its manufacturing
power. For, obviously, the continued provision of a country with foodstuffs
depends upon a number of factors over which it usually has little or no control.
Such provision depends upon its ability to pay for its imports, which in turn
depends upon its ability to sell its manufactured products (or other goods and
services) abroad at profitable prices. Such ability to sell, and sell at a profit, obviously cannot be taken for granted. Moreover, a nation which relies on imports to
meet a substantial portion of its food requirements depends on the continued

ability and willingness of the exporting country to maintain an adequate volume of exports at reasonable prices, not to mention the danger of supplies being cut off completely in times of war. It is, of course, possible to ignore these and similar contingencies or to classify them as political and therefore "non-economic." Past experience has shown, however, that however these dangers are classified, they are certainly real enough to warrant the attention statesmen have given them.

It seems reasonable to believe that List would have argued for tariff protection of Europe's declining agriculture had he witnessed the effects of overseas and Russian competition on it after 1870. His insistence on the development of the manufacturing power in predominantly agricultural countries reflected merely his general realization of the importance, in the interest of a nation's continued independence and existence, of establishing and maintaining a balanced economy that combined, "within its own territory agriculture, manufactures, shipping and commerce."[20] Just as the United States and Germany needed protective tariffs to develop their manufacturing powers during the nineteenth century, for example, Great Britain may eventually find it necessary to adopt protective measures to avoid becoming, as Beveridge put it, "a country of factory and office workers without agriculture."[21]

It is evident, of course, that the social goal of a balanced economy which combines agriculture, manufacture, and commerce may in some instances be attainable only at the cost of a lower standard of living. Smaller nations in particular may find the price to be paid for establishing a balanced economy prohibitive, especially if their protective resources are inadequate or highly specialized. More importantly, advances in military technology have made it clear that a balanced economy no longer protects the small state in the instance of an attack by a powerful neighbor.

> Since effective military power now rests to such an unprecedented degree upon the possession of vast supplies of an almost bewildering variety of heavy arms and equipment, it follows that the small state can no longer enjoy its former importance as a buffer, capable of holding off a more powerful opponent until the allies of the smaller state can come to its assistance. It cannot cope with the swift attack of fast mechanized equipment. The difference of the effectiveness of Belgian resistance to the German armies in 1914 and in 1940 provides a striking illustration of the fundamental change in the role of the smaller states. Now, more than ever before, they are at the mercy of their larger neighbors.[22]

The declining military power of the smaller states may merely be the prelude to their ultimate integration into larger regional political and economic units; yet it would be mistaken to believe that such considerations refute the validity of the doctrine of productive forces and protectionism. As long as the "union" of nations is as imperfect as it is today, and in the absence of some form of world government, the goal of a balanced economy combining agriculture, manufacturing, and commerce is likely to remain that of political units as large as the United States, Great Britain, and Russia. For, ultimately, universal free trade would only be possible and equally desirable for all under a system of world government which has eliminated the danger of war. To deny this fact, to advocate free trade in a world in which the problem of peace has not been solved, and to argue (as some liberal economists have) that free trade will in fact be conducive to peace, is to use the results of abstract speculation as maxims of practical policy, while ignoring the political aspects of the equation. And yet it is in this so-called non-economic sphere that we find the social returns which have motivated the formulation of the international economic policies of many countries. [...]

Summary and conclusions

[...] The further ramifications of the above analysis can only be touched upon here. They include the fact that international economic policies cannot be formulated in a political vacuum, and in accordance with purely "economic" criteria; they must inevitably be shaped by considerations of national interest and the distribution of power in the world. More specifically, commercial and investment policies, as well as methods of trade, must take into account such factors as: political and economic conditions in foreign countries; these countries' policies, institutions and trading methods; the distribution of military and political power abroad; existing alliances; and the immediate and long-term objectives of diplomatic policies. It is not merely, as Adam Smith notes, that defense is much more important than opulence, but also that it is more important to sell to one's friend than to an enemy.[23] This is especially true in a world in which the balance of power is precarious, and where military insecurity confronts each nation with considerable dangers. Under these circumstances it may become necessary, as Herbert Feis points out,

> to gauge afresh every aspect of our economic and financial relationships. In respect to each of our exports we should have to ask: first, will possible defense needs enable us to spare them; second, will the country that is securing them prove to be a friend or a possible enemy; third, can we directly secure in return for them any commodity that will contribute to our military strength? In regard to our imports we should have to ask: first, do they contribute to our military strength; second, are we buying them in those places where we wish to encourage production; and third, will the dollar that we may pay be used for a friendly or unfriendly purpose?[24]

Economists brought up in the tradition of pure economic analysis may consider the formulation of commercial and financial policies with reference to political objectives as evidence of economic nationalism. They are likely to deplore such a development as the final step in the gradual process of the submerging of economics under politics. And they will be inclined to see in this economic nationalism the cause of international conflicts and wars. Such a conclusion, however, confuses cause with effect. It is not the policy of economic nationalism (a highly ambiguous term in any case) that leads to wars; it is rather the danger of war that makes it necessary to form international economic policies in the context of the prevailing political conditions of the world. This circle cannot be broken by ignoring political realities, or by simply identifying the interest of each state with a hypothetical and universal "common good." The belief in the existence of a fundamental and universal harmony of interests belongs to the endeavors of the utopian, who believes he has solved the problems of real life merely by *assuming* them to have been solved, when the fact is that

> the utopian, secure in his understanding of [the] common good, arrogates to himself the monopoly of wisdom. The statesmen of the world one and all stand convicted of incredible blindness to the interest of those whom they are supposed to represent.[25]

The events of the twentieth century have made it clear that, in international relations even more than in other spheres, the political and the economic are inseparable, and that any departmentalization of the two is a denial of reality. The sooner this is realized and the sooner foreign trade and international financial relations are conceived as economic problems as well as integral parts of foreign affairs in general, the greater will be the contribution of the economist to the understanding and resolution of international problems.

Transportation and social returns

The subject of transportation is another example of the principle of social returns, in that its significance in production cannot be measured merely by the fact that it "facilitates" the production and distribution of commodities. Improved means of transportation have the farthest-reaching social and political consequences, which place it in a special category among productive activities. The following discussion attempts to trace the social returns of transportation, and to demonstrate that neither free competition nor the present system of publicly-regulated but privately-owned facilities guarantee that investments in transportation will yield the maximum benefit at the lowest cost. Our examination of transportation begins with a brief summary of the evolution of its policies and doctrines.

The evolution of transportation policies and doctrines

The social returns of transportation have always made it necessary for governments to play a major role in their construction and operation. Rome's military roads, for example, connected the far corners of its empire, and in the Middle Ages, the provision of adequate roads was considered an element of sovereignty. For it was axiomatic that sovereignty [...] can be preserved only if the state and its citizens alike possess mobility. The minimum requirement on the one hand is that the state and its agents have access to all parts of the territory over which authority is to be exercised, and on the other, that the citizens be guaranteed avenues of egress from and ingress to their homes, places of business, and places where government functions are carried on. Early Saxon law recognized these requirements of sovereignty by imposing upon all lands an obligation to perform three necessary public duties [...] to repair roads and bridges; to maintain castles and garrisons; and to aid in repelling invasion.[26]

In sharp contrast to such farsighted policies in early Saxon law is the general backwardness of the state of transportation during the Middle Ages. This backwardness, which blocked the growth of trade, production, and national productivity, was only partly the result of a backward state of technical knowledge; to an even greater extent, it was caused by various man-made hindrances, such as the medieval toll system, town dues, and other features of medieval particularism and feudal life. These obstacles—which, as E.F. Heckscher notes, restricted medieval trade "much more than was warranted by purely technical difficulties"—assumed such proportions in the German states that during the second half of the sixteenth century, "[river] tolls had to be paid at thirty-six points along the route from Basel to Cologne alone—roughly one for every fifteen kilometers."[27] Because of river tolls, trade was forced to use the less convenient and considerably more expensive land routes, despite the fact that here too they were often subject to special taxes.

It is only against this background of a completely disrupted transportation system that the enthusiasm of mercantilist writers and statesmen for the development of better means of transportation, such as roads, canals, and shipping, can be fully appreciated. This enthusiasm, which Colbert put into practice in his celebrated road-building program during the seventeenth century, clearly demonstrates the mercantilists' realization of the social returns of improved transportation. The mercantilists were perhaps not fully aware that better means of communication were the basis for any successful effort to establish greater national unity and to overcome other shortcomings resulting from medieval neglect; they were, however, fully conscious of the effects that improved transportation would have on national productive efficiency.[28] The mercantilists' understanding of the social benefits of transportation has left a definite mark in the literature dealing with transportation problems and policies. In the United States and Germany, respectively, Hamilton and List preserved a kind of neo-mercantilist attitude towards transportation. Thus, Hamilton's "Report on Manufacturers" in 1791 contains the following passage on the benefits of improved transportation, which in some respects must be regarded as a link between mercantilism and several contemporary transportation doctrines:

Good roads, canals and navigable rivers, by diminishing the expense of carriage, put the remote parts of a country more nearly upon a level with those in the neighborhood of the town. They are, upon that account, the greatest of all improvements. They encourage the cultivation of the remote, which must always be the most extensive, circle of the country. They are advantageous to the town, by breaking down the monopoly of the country in its neighborhood. They are advantageous, even to that part of the country. Though they introduce some rival commodities into the old market they open many new markets to its produce. Monopoly, besides, is a great enemy to good management, which can never be universally established, but in consequence of that free and universal competition which forces everybody to have recourse to it for the sake of self-defence. It is not more than fifty years ago that some of the counties in the neighborhood of London petitioned the Parliament against the extension of the turnpike roads into the remoter counties. These remoter counties, they pretended, from the cheapness of labor, would be able to sell their grass and corn cheaper in the London market than themselves, and they would thereby reduce their rents, and ruin their cultivation. Their rents, however, have risen, and their cultivation has improved since that time.[29]

It was partly under the influence of American experiences and partly as a result of the backward state of economic development that some of the founders of the German historical school developed a doctrine of transportation which reflects a more or less complete realization of the social returns obtainable from transportation facilities.[30]

In contrast with their mercantilist predecessors, the majority of economists in the late eighteenth and nineteenth centuries tended to neglect the benefits of improved transportation. In their preoccupation with such narrower problems of manufacturing as market prices and production, classical economists either failed to consider transportation problems completely or tried to express the utility of transportation in terms of exchange values.[31] Whatever the reason, it was the philosophy of *laissez-faire*, rather than Hamilton's and List's understanding of the social character of the benefits of transportation, which determined public policy in the area of railroad development. This phase of railroad development in England, and to a degree also in the United States, was marked by the absence of any overarching developmental plan. In response to individual applications to Parliament, private companies were given special charters to construct and operate railway lines, a procedure that led not only to the construction of a great number of uncoordinated short routes, but was also accompanied by speculative overexpansion and subsequent losses, as well as unnecessarily high fixed and operating costs.[32]

The neglect of the social benefits of transportation which marked the *laissez-faire* era of railroad development, along with the excessive and discriminatory rates railroads charged for their services, led to a departure from the early policy of non-intervention in railroad construction, and in transportation in general. In many countries (including even the United States, where private ownership and competition have always been more important than in other nations), the recognition of the social benefits of railways and other means of transportation has led to the undisputed role of government in the construction and operation of those forms of transportation with predominantly social returns, and in substantial public aid being granted to virtually all branches of transportation. In fact, the development of all privately-operated forms of land, water, and air transport would have been impossible without the active intervention and public aid given by government authorities. [...]

The present system of transportation in the United States may thus be said to be the result of substantial public investment, with a public sector (roads, highways, bridges, waterways, harbor facilities, etc.) under government management and a "private" sector (railroads, motor transport, etc.) subject to public regulation. Before assessing the shortcomings of this mixed system of transportation, it is necessary to inquire into the effects of transportation, in order to make clear the predominantly social character of the benefits derived from investments in new and improved transport facilities.

The social returns of transportation

As has been illustrated above, the effects of transportation go far beyond those that can be expressed in terms of exchange values. Even the so-called economic effects of transportation cannot be measured simply in terms of dollars and cents. Generally speaking, it is, of course, possible to state that improved transport facilities reduce the costs of transportation, or that transportation increases the efficiency of production by removing "the obstacles which time and space impose upon productivity of all our resources."[33] The generally accepted statements regarding the beneficial effects of transportation fail, however, to make it sufficiently clear that many of these benefits cannot be easily appropriated by private producers, but rather accrue to society as a whole. This becomes increasingly clear when the effects of transportation are traced in greater detail.

It is true that roads, waterways, ships, carriages, railroads, and airplanes have reduced the costs of transportation, and that whoever is able to offer better and cheaper transport facilities is capable of appropriating at least some of the resulting benefits by attracting traffic and charging appropriate prices for his products. But these are only the most superficial effects of transportation. Lower transportation costs also equate to lower production costs, which in turn widen the "extent of the market" of all producers, who are thus enabled to enlarge their scale of production. At the same time, the scale of production, by determining the demand for transportation, influences the optimum scale of transport facilities, through the optimum investment in transportation. Thus, transportation and the scale of production influence each other symbiotically, and it may be said that improved means of transportation pave the way for the increasing capital intensity, or "roundaboutness," of economic life.[34] Lower production costs also promote competition between producers in formerly non-competitive parts of the country. Separated from each other and protected by high transportation costs, individual producers (and often entire areas of production) enjoy monopolistic positions relative to each other—but better transport facilities tend to eliminate these monopolies of location. Supply and demand, and consequently prices, are thus equalized over wider areas. Transportation also affects labor, as improved facilities make it easier to shift workers to where they are most needed, creating a more competitive labor market. Agricultural production is improved as well, as better transportation not only widens the areas from which consumers are able to obtain food, but also lengthens the period during which seasonal products are available in any area. By increasing the speed of shipment of perishable goods, better transport facilities have also been instrumental in making new commodities available to those who formerly had to go without them.

Perhaps most importantly, though, transport facilities and rates determine the relative competitiveness of different geographic areas, and thus exercise a great influence on the locations of industrial production. Once established, entire industries and the welfare of entire communities may depend completely upon the continued existence and operation of their transport service. New and cheaper transportation also has far-reaching effects on land values and rents. By furnishing access to formerly remote areas, or merely by reducing costs, new roads make production feasible and profitable on land which was formerly inaccessible. The values and rents of such land then increase.[35] Such dependence of land values and rents upon roads and other transportation facilities is perhaps best illustrated by the great importance of the many unimproved secondary roads to rural landowners. In the United States, these roads "furnish the only means of access to about half of the country's farms and 35 percent of the rural dwellings. [...] The true worth of these access roads derives from the fact that without them, land would be valueless."[36]

In addition to facilitating the production and exchange of commodities, transport facilities have far-reaching effects on rural social life, and on national integration. By providing access to markets and sources of supply, by connecting centers of population with recreational areas, and by bringing formerly inaccessible regions into closer contact with more developed areas, improved methods of transportation and communication have been instrumental in creating the basis of modern civilization.[37] This phenomenon can be seen most clearly in the expansion and development of the United States in the nineteenth century. Before the advent of railroads, the development of the country depended exclusively on the construction of roads and waterways, both of which played a pioneering role in the opening of the American frontier. River improvements and waterways such as the Erie Canal, for example, contributed greatly to the settlement of the Midwest. It was the railroads, however, which opened up the farther western reaches of the American continent: "Reduced transportation costs and a greatly improved service bred traffic, permitted settlement, promised national unity, and contributed greatly to the increase of the national wealth."[38]

The provision and maintenance of adequate road transportation was also important to American development, if for no other reason than that it made the entire system of rural education possible. The operation of rural schools at reasonable costs requires an enrollment of a certain minimum number of pupils per school, and

in order to operate an efficient rural school, the pupils must be assembled from a relatively large area. Consequently, those living long distances from the school must use a disproportionate part of their day walking to and from school, they must be transported by their parents, or they must be transported by the school authorities. [...] [In the United States, almost four million pupils are transported to rural schools at public expense,] requiring the operation of some 93,000 buses over more than a million miles of school bus routes.[39]

The importance of transport facilities for defense and national security has never been more important. Modern warfare, with its increasing emphasis on mobility and its motorization of armies, makes the provision of adequate land, water, and air transportation facilities an integral part of any defense system. Without a well-coordinated network of highways, railroads, shipping, and airways, it is impossible to assure the effective mobilization and training of the armed forces, to carry out maneuvers and war games, or to move troops and supplies to military centers and to the front. Just as important as the distinctly military significance of transport facilities is their economic role in the war effort. A country's ability to mobilize its economy for war depends on the adequacy of its transportation system; in the course of mobilization, materials will need to be moved in ever-increasing quantities to war-production centers, and finished war products will need to be distributed to military supply centers—all in addition to the commercial demand for transportation services resulting from the need to supply civilian consumers with essential goods and services.

It should be obvious, then, that

roads (and transportation in general) belong to that unappreciated class of blessings of which the value and importance are not fully felt, because of the very greatness of their advantages, which are so manifold and indispensable, as to have rendered their extent almost universal and their origin forgotten.[40]

The larger benefits of transportation—those that are available to all members of society—remain largely inappropriable to either private producers or consumers. As J.B. Clark has observed, for example,

in the case of railroads the inappropriable utilities are so great as almost to overbalance those which can be retained by the owners. The railroad creates a value far in excess of that which its projectors can realize; and this distributes itself among the adjacent population and appears in the enhanced value of lands and the increased rewards of general industry.[41]

The same probably holds true with respect to all other means of transportation and communication. However, more important than any attempt to determine the relative importance of the private and social utilities created by transport facilities is the fact that the appropriable (private) utilities of transportation are intrinsically connected with, and inseparable from, the social returns of transportation. The same railroad that reduces the cost of production, widens the extent of the market, and determines the location of industries also serves military purposes. This same intrinsic connection between "economic" and "non-economic" returns can be observed in all other transportation agencies as well.

Non-competitive factors in transportation

In addition to the social character of many of the benefits of transportation, there are several features of their construction and operation which the competitive calculus cannot adequately explain. First, modern transportation requires heavy initial investments of capital, making it an industry with a particularly high percentage of fixed costs. This is due not only to developments in technology, but also to the fact that transportation centers on the *movement* of commodities and not their *transformation* from one form into another, as manufacturing does; since transportation does not require the same magnitude of investment in materials as manufacturing does, the proportion of overhead costs in transportation is usually higher.[42] As long as the demand for transportation between two points is great enough for one initial investment (one railroad track, one canal, one tunnel) to provide the required services, it would be wasteful to erect more than one facility merely in order to stimulate competition between independent businesses. Such duplication of facilities would make it impossible for either to operate at full capacity, and thus to spread its overhead costs over the greatest possible number of services. Even if demand calls for an expansion of the existing facilities, it is usually more economical to enlarge the scale of operation (say, by adding another track alongside the old, or increasing the width of the road) and to operate the new and old equipment as a single unit than to construct and operate additional facilities under separate management.

Second, it is important to note that the operational efficiency of any single means of transportation

> depends also upon the extent of its integration with all other transport facilities. That is to say each transportation facility must form part of a transportation system in order to yield the greatest possible benefits. Every road has to be properly connected with other roads, every railway, every canal has to be conceived *a priori* and planned as a part of the total transportation net, and railroads, inland waterway, and highways must be systematically coordinated if they are to yield the highest possible utility. If the establishment of the transport net were left to freely formed private enterprises only profitable lines would be constructed which would be highly inadequate as far as the consideration of all collective objectives is concerned.[43]

Such coordination is not confined merely to the national sphere; there exists at the same time a genuine need for international integration and coordination of railroads, canals, shipping, and most importantly, airports and planes.

While the social character of the returns of transportation are an obvious matter of public concern, the high amount of initial investment and high overhead costs of transportation are an even more important consideration. Since these characteristics give most transport facilities a "natural monopoly," and since all transport facilities need to be conceived as integral parts of a well-coordinated system, it is imperative that the construction and operation of the transportation industry be placed under public auspices if it is to yield the greatest possible benefits. This raises the final question of how adequate the present "mixed" system of transportation, and the related public-utility concept, are to the optimal solution of the transportation problem.

The limitations of the present system of transportation to the realization of social returns

The most crucial limitations of the present "mixed" system of transportation prevent it from achieving a sufficient degree of physical and technical integration of existing facilities. In the absence of such integration, costs have remained unnecessarily high, and certain social returns have not been realized. Even in public-sector transportation under government management, the emphasis has been much more on the promotion of new facilities than the effective integration of the new with the old. The federal government, "operating through separate public agencies each acting as the special advocate of one form of transportation [...] spends an average of more than a billion dollars a year for transportation facilities without comprehensive plans."[44] As one student of public promotional policies notes,

> there has been a complete absence of broad plans to include all forms of transportation [...] and non-transportation as well as transportation objectives. The airport plan has no connection with the highway plan and the latter is unrelated to railroad plans, in spite of the fact that tremendous savings and improved services could both be achieved through coordination.[45]

As a result, public action in transportation has been marked by "waste of public funds; vague and conflicting objectives; the absence of criteria to guide expenditures; and questionable methods of financing, cost allocation and administration have all furnished evidence of serious shortcomings."[46]

The most noticeable evidence of diseconomies resulting from the absence of an integrated and coordinated transportation plan is the existence of costly and unnecessary competition between different transport agencies and, concomitantly, the great duplication of facilities.

> Each transport agency attempts to share traffic more logically belonging to another. The railroad, struggling desperately to regain its former position,

attempts to retain the short-haul and less-than-carload business despite heavy terminal expenses which must often result in handling at a loss. The motor truck invades the long-haul fields by attracting the more lucrative traffic from the rails, despite the greater economy of the latter. The inland waterway diverts traffic over circuitous routes in order to share in the haul.[47]

In addition to the multiplication of services, the lack of integration between existing facilities leads to the absence of unified and central terminals. Under present conditions, freight must be received at, transferred to, and delivered from widely scattered terminal facilities under diverse ownership, resulting in loss of time, wasteful transfers, and duplication of delivery, all of which increase costs.

> It has been estimated, for example, that approximately two-thirds of the typical completed car movement, involving about fifteen days on the average, is spent within terminal areas. The fact that the terminal accounts for one-third of railroad freight operating costs emphasizes further the possibilities of terminal improvement as a means of restoring railroad profitability and reducing costs to travelers and shippers.[48]

According to appraisals made by the Federal Coordinator of Transportation, the annual savings likely to result from the unification of freight terminals alone would amount to at least fifty million dollars. Other estimates of the potential annual economies obtainable from better coordination of railroad transportation in the United States are: one hundred million dollars from the pooling of freight cars; one hundred million from the integration of merchandise traffic; and one hundred million or more by various changes in passenger traffic.[49] Estimates of the total annual savings possible from specific schemes of consolidation or coordination of railroads alone range from a minimum of about two hundred million dollars to a maximum of one billion, with some consensus centering on about half a billion dollars.[50] The significance of these estimated savings is amplified by the fact that

> each $100,000,000 of economy achieved through railroad unification would be equal to about 3 percent of the operating expenses of all operating steam railways for the year 1939. Savings of about $500,000,000 would amount to about one-sixth of the operating expenses for that year and would have reduced the operating ratio from 0.729 to 0.608. Savings of half a billion dollars also would have increased net railway operating income from $638,766,000 to $1,138,766,000 for 1939, and would have been equal to more than 75 percent of the fixed charges of the carriers.[51]

(It should be noted that these are the anticipated results of railroad consolidation only; estimates of the total economies obtainable from the coordination and integration of the entire transport system in the United States are not available.)

Another limitation of the present mixed system of transportation is that it creates unequal competitive conditions, and thus contributes to an uneconomic utilization of existing facilities. For example, air, water, and highway facilities are currently financed in varying degrees through general funds, while railroads currently receive no direct support from general taxation.[52] While some carriers have to cover only part of their costs, then, railroads are forced to charge rates high enough to cover all their costs.[53] Because of such differences in financing,

> sufficient volumes of passenger and freight business have been taken from the rails, or kept from them, to result in serious financial consequences for rail operation. And it is not merely the traffic lost, but also the necessary lowering of the rates to retain traffic, which has spelled diminishing revenues. Furthermore, in the case of air and water transportation the fact that carriers pay little or nothing for these facilities establishes the conclusion that railroads have been the victims of subsidized competition to the extent that traffic moving by air and water would have moved by rail save for lower rates made possible through appropriations from general funds.[54]

The uneconomic character of such a shift of traffic away from existing railroad facilities requires no detailed explanation; it is verified by the underutilization of existing transport facilities at the same time that scarce resources are being used for the construction of new and additional ones.

Even more fundamental limitations of the American mixed transport system are caused by the public-utility status of the private sector of transportation. As has been noted, the present system of public-utility regulations is based on the doctrine of fair return on fair value. This doctrine is merely an adaptation of the principle of self-liquidation in private industry, which regulates production under competitive conditions. The operation of all public utilities, then, is regulated in such a manner that their operating revenues are sufficient to cover the total costs of operation, including a fair return on private investments. This principle, which makes railroads the victims of unequal competition from other subsidized transport agencies, is also vulnerable to criticism for a number of other reasons. First, it results in commercial users being charged for the full cost of transport facilities, despite the fact that these facilities yield substantial social benefits for all members of society. Second, under the influence of the principle of self-liquidation, private investments, as well as the operation of the railroad business, are likely not to take into account the broader social benefits of transportation. In fact, social benefits and objectives lie entirely beyond the scope of traditional public-utility regulation, which in its concentration on the protection of the consumer and private owners "fail[s] to impose definite responsibility for socially desirable action."[55] Railroads are under no obligation to construct and operate their facilities with a view to their effects on national defense, the development of new industries, the stabilization of business and employment in either general or specific areas, or the promotion of social integration, nor can they be expected to do so.

These specific shortcomings, and the general failure of the present system of public-utility regulation, are, of course, not confined to railroads but hold true for all public-utility industries. As Gray pointed out,

> public utility companies are under no legal compulsion to conserve national resources, to utilize capital efficiently, to employ the best known techniques and forms of organization, to treat labor fairly, to extend service to non-profitable areas, to improve public health, to strengthen national defense, to promote technical research, to provide service to indigent persons, to institute rate and service policies that will foster cultural and social values, to develop related benefits such as navigation, flood control, and irrigation. This being the case private utility monopolists will have regard for these broad social objectives only when by so doing they can increase or maintain their own profit. Experience has shown that they will not voluntarily strive to attain these ends; moreover, it is clear that public utility regulation, as at present constituted, cannot compel them against their own interest to do so. Thus, the public utility concept is functionally impotent in the sense that it is incapable of securing the social objectives that are essential in a modern economy.[56]

Thus, the major weakness of the present mixed system of transportation in the United States is due to the promotion of transport facilities without sufficient coordination, and the absence of an integrated approach under which all forms of land, water, and air transportation are treated as constituent parts of a unitary system. Different local, state, and federal authorities are responsible for the formulation of policies, and different transport agencies compete for traffic which could be carried more economically by others. Wasteful duplication and uneconomic utilization of transport facilities are the consequences of this lack of coordination. The principle of self-liquidation which guides the system of public-utility regulation is also inadequate and incapable of maximizing the social returns of transportation.

Summary

Transportation provides another example of the principle of social returns. Virtually all means of transportation yield utilities which are not exchangeable and tend to diffuse themselves among all members of society. Improved transportation not only provides greater opportunities for the division of labor; it also reduces the cost of production, influences the location of production, and has an important influence on national defense, rural life and education, and overall social integration. Although the social character of the benefits of transportation has been acknowledged and manifested in economic policy, as seen by the promotion of new transport capacity through extensive grants of public aid and the public regulation of the private sector, the present "mixed" system of transportation, and especially the principles which govern the public recognition of the private sector, offer no plan for the adequate integration of existing facilities and no way to account for the broader social objectives and returns of new ones.

Social returns and multiple-purpose projects

Based on the evidence we have already examined, it would appear that the phenomenon of neglected social returns is likely to occur whenever productive activities serve more than one purpose and are capable of yielding more than one type of benefit. The satisfaction of collective needs, transportation, international economic policies, and scientific research all create a multiplicity of benefits, some of which are privately appropriable and exchangeable, while others tend to accrue to society as a whole. Under such circumstances, it is probable that the market mechanism will generate a one-sided emphasis on the production of those utilities that are privately appropriable and remunerative, with the result that the social utilities that are less easily appropriated are often sacrificed. This raises the question of whether there are multiple-purpose projects which generate important returns, some of which are social in nature.

Among the most typical, and at the same time most important, multiple-purpose projects are those which are designed to improve or conserve available land and water resources. Such land- and water-use projects include various schemes of land reclamation, soil conservation, flood control, and stream- and water-control projects. Almost all land- and water-use projects, in fact, have multiple purposes, because of the intrinsic connection between both entities in any given area—a river and its drainage basin, for example. Consequently, most measures designed to improve and conserve available land and water resources often have effects which are felt at a considerable distance from the place at which they are actually undertaken. A brief examination of these interrelationships follows, in which the nature of the social returns which are likely to be neglected by the competitive calculus, and which could be produced only by adequate planning and organization, are also considered.

Land reclamation

As has already been seen in the discussion of the social costs of agriculture and private forestry, the drainage of wetlands and the elimination of swamps may have the most far-reaching negative effects on ground-water supplies, stream flow, and wildlife in surrounding areas. Not only may ground-water stores be depleted by drainage, but streams, ponds, and lakes in more distant areas may also become dry or even disappear entirely, creating serious shortages of water supply, stream pollution, and wildlife destruction. If properly planned, however, drainage and irrigation projects may serve several useful purposes, such as flood control and the generation of power, in addition to their immediate objective of increasing soil fertility and crop yields in areas with insufficient or irregular rainfall. The positive and negative consequences of drainage and irrigation projects, then, must be properly seen not merely as local, but as regional and sometimes even national problems. This makes it necessary to evaluate any new projects of this nature not merely for their local consequences, but also for their farther-reaching benefits and drawbacks. Just as "new projects which might appear feasible from a local standpoint may be unjustified when viewed from the standpoint of regional or national economy,"[57] so may the "social benefits from unified developments [...] justify outlays which private interests could not be expected to make because they would not yield direct and tangible profits."[58]

A number of other factors place land reclamation outside the range of the competitive calculus of private enterprise. First, drainage and irrigation projects, once established, may become the basis of the livelihood of large groups of people, to the extent that they determine these peoples' patterns of life and their welfare. Both the agricultural settlements in the immediate neighborhood of irrigated land and the prosperity of urban communities may become dependent on the maintenance and continued operation of the project, for "these communities owe their existence, the business which maintains them, and their future prospects to construction of irrigation works which provide water for the farms beyond their limits."[59] However, irrigation projects, like drainage facilities, often require expensive maintenance works to prevent their destruction by premature silting.

> Irrigated land is a good example of a factor of production which can be kept in a productive state only with the constant application of labor and capital. If silting is not prevented, the dams, the flumes and the thousands of acres "under the ditch" may have to be scrapped like a worn-out machine or a depreciated building. Hence the need for a coordinated land policy embracing not only the irrigated land, but also the range land, the dry farming areas and the forests.[60]

Similarly, "if the drainage works are not maintained, the areas will revert in a comparatively short time to their previous swampy or marshy condition."[61]

Second, irrigation projects have been so widespread in the Western United States that the point has been reached where

> no additional developments of the simple low-cost-per-acre type remain. All large projects undertaken in the future will be complex, with comparatively high costs per acre for the land irrigated. Many of them will not be irrigated projects solely, but will serve in addition various other valuable functions.[62]

According to the 1934 Report of the National Resources Board, there are only 3.8 million acres which can be irrigated at less than $50 per acre; an additional 3.2 million acres that would require expenditures of $50 to $100 per acre; another 3.2 million acres with costs ranging from $100 to $200 per acre; and about 1.3 million acres that would require expenses of more than $200 per acre.[63] The costs of constructing and operating such extensive and expensive projects obviously exceed the means of individual farmers.

Finally, the predominantly social and non-exchangeable character of the benefits of drainage works is emphasized by the fact that, while they were formerly designed to increase soil fertility and to promote agriculture, settlement, and crop production, one of the chief objectives of all drainage works inaugurated in the United States in recent years has been the elimination of public-health hazards, through the eradication of the insects that spread malaria.[64]

Soil conservation

Soil-conservation practices are another important example of multiple-purpose projects. That such practices may serve more than one purpose, and that they are likely to yield important social returns, is particularly evident in their effects on the social costs of agriculture and private forestry. Both of these productive activities may create a wide variety of social losses, in the forms of soil erosion, reduced soil fertility, greater frequency of floods, sedimentation of rivers and reservoirs, and the destruction of wildlife. The promotion of such soil-conservation practices as simple crop rotation, strip cropping, vegetative control of gullies, the replenishment of the humus supply, the growth of soil-building crops, contour plowing, terracing, the construction of run-off channels and reservoirs, the rational assignment of land to forests, and reforestation, serves several purposes, many of which are social in character. In fact, the reason that the individual farmer or lumber company often shows insufficient interest in the adoption of these and similar conservation measures is because their beneficial effects accrue to other people, or to the community as a whole. The individual entrepreneur has no way of getting repaid directly for the cost of conservation practices on his own land; yet these practices can help retard the run-off of rainfall, prevent soil erosion on adjoining land, maintain ground-water stores, equalize stream flow, protect wildlife, avoid the sedimentation of rivers and reservoirs, and reduce the frequency and crest of floods. The results of such practices benefit all members of society, but represent inappropriable social returns to which individual entrepreneurs can hardly be expected to pay adequate attention. The realization of these social benefits depends, therefore, on the formulation of public policies regulating land use. The specific practices required in each case depend on the topography of the land, climate conditions, the character of the soil, and the demand for farm crops. The technical challenges posed by such factors, while interesting, lie outside the scope of the present inquiry.

Flood control

While it is impossible to prevent floods completely, the frequency of their occurrence and severity may be lessened by the construction of levees, the improvement of stream channels, the diversion of water into spillways and overflow basins, and the building of reservoirs. Most such measures offer a striking example of multiple-purpose projects and their social returns, since floods are almost invariably regional problems, and their solution requires the use of techniques extending over an even greater area than that of most land-reclamation and soil-conservation projects. Also, "local improvements in the [river] channel planned to protect only adjacent property may actually increase the flood hazard downstream."[65] The regional and sometimes national character of flood control is perhaps best illustrated by the fact that the flood hazards of the Mississippi can be mitigated only if the stream flow in the tributaries of the master stream are likewise regulated and controlled.

In addition to protecting life and property from damage and destruction, flood-control projects can also be made to render important services in navigation, irrigation, the maintenance of communication and transportation facilities, national defense, the development of electric power projects, the maintenance of adequate water supplies for domestic and industrial purposes, the conservation of health, the preservation of wildlife, recreation, and the stabilization of land values. The inappropriable nature of such benefits, and the fact that flood hazards are causally related to the misuse of farm and forest land throughout the drainage basin, underlines the fact that the problem of flood control can be solved successfully only if it is approached as a regional or national, not merely local, question. Only then can it be assured that land and water resources are used properly through the entire river basin.

Stream and water projects

As in the examples cited above, "every water project of magnitude may be made to contribute to the solution of more than one problem."[66] For instance, the construction of dams and reservoirs for the purposes of irrigation and flood control may also, "in conjunction with the available flow of water [...] be used in the development of power."[67] The same dam or reservoir may be used to regulate the flow of the stream as well, thus increasing its usefulness for navigation and other purposes, such as better recreational opportunities and the conservation of wildlife. Conversely, dams and reservoirs planned primarily for the development of marketable power may also afford opportunities for irrigation and flood control. Such inland waterway improvements as the deepening, widening, and straightening of stream channels for navigation purposes, if properly planned, may contribute to pollution abatement, flood control, and power development as well. Or, irrigation projects may be used to contribute to flood control, navigation, or resettlement.

This is not to claim, however, that the various potential purposes of water projects do not sometimes conflict with each other; on the contrary, the construction of dams and reservoirs may hinder the navigability of the stream on which they are built, and similarly, "economical power production [...] requires that water storage be related to variation in power load," whereas "irrigation water [in contrast] must be stored during periods of high flow for release to satisfy the demand during the growing season."[68] These and other conflicts, however, can be solved through the construction of locks and other such structures, the provision of additional dams, the re-regulation of ponds, or the adequate allocation of a definite irrigation surcharge storage space in power reservoirs. The existence of these conflicts between the purposes of water projects, and the possibility of their solution by appropriate planning, add weight to the conclusion that

> a large dam and storage reservoir built and used mainly for flood control is a wasteful maladjustment socially if not economically, provided it could have been practicable to design, construct, and operate the dam to regulate the flow of the stream for other purposes as well as flood control, to develop marketable power, or to realize incidental reservoir values in connection with recreation and wildlife conservation.[69]

In short, even if some of the benefits of river and water projects were privately appropriable and could be offered for sale by private producers (as in the case of electric power), the private and competitive development of such multiple-purpose projects would still be liable to defeat the principle of economy in making the best use of available resources. For private enterprise would concern itself only with the development of the part of the project which yields an appropriable financial surplus, in neglect of all other potential benefits and purposes. (A more detailed case study of the social benefits produced by outstanding examples of land- and water-use projects in the United States is made unnecessary by the rapidly growing literature on one of the most successful multiple-benefit projects: The Tennessee Valley Authority.[70])

Summary

The multiple purpose of the different projects discussed rests upon the natural interrelationship which exists between the land- and water-use problems within any given drainage basin. As a result, the effects of any of the aforementioned land- and water-development schemes are felt over so wide a region, and affect so great a number of people, that none of them can be economically planned, operated, and maintained locally. Whenever these schemes are operated by private enterprise, the fact that some of their returns are exchangeable and sufficient to cover the costs of construction and operation leads to the neglect of the potentially broader but less appropriable returns obtainable from them, despite the fact that these returns would be highly worthwhile in terms of additional costs and social benefits. It is these social benefits of multiple-purpose projects which make the competitive calculus of exchange values unsuitable for determining the efficacy of their production and operation.

Notes

1 This is the title of the unpublished manuscript on social returns (later referred to as social benefits) which was developed as part of Kapp's original project but must be seen as abandoned by 1946. The most recent references in the footnotes date from 1942 and the original manuscript title which included Social Returns still appears in the correspondence with J.M. Clark in 1945 but not thereafter. See Sebastian Berger,

"The Making of the Institutional Theory of Social Costs: Discovering the K.W. Kapp and J.M. Clark Correspondence," in *American Journal of Economics and Sociology*, Vol. 72 (5), 2013: 1106–1130.

2 This table of contents is contained in the unpublished manuscript. The individual chapters are of different qualities and the editor decided to not publish Chapter 19 on "Science and Social Returns" and Chapter 21 on "Social Minima and Social Returns" due to their very preliminary character. Both themes are developed by Kapp in the other publications, e.g., the chapter on the social costs of privatized science in *The Social Costs of Private Enterprise* (1950) but also *Governmental Furtherance of Environmentally Sound Technologies as a Focus of Research and Environmental Policies* republished in *The Foundations of Institutional Economics* (2011). Chapter 16.2 is missing in the manuscript.

3 The fact that epidemics do not respect political boundaries, and that their effective elimination requires action on both a national and an international scale, makes their prevention by measures of public health control a genuine and widely accepted "international need." The wide recognition of common interest in the prevention and containment of contagious diseases doubtless accounts for the fact that international public-health organizations have been more effective than those in the political and economic fields.

4 Adolf Wagner, *Allgemeine oder Theoretische Volkswirtschaftslehre*, Leipzig: C.F. Winter'sche Verlagsbuchhandlung, 1876, p. 260.

5 G. Colm, "Is Economic Planning Compatible with Democracy?" in *Political and Economic Democracy*, M. Ascoli and F. Lehmann (eds), New York: W.W. Norton, 1937, p. 35.

6 Royal Institute of International Affairs, *Nationalism*, London, New York, Toronto: Oxford University Press, 1933, pp. 24–25.

7 W. Röpke, *International Economic Disintegration*, London, Edinburgh, Glasgow: William Hodge and Company, 1942, p. 88.

8 F.D. Graham, *Social Goals and Economic Institutions*, Princeton: Princeton University Press, 1942, p. 8.

9 R. W. Souter, "The Nature and Significance of Economic Science in Recent Discussions," *Quarterly Journal of Economics* 47, 1933, p. 393.

10 Herbert Feis, *The Changing Pattern of International Economic Affairs*, New York and London: Harper & Brothers, 1940, p. 20.

11 E.H. Carr, *The Twenty Years' Crisis 1919–1939: An Introduction to the Study of International Relations*, London: Macmillan and Co. Ltd., 1939, p. 59.

12 Ibid., p. 70.

13 A. Hamilton, "Report on Industry and Trade," in *The Works of Alexander Hamilton*, Vol. 4, pp. 135–136.

14 F. List, *Introduction to the National System of Political Economy*, 1841, quoted in M.E. Hirst, *The Life of Friedrich List and Selections from His Writings*, New York: Charles Scribner's Sons, 1909, pp. 301–302.

15 Ibid., pp. 292–293.

16 F. List, *The National System of Political Economy*, London: Longman's Green and Co., 1904, p. 108.

17 F. List, "Introduction to the National System of Political Economy," op. cit., p. 307.

18

It is true that protective duties at first increase the price of manufactured goods; but it is just as true, and moreover acknowledged by the prevailing economical school, that in the course of time, by the nation being enabled to build up a completely developed manufacturing power of its own, those goods are produced more cheaply at home than the price at which they can be imported from foreign parts. If, therefore, a sacrifice of value is caused by protective duties, it is made good by the gain of a *power of production* which not only secures to the nation an infinitely greater amount of material goods but also industrial independence in case of war.

Ibid., pp. 117–118

19 Ibid., chapter 28, pp. 170–180.
20 Ibid., p. 54.
21 The reference to this quotation by Beveridge is missing from the manuscript and could not be located.
22 G.L. Kirk, "Post-war Security for the United States," *American Political Science Review* 58, no. 5, p. 948.
23 *"Il vaut mieux vendre a son frere qu'a son enemi."* See F. Galiani, *Dialogues sur le Commerce des Grains.*
24 Herbert Feis, *The Changing Pattern of International Economic Affairs*, New York and London: Harper & Brothers, 1940, p. 126.
25 E.H. Carr, op. cit., pp. 70–71.
26 C.L. Dearing, *American Highway Policy*, Washington: The Brookings Institution, 1941, p. 10.
27 See E.F. Heckscher, *Mercantilism*, London: George Allen and Unwin, Ltd., 1935, pp. 45. The above quotations are from pp. 45 and 57.
28 This mercantilist emphasis on the effects of transportation on national productive efficiency is perhaps best illustrated in the writings of Nehemiah Grew, who computed the benefits of improved roads as follows: "If only one horse could be eliminated from every gang of horses, and if on the average, each market town possessed 20 gangs, and each village four; then, if the cost of keeping each horse be five pounds a year, the net national economy would be 230,000 pounds annually." In addition, "once every 5 or 6 years, over 45,000 horses would be available for exportation." See E.A.J. Johnson, "Nehemiah Grew: A Forgotten Mercantilist," *American Economic Review* XXI, 1931, p. 466.
29 A. Hamilton, "Report on Manufacturers," *Papers on Public Credit, Commerce and Finance*, New York: Columbia University Press, 1934, p. 246.
30 F. List, "Eisenbahnen und Kanäle, Dampfboote und Dampfwagentransport," *Staatslexikon* 4, 1834–1843, pp. 650–778; K. Knies, *Die Eisenbahnen und ihre Wirkungen*, Braunschweig: C. A. Schwetschke und Sohn, 1853.
31 M. Dupuit, "De la Mesure de L'Utilité des Travaux Publics," *Annale des Ponts et Chausses*, Memoires et Documents, vol. 8, 1844, pp. 332–333.
32 For a more detailed account of the early stage of railroad development, not only in England and the United States but also in France and Germany, see E. Sax, *Die Verkehrsmittel in Volks- und Staatswirtschaft*, Vol. 3: Die Eisenbahnen, Berlin: Julius Springer, 1922, pp. 431–532.
33 National Resources Planning Board, *Transportation and National Policy*, Washington: US Government Printing Office, 1942, p. iii.
34 E. Sax, *Die Verkehrsmittel in Volks- und Staatswirtschaft*, Vol. I: Allgemeine Verkehrslehre, Berlin: Julius Springer, 1922, p. 62.
35 At the same time, new transport facilities may, of course, cause lower land values and rents in areas nearer to markets, due to the competition from more distant regions. See D.P. Locklin, *Economics of Transportation*, Chicago: Business Publications, Inc., 1938, pp. 2–4.
36 C.L. Dearing, op. cit., p, 123.
37 Two prime examples of this phenomenon in the United States are the influence of radio and the system of rural free delivery, which serves more than 26 million people and which is based largely on the maintenance of a system of improved rural roads. The great social benefits resulting from adequate postal service in rural districts was summarized by President Theodore Roosevelt: "[Rural free delivery] is justified both by the financial results and by the practical benefits to our rural population; it brings the men who live on the soil into close relations with the active business world; it keeps the farmer in daily touch with the markets; it is a potential educational force; it enhances the value of farm property, makes farm life far pleasanter and less isolated and will do much to check the undesirable current from

country to city." *A Compilation of the Messages and Paper of the Presidents*, Vol. XV. Second Annual Message, p. 6764.

38 *Public Aids to Transportation*, op. cit., Vol. I, p. 53.
39 C.L. Dearing, op. cit., pp. 143–4.
40 W.M. Gillespie.
41 J.B. Clark, op. cit., pp. 215–6.
42 See E. Sax, op. cit., vol. O, p, 61.
43 Translated from ibid., p. 139.
44 *Federal Aid to Transportation*, p. 9.
45 Ibid., p. 275.
46 Ibid., p. 9.
47 Ibid., p. 7.
48 Ibid., p. 3.
49 These estimates are based upon studies of the Federal Coordinator of Transportation and are quoted from National Resources Planning Board, *Transportation and National Policy*, op. cit., p. 166.
50 Ibid., p. 162. See also B.H. Behling, *Railroads Coordination and Consolidation—A Review of Estimated Economies*, Interstate Commerce Commission, Statement No. 4023, Washington, 1940.
51 Ibid., p. 162.
52 Ibid., p. 258.
53 The argument that roads received public support in the past is irrelevant in this context, since profits and business policies are determined by present costs and estimates of future costs, not by past ones.
54 Ibid., p. 259. "As for motor transport which contributed large sums of user revenue for financing highways, it is believed that the multiple nature of the highway function and the predominance of overhead costs combine to make it more a matter of conjecture whether vehicles as a class, or specific types of vehicles, pay a proper share of the highway bill in a particular state."
55 H.M. Gray, "The Passing of the Public-Utility Concept," *The Journal of Land and Public Utility Economics* XVI, 1940, p. 16.
56 Ibid., p. 16. In addition to the "obsolescence" of the public-utility concept, Gray emphasizes its recent "perversion" from "a system of social restraint designed primarily, or at least ostensibly, to protect consumers from the aggressions of monopolists" to "a device to protect the property, i.e., the capitalized expectancy of these monopolists, from the just demands of society and to obstruct the development of socially superior institutions" (ibid., p. 15). Evidence of such a perversion may be found not only in various familiar abuses and financial manipulation, but also in the attempt by various public-utility industries to protect their own privileged domain against competitors by securing "their inclusion within the restrictive confines of the public utility status" (ibid., p. 11; see also pp. 11–15).
57 National Resource Committee, *Drainage Basin Problems and Programs*, Washington: US Government Printing Office, 1938, p. 13.
58 Ibid., p. 9.
59 Ibid., p. 84.
60 R.T. Ely and G.S. Wehrwein, *Land Economics*, New York: The Macmillan Company, 1940, p. 258.
61 *Drainage Basin Problems*, op. cit., p. 131.
62 Ibid., p. 83.
63 National Resources Board, Report December 1, 1934, op. cit., p. 129.
64 *Drainage Basin Problems*, op. cit., p. 11.
65 A.E. Perkins and F.R. Whitaker, op. cit., p. 380.
66 *Drainage Basin Problems*, op. cit., p. 7.
67 Ibid., p. 92.

68 Ibid., p. 93.
69 Ibid., p. 8.
70 See J.S. Ransmeier, *The Tennessee Valley Authority, a case study in the economics of multiple-purpose stream planning*, Nashville: Vanderbilt University Press, 1942; C.H. Pritchett, *The Tennessee Valley Authority, a study in public administration*, Chapel Hill: University of North Carolina Press, 1943; and *The Widening of Economic Opportunity Through TVA*, Knoxville, 1940.

6 Towards a new science of political economy

Conclusions and implications

Despite the fact that the preceding analysis has not covered all the instances of social costs and social returns, it is nevertheless possible at this point to discuss its results and broader implications. An appraisal must first be made, however, of the overall rationality of the unplanned market economy; afterwards, the thread of our argument will be resumed with an introductory discussion of the present scope and limitations of economic science, which will then lead to the forming of conclusions for the future of economics.

The social inefficiency of the unplanned market economy

We have attempted to determine the validity of three of the basic assumptions of economic science: that human conduct is rational; that entrepreneurial outlays measure the total costs of production; and that private returns are an adequate measure of the total benefits obtainable from production. These are the traditional abstractions of neo-classical equilibrium theory—yet the results of our inquiry were that the aspects of economic reality from which these assumptions were abstracted actually tended to invalidate the conclusions drawn from these basic premises. Thus, these premises must be considered incorrect, and untenable as tools for the comprehension and interpretation of modern economic life.

The assumption of rational economic conduct, for example, was revealed to be invalid due to the obstacles to reasoned choices in modern industrial society. The entrepreneur and seller cannot be said to possess the knowledge of the conditions of supply and demand necessary to determine the most profitable level of output; he has only the vaguest notion of the elasticity of demand for his product and no more than an approximate idea of the supply curve and future costs of the raw materials and labor he needs. Nor can he predict with any reasonable degree of certainty the reactions of his competitors, which (especially under monopolistic competition) are of paramount importance in determining the highest profit combination of the factors of production. Obstacles also stand in the way of rational choices by the consumer; the complexity of modern civilization and the institution of sales promotion in a monopolistic economy subject the individual to pressure and modes of persuasion that defeat his attempt to make the best use of his limited income. Instead of producing the goods and services which consumers prefer, and which it would be feasible and economical to produce, the business community tends to produce what it finds most profitable to sell by means of an elaborate and often costly system of sales promotion. Thus prevented from giving direction to the productive process through reasoned and intelligent choices, consumers must choose among alternatives which have been either artificially limited or confusingly proliferated through product differentiation, advertising, and other forms of monopolistic competition.

The tacit assumption that entrepreneurial outlays measure the true total costs of production was also refuted by the fact that private productive activities under modern conditions tend to create social losses and damages for which the private entrepreneur is not, and often cannot, be made fully accountable. Among these losses are the effects of air and water pollution, the premature depletion of natural wealth, technological changes, economic depressions, monopoly, urban land utilization, and industrial location. Such social costs of production are not reflected in entrepreneurial outlays but are shifted to third persons, or to the community as a whole.

Finally, another implicit assumption—that private returns provide an adequate measure of the total benefits obtainable from production—was refuted as well, by the phenomenon of inappropriable, non-exchangeable utilities. These utilities, which play a much greater role than is usually assumed, diffuse themselves among all members of society and thus cannot be separated into specific advantages or damages. Market prices and private returns fail completely to measure the relative importance and magnitude of these broader social returns.

In eliminating social costs and social returns from its investigations on the grounds that they are "non-economic," then, economists not only evade one of the most important economic issues but also overlook two important facts: that most of the social costs lead to greater private or public expenditures, and that the production of inappropriable utilities necessitates the use of scarce resources in much the same way that the creation of appropriable utilities consumes the limited means of society. So, even in the narrow sense in which economists traditionally employ the term, social costs and social returns are very much "economic" phenomena.

The obstacles to rational behavior in modern industrial society and the existence of social costs and social returns do more than merely undermine the basic assumptions of classical and neoclassical equilibrium economics, however; they also invalidate the metaphysical preconceptions from which the assumptions were originally derived. As soon as we include in our speculations not only the abstractions of economic science and the business world, but also the omitted truths of irrational behavior and social costs and returns, the allegedly natural and beneficial orderliness of the capitalist exchange economy begins to crumble. For example, the so-called market test—the system of economic calculation in terms of exchange values—is exposed as a highly misleading regulator of production once the effect of social costs and returns upon it is considered. In fact, if strictly observed, the market test of production, in terms of entrepreneurial outlays and private returns, would make modern life virtually impossible. For, if the criterion of worthwhile production is the realization of a surplus of private returns over private costs measured in terms of exchange values, then government services, educational facilities, social services, and the like could not be provided "except to consumers who are willing to pay the full costs of them."[1] Under the criteria of the market test, then, the great majority of people in modern society would have to go without such services.

However, even if the market test is *not* strictly adhered to, and even if public authorities assume responsibility for the creation of some of the more essential social returns regardless of the monetary returns obtainable from them, the neglect of social costs in the competitive sector of the capitalist exchange economy inevitably leads to economic maladjustments, with far-reaching consequences. For if it is possible for private producers to shift a substantial portion of their production costs to others or to the community, some industries are likely to expand production to a level which would be unjustified under a more comprehensive method of socio-economic calculation.

If the above considerations effectively refute the belief in the hidden orderliness of the economic process, they also challenge the optimizing effect of competitive equilibrium. Indeed, it is impossible to claim that the equilibrium of supply and demand achieves a maximum aggregate satisfaction, even in a perfectly free market. If consumers are unable to make the best possible use of their income, if entrepreneurial outlays fail to measure the true total costs of production, and if important social returns are omitted from private returns (and thus also from the economic calculation of the capitalist exchange economy), the competitive equilibrium of supply and demand is revealed as an arbitrary, and highly wasteful, use of resources. What is optimized is not "aggregate satisfaction" in any comprehensible sense of the term, but at best only private exchangeable utilities. Similarly, what are minimized are not total costs but merely entrepreneurial outlays; social costs and returns are omitted from the equilibrium equation entirely. Competitive equilibrium (and monopolistic equilibrium even more so) is not equilibrium at all; it cannot preclude the use of scarce resources for relatively unimportant purposes and at the expense of more important ones, nor can it guarantee that production costs will not exceed the costs of the benefits available from it.

The concept of competitive equilibrium becomes a veritable caricature of "economic optimum" if used to appraise the overall rationality of the economic process, and as a standard of economic policy. It is obvious that the power of scarce resources to satisfy wants cannot be maximized merely by creating a maximum of exchangeable utilities, nor can it be claimed that a maximum of productive efficiency is achieved without accounting for the social costs of production. If the concept of economic optimum has any place in economic discussions—and we believe that it has—it cannot be conceived solely in terms of some of the costs and some of the returns, but must include *all* the costs and *all* the gains. Exchange values (i.e., private costs and returns) do not provide such a comprehensive standard for the measurement of the overall rationality of the economic process.

Reputable economists and laymen alike frequently attempt to refute criticisms and doubts of the hidden orderliness and rationality of production in the capitalist exchange economy with the empirical evidence of the history of capitalism over the past 150 years, especially its achievements in raising standards of living. While it is undoubtedly true that the past century and a half have seen substantial and progressive material advances in the European and American capitalist exchange economies, it is one thing to note these advances and another matter completely to account for them. In particular, the familiar argument that the economic progress of the past 150 years must be credited to capitalistic economics, and more specifically the beneficent and orderly character of the latter, bears all the superficiality of similar conclusions based upon experience and sense perception. And, like many such other conclusions, it is not merely superficial, but a wholesale misinterpretation of reality. Such arguments overlook the fact that ever since capitalism has become the prevailing economic mode in the regions under scrutiny, it has been marked by a more or less periodic recurrence of economic crises and depressions. These recurrences are perhaps the strongest proof of the absence of any inherent orderliness in the capitalistic process.

The empirical arguments which attribute the economic advances of the past century and a half to capitalism also neglect the economic effect of the many discoveries made in the seventeenth and eighteenth centuries. In fact, a substantial portion of the economic progress usually credited to the growth of capitalism was actually made possible by achievements in the natural sciences and the resulting new techniques of production, which, for the first time in the history of mankind, permitted the full and systematic exploitation and utilization of the earth's resources. The rapid economic advances these discoveries made possible would have been made under almost any form of economic organization. This is not to deny that the free-enterprise system provided a more efficient organization and a more powerful stimulus for the application of such discoveries than mercantilism, or indeed any other preceding economic order, would have; however, to conclude that the private-enterprise system is responsible for the rapid economic progress that resulted would be just as illogical as attributing the considerably more rapid industrialization and economic advances of the Soviet Union during the last twenty years to socialism. The Soviets, while handicapped by the lack of a skilled labor force, were able to make use of technical knowledge which early capitalism did not possess. In both cases, then, it is necessary to consider the state of technological development and its effect on the final result to arrive at a balanced judgment of the performance of different economic systems.

Finally, those who promote the record of the capitalist exchange economy should not forget that a substantial portion of the economic achievements of the past and present century has been bought at the price of unrecorded social costs. These costs have been borne mainly by labor, in the form of impaired physical and mental health, reduction of skill requirements and lowering of social status, loss of security, the compulsory submission of costly changes of residence and retraining, monotony of work, and the like. The rapid expansion of industrial production, particularly the economic development of the American continent in record time, was also purchased at the cost of an overly rapid depletion of natural wealth. Indeed, it is only recently that people are beginning to realize that the capital they have been living on was actually obtained in substantial measure by the "consumption" of capital, including manpower and natural resources.[2]

It should be evident, then, that the familiar empirical conclusions about the fundamental orderliness and beneficent results of the unplanned market economy collapse under close analysis. They reflect the rationalizations of the same pre-conceived social and political philosophy which shaped and colored the assumptions and development of orthodox and neoclassical economic theory. When we abandon the traditional presuppositions of equilibrium economics, its explicit assumptions collapse as well, and the seemingly impressive philosophical foundation of theoretical conclusions which form the basis of classical and neo-classical economic thought crumbles. In order to understand more fully the implications of our investigation of the future of economic science, we will return to the beginning of our analysis and take up once again the thread of the argument presented in the introductory chapter.

The normative-apologetic character of orthodox and neoclassical equilibrium economics

As was emphasized above, the origin and development of economic science can be understood only in the context of the tacit philosophical presuppositions of the seventeenth and eighteenth centuries. The essence of these tenets is the unquestioned belief in a rational and beneficent order in social affairs, a belief which can be traced to the political thinkers of the age, who shared the precon-ceptions of the natural sciences. Congruent with their general social philosophy and the prevailing anti-mercantilistic aspirations of the time, the political econo-mists of the eighteenth century envisioned the manifestation of this "natural" order in economic life as a system of natural liberty, based on private property and free competition. The physiocrats and Adam Smith considered it their task to correlate the detailed phenomena of economic life within a coherent concep-tual system, in such a manner as to reveal the orderly character of the economic process under conditions of free competition, and to prove its beneficent results for society as a whole.

Succeeding generations of economists have been influenced by this belief in a rational order of things, revealed by systematic research. It has given economists a scientific mentality which accounts for the teleological search for levels of equilibrium, in keeping with the tenets of classical and neoclassical economics, and the neglect of the less harmonious aspects of economic life. The search for levels of equilibrium, in terms of exchange values, has in turn shaped the scope of economic investigations. Indeed, it was perhaps inevitable that many theoret-ical economists, in their search for the hidden orderliness in economic life, should have concentrated their attention on those phenomena which could be shown to serve the equilibriating tendencies of free competition and the beneficent purpose imputed to the system. Philosophical presuppositions and the search for levels of equilibrium also account for the more explicit assumptions of economic science, such as perfect competition and perfect mobility of the factors of production. And they are responsible for the original emphasis on static analysis and the neglect of dynamic changes, as well as for the assumption of rational human conduct. Such assumptions have led to the simplification of economic theory, the distortion of the complex reality of economic life, and the elimination of the less congenial aspects of reality from the sphere of economic theory—namely, those aspects which would be impossible to construe as contributing to the orderliness of the economic process in the unplanned market economy. This shortcoming is particularly acute in its assumption of rational human conduct, transforming an indeterminate, autonomous, and possibly disruptive factor into one sufficiently determinate to make it an integral part of economic theory. The assumption of economic rationality also provides an apparently objective justification for judging indeterminate human behavior as "non-economic," and thus excluding it from consideration.

A similar excision of the less harmonious aspects of socio-economic reality is employed in some of the more implicit assumptions of classical economic theory; for example, the assumption that economic behavior can be neatly separated from non-economic behavior, and that exchange values provide an adequate measure of the former. It is this implicit assumption that explains the acceptance of entrepreneurial outlays as an adequate and significant measure of the true total costs of production, and provides the basis for the tacit recognition of market prices and private returns as exclusive standards for the measurement of the benefits obtainable from production.

Finally, it is important to note that the tacit presuppositions and the search for hidden orderliness in the capitalist exchange economy have shaped the basic concepts of classical economics: wealth, utility, production, productive labor, and of course economy itself (in the smaller sense of the word). We might do well, then, to investigate briefly just how well these fundamental concepts have been adapted to, and serve the traditional search for, orderliness in economic life.[3] To begin, no elaborate analysis is required to show that wealth is conceived entirely in terms of appropriable (i.e., exchangeable) utilities only as measured by market prices. The concept of wealth hinges in turn on that of utility, which considers the qualities of goods and services which can be taken into exclusive possession, and as such can be measured in terms of exchange values. Goods and services without these qualities are judged to be without utility or to possess submarginal utility, and are consequently not considered as wealth. Utility, then, is not merely a function of physical and economic appropriability and technical exchangeability, but is also dependent on effective demand. Commodities for which there is no demand are said to be without utility, and are therefore not classified as wealth.

Production and productive labor are conceived in the same narrow manner as wealth; the concept of production, in fact, has always been dependent on the meaning of wealth. Disagreements between earlier economists over the "productiveness" of certain human activities can be understood only in the context of their differing definitions of wealth. Adam Smith, for example, regarded the labor of doctors, lawyers, and domestic servants as unproductive because he conceived of wealth in an exclusively material sense. Unlike his predecessors, who defined wealth either in terms of gold and silver (mercantilists) or the produce of the earth (physiocrats), Smith considered as wealth only capital equipment and consumption goods ("permanent objects or vendible commodities"), and excluded services from his definition. Today, wealth is the equivalent of exchangeable utilities in effective demand, and production is simply the creation of utilities for which there is a demand. "Labor is, in fact, productive when it satisfies a demand—when people are willing to pay for it."[4] No matter how important or essential goods and services may be, if they are not exchangeable, and consequently not measurable in dollars and cents, they are not wealth, and their creation (under government auspices, for example) is "unproductive" according to the theory and terminology of traditional value theory.

The traditional definition of these terms, however, restricts their validity and relevance outside the capitalist market economy. In an economic system in which the categories of market, exchange, and demand do not exist (as, for example, in the manorial economy), labor would be judged unproductive according to the traditional concepts of production and wealth. Similarly, the idea of economy or economic optimum is conceived solely as a function of the capitalist exchange economy—that is, in terms of private costs and returns, and thus in terms of exchange values—and is useless in the analysis of any other type of economy. Some economists have even gone so far as to assert that the capitalist exchange economy and the competitive calculus are thus prerequisites for the achievement of economy and economic rationality, and that all other forms of economic organization are incapable of allocating resources in a competitive or rational manner.

It is true that the implicit and explicit abstractions of value theory did succeed in coordinating a substantial number of detailed economic phenomena into a coherent whole, thus lending credibility to the assumption of orderliness in the economic process of the capitalist exchange economy. Given its aims, concepts, and assumptions, the theoretical conclusions of modern economic science in support of the system of natural liberty follow tautologically. Economic science was thus destined to become mere "methodology," a "technique of thinking," to use a phrase of Schumpeter's.[5] Once the individual economist accepts the methodology and masters the technique of thinking, it is difficult if not impossible for him to realize the philosophical presuppositions, and hence the limitations, of the conceptual system of economic science.[6] Having accustomed himself to the methodology, he tends to classify every phenomenon of economic reality according to the traditional scheme of logical categories,[7] and even the most penetrating deductions and the most earnest desire for objectivity cannot help but produce normative and apologetic conclusions in support of *laissez-faire* and against any positive regulation and control of the economic process by public authorities. Indeed, he will believe that only a fallacious interpretation of the basic propositions and conclusions of economic theory can justify any other course of public policy than that of non-interference with economic life.[8] It is, in fact, such narrow efficiency of the scheme, to borrow a phrase with which Whitehead refers to physical science, which was the very cause of its methodological supremacy.[9]

It should be emphasized here that in our characterizations of the conclusions of economic science as narrow and apologetic, we do not wish to imply any conscious dishonesty on the part of individual economists. The apologetic and normative character of the conclusions of value theory is not necessarily the result of an apologetic attitude consciously assumed and maintained by each economist in the course of his deductions. The apologetic-normative element is, rather, inherent in the philosophical presuppositions of the science, and in the resulting imputation of rational order into economic life; it is expressed in the search for levels of equilibrium and in the corresponding delimitation of the scope of economic analysis, and hidden in the basic assumptions and concepts of economic theory. Indeed, the economist would probably answer any challenge to his impartiality by asserting that he is speaking from a purely "economic" perspective. It will not (and cannot) occur to him that it is precisely this perspective that introduces the normative-apologetic element into his supposedly objective and neutral judgments. He also will not see that in his attempts to draw conclusions and offer solutions to concrete political problems in purely economic terms, without political premises, he will perpetuate (even in modern equilibrium theory) the old illegitimate union between pure economics and economic liberalism, and as such will produce a strange mixture of scientific conclusions and subjective value-judgments, arrived at by the rationalizing of preconceived socio-political ideals, ideologies, and metaphysical preconceptions.[10] This tendency to deal with political problems and draw political conclusions without using political premises also accounts for the traditional tension between abstract equilibrium theory and economic practice, and makes the former increasingly irrelevant to the comprehension and solution of current problems. In some instances, theoretical economists have helped to advance the interests of private groups by using their "pure" economic conclusions to supply an apparently objective critique of any form of government regulation of economic life. The inevitable result of such subordination of economic science to partisan causes has been a growing distrust of economics and the professional economist by both statesmen and the general public.[11]

This is not to deny in the least the great positive contributions of classical economics, merely to critique its shortcomings. The classical economists fought against a social philosophy and a system of restrictive regulations which were thoroughly inadequate to make full use of the technical advances made possible by the inventions and discoveries of the natural sciences in the seventeenth and eighteenth centuries. By introducing into the study of social affairs the rationalistic concepts of natural order, and by demonstrating that free competition was the "natural law" of such an order, the economists of the eighteenth century "supplied the necessary framework of ideas to meet the need of a new social philosophy adapted to the early days of the industrial revolution."[12] In their struggle against the shackles of mercantilism, the classical economists also expressed in "scientific" terms the prevailing aspirations and ideals of economic and political liberty, thus serving the positive purpose of promoting a development which, under the circumstances, must be regarded as progressive both in respect to the process of production and its scientific interpretation.[13] By introducing the concept of natural order into the study of economic and social affairs and combining it with the prevailing utilitarian doctrines, the classical economists also protected economic science, as Myrdal has observed,[14] against the specifically German philosophy of society which conceived of the state as a metaphysical super-organism that the individual was subordinated and bound to by various duties.

Today, however, it is increasingly evident that neither German state metaphysics nor the preconceptions of a beneficent natural order and harmony of interests in political affairs (those curious products of seventeenth century French rationalism and Anglo-Saxon empiricism) provide an adequate foundation for economic science. On the contrary, these philosophical presuppositions of political economy have become the biggest obstacles to the scientific comprehension and interpretation of social reality. At the same time, it appears that modern economic theory has reached the point where very little additional knowledge can be obtained from its present abstractions; indeed, with the help of mathematical methods, economists seem to have squeezed every last drop of useful information from their assumptions, and the achievements of mathematical equilibrium theory seem limited to the refinement and elaboration of old solutions and conclusions, without throwing much or any new light on the problems under discussion.

The exhaustion of the possible content and meaning of its assumptions makes neoclassical equilibrium theory a perfect illustration of Whitehead's dictum that

> systems, scientific and philosophic, come and go. Each method of limited understanding is at length exhausted. In its prime each system is a triumphant success; in its decay it is an obstructive nuisance. The transitions to new fruitfulness of understanding are achieved by recurrence to the utmost depth of intuition for the refreshment of imagination.[15]

Such a point has indeed been reached, at which it becomes possible to make positive and constructive suggestions for a reorientation of economic science.

Notes

1 B. Wootton, "Economic Planning," in W.E. Spahr (ed.), *Economic Principles and Problems*, Vol. II, New York: Farrar and Rinehart, Inc., 1940, p. 609.
2 The possibility—indeed the probability—of such capital consumption in the capitalist exchange economy emphasizes some of the limitations of the use of exchange values as the exclusive measurement of national income and national wealth. Such measurements

not only exclude the possibility of capital consumption, but are also incapable of measuring non-exchangeable utilities such as social returns. The growing proportion of resources used for the production of such social returns (government services, public health, national and social security among them) in modern society strongly suggests the need for broadening current concepts and estimates of national income, which fail to make appropriate allowance for social costs and many social returns.

3 The following analysis of basic economic concepts is based largely on L.M. Fraser, *Economic Thought and Language*, London: A. and C. Black Ltd., 1937.

4 Ibid.

5 See J. Schumpeter's Introduction to Enrico Barone, *Grundzüge der Theoretischen Nationalökonomie*, Bonn: Kurt Schröder Verlag, 1927, p. 7.

6 G. Myrdal, op. cit., p. 34.

7 Ibid.

8 Cf. C. Sutton, "The Relation Between Economic Theory and Economic Policy," *The Economic Journal* 47, 1937, p. 51.

9 A. N. Whitehead, *Science and the Modern World*, p. 26.

10 For a more elaborate analysis of the normative-apologetic character of economic science, see G. Myrdal, op. cit., especially Chapter 1; and B. Wootton, op. cit., pp. 132–182.

11 Winston Churchill has given conservative and restrained expression to this distrust of classical economic doctrine:

> Whatever we may think of these doctrines we can clearly see that they do not correspond to what is going on now. […] It is certain that the economic problem with which we are now confronted is not adequately solved, indeed, is not solved at all, by the teachings of the textbooks, however grand may be their logic, however illustrious may be their authors.
> *Amid These Storms*, New York: Charles Scribner's Sons, 1932, pp. 234–235

12 L.K. Frank, "The Principle of Disorder and Incongruity in Economic Affairs," *Political Science Quarterly* 47, 1932, p. 521.

13 See G. Myrdal, op. cit., p. 85.

14 Ibid., p. 86.

15 A.N. Whitehead, *Adventures in Ideas*, pp. 203–204.

7   Social costs and social benefits—a contribution to normative economics[1]

Social costs and social benefits are phenomena which transcend the traditional scope of economic theory. For this reason they have remained at the periphery of economic analysis. Indeed, they raise issues which can only be disturbing to those who are convinced of the fundamental efficiency of the economic process in a system of business enterprise. For the neglect of social costs and social benefits by the price mechanism sets the stage for considerable social inefficiencies in the allocation process which go far beyond the limitations usually conceded by neoclassical economics. The theory of social costs and social benefits raises some of the most fundamental and critical issues not only with regard to the substantive rationality of the price system but also with respect to the use of formal concepts and formal optima, the importance of quantification in monetary terms and the relevance of pure economics for the formulation of economic policies, and economic planning in general. In fact, the theory of social costs and social benefits lends support to those who have long argued in favor of an integrated institutional approach for the study of economic phenomena.

The present essay is concerned with a number of questions which deal with such issues as the proper classification and definition of social costs and social benefits as well as their quantitative measurement. In addition, we shall discuss some of the normative implications of social costs and social benefits for the formulation of economic policies and economic planning.

Problems of definition and classification

Definitions and classifications are never of secondary importance. They are basic and usually of far-reaching significance in their ultimate theoretical and practical implications. Concepts are tools which permit us to organize social facts into a general pattern. They guide our observations and experiences and help us to establish some preliminary order. At first our original notions reflect the uncertainty and indefiniteness which surrounds the beginning of all scientific thought. It may be said that such indefiniteness is unavoidable in new concepts and may even account for their fruit-fullness as a tool of analysis. As the concepts are used and developed in the study of concrete social phenomena they gain in precision. Clearly defined concepts are prerequisite tools for the intellectual preception of reality and the formulation of satisfactory hypotheses.

The concepts of social costs and social benefits are not freely invented fictitious notions that have no counterpart in reality. On the contrary, they have their origin in observable social phenomena. As a matter of fact, they refer to a variety of disutilities and "external" economies with identifiable common characteristics. While these concepts are based upon a critical examination of empirical phenomena they are not simply descriptions of such phenomena and experiences. They are carefully formulated "images" or representations of reality created for the purpose of theoretical interpretation. They abstract by simplifying or "condensing" common characteristics of phenomena grouped as a class and render more precise what otherwise would remain ambiguous and obscure.

It might be argued that if the concepts of social costs and social benefits refer to a variety of social diseconomies and (external) economies which arise under different circumstances they lack a sufficiently clear meaning or definition. Such, however, is not the case. Indeed, the fact that social costs and social benefits arise under different conditions does not mean that the concepts are necessarily imprecise or vague. The precision of an analytical concept depends upon the clarity with which it is possible to define the common characteristics of the empirical instances to which the concept refers. If uniqueness of empirical conditions and quantification were to be made the prerequisites of all scientific concepts we would have to abandon any attempt at generalization in the social sciences. Or, more specifically, we would have to develop separate concepts for each kind of social disutility and social benefit depending upon the specific situation in which they may arise. This would be equivalent to a concentration on particular events or the end of theory in social inquiry. It would involve a return to a radical and naive empiricism which lacks generic terms and concepts and which develops different verbal expressions for each particular process. No doubt, it will be difficult and sometimes impossible to attribute an unequivocal quantitative value or importance to disutilities or benefits under consideration but this is a problem of quantification which must be distinguished from the need for clarity in the formulation of concepts.

Specifically what are social costs and social benefits? What are their common characteristics? Do we possess as yet a satisfactory classification of social and private costs and of social and private benefits? Is such a classification possible? Social costs can be defined as harmful effects and damages sustained by the economy as a result of private productive activities. Social costs may take the form of a variety of "diseconomies", increased risks and uncertainties which may extend far into the future. What makes these diseconomies social costs is the fact that they are borne by third persons or by society. In this sense they are indeed "external". Of course, the term external is relative. What is "external" depends upon the degree of consolidation of industry. Furthermore, if production becomes centralized the unit of investigation is the entire economy; in this case the term "external" loses its meaning altogether for all costs would be internal. However, even under these circumstances we may speak of social costs in the sense of wasteful outlays, avoidable inefficiencies, and harmful effects on public health and public wealth.

These considerations also throw light on another aspect of social costs: the general interdependence of all parts of the economy makes it likely that, with any given level of vertical and horizontal integration, social costs caused by a particular firm may adversely affect not only third persons but other entrepreneurs and may even adversely affect the firm originally responsible for their occurrence. For instance, the social costs of air pollution are borne by everybody, including the entrepreneurs who originally contributed to it. They, as well as other firms, will see their private costs increased by the negative effects which air pollution may have on the health of their workers and the value of their property. In this way part of the "social" costs are absorbed into private costs. In still other cases the social costs may assume the form of unnecessarily higher private costs of production. This happens, for example, when the competitive race to exploit an oil pool leads to a technically inefficient spacing and multiplication of oil wells. In this case the social diseconomies take the form of unnecessary capital inputs which, together with the subsequent loss of natural gas and reservoir pressure, constitute an increase of production costs. Similarly, in the case of soil depletion and erosion the attempts by farmers to minimize *current* costs has the effect of increasing future costs of cultivation. In all these instances, at least part of the social costs take the form of higher private costs. However, do these examples affect the usefulness of the distinction between private and social costs? If private enterprise internalized the total or a major share of the social costs caused by its productive activities the distinction would be less than fully satisfactory, although even then it would not entirely lose its significance. We would be faced with a kind of joint costs—that is, social costs—which due to economic and technical interdependencies of the productive process, are at least in part reflected in higher private costs of production. Actually, however, we are confronted with a different situation. For example, that part of the social costs which are caused by air and water pollution and borne by the firm whose productive activities contributed to the pollution of the atmosphere (or river) is rather small—if compared with the total of the social losses sustained by the community. Admittedly, the proportion of "internalized" social costs may be higher in the case of duplication of capital costs and the losses of reservoir pressure in the oil industry or the depletion and erosion of the soil in agriculture. But even in these cases the original distinction does not lose its usefulness if we consider that the increased private costs are avoidable and are actually passed on to the community in the form of higher prices. They are damages or diseconomies sustained by the economy in general which could be avoided under different institutional conditions. For, obviously, if these costs were inevitable under any kind of institutional arrangement they would not really present a special theoretical problem. We are thus led to the conclusion that in order to reveal their origin, the study of social costs must always be an institutional analysis. Such an analysis raises inevitably the question of institutional reform and economic policy which may eliminate or minimize the social diseconomies under discussion.

Turning to the problem of social benefits, we are faced with similar issues of definition and classification. For the term social benefits refers to all those utilities and "returns" which tend to accrue to society either as a result of institutional arrangements or are due to private productive activities. Like social costs, these broader social benefits belong to those omitted aspects of reality which classical political economy did not succeed in incorporating into its theoretical framework. It is true that Adam Smith developed a theory of social benefits in connection with his doctrine of public institutions and public works which,

> though [...] in the highest degree advantageous to a great society, are, however, of such a nature, that the profit could never repay the expense to any individual or small number of individuals and which it, therefore, cannot be expected that any individual or small number of individuals should erect or maintain.[2]

Lord Lauderdale and Friedrich List pointed to essentially the same kind of social benefits in their critical doctrine of "public wealth" and "productive forces." Later, Henry Sidgwick called attention to useful services which were "incapable of being appropriated by those who produce them or who would otherwise be willing to produce them."[3] J.B. Clark developed a theory of non-competitive economics based upon the principle of "inappropriable utilities" which "flee from him who creates them and diffuse themselves among the members of the community."[4] Even Marshall's "external economies" may be considered as social benefits which accrue to every firm and for which no remuneration can either be charged or need to be paid.[5] These earlier discussions of social returns remained isolated attempts which moreover were never systematically developed.[6]

Social benefits differ from private utilities and private returns by virtue of the fact that they cannot be divided or withheld. Once produced, everybody benefits and nobody can be excluded. In short, social benefits accrue to all members of society. This inability to divide or to "monopolize" even a share of social benefits reflects not only the existence of basic economic and technological interdependencies within the economy but is also due to the fact that some of the most important internal and external security needs as well as cultural requirements are collective in character. That is to say they concern all members of society and their gratification automatically benefits every individual. Whenever we are confronted with social needs or public interests or purposes we enter the field of social benefits and the legitimate sphere of government, which is "to do for the people what needs to be done, but which they cannot by individual effort, do at all, or do so well, for themselves."[7]

Without taking account of these indivisible social needs and social benefits it is impossible to arrive at an understanding of the scope of the public economy and public investments and of the formulation of economic policies, whether in economically advanced countries or in the underdeveloped world. While we cannot enter into a detailed discussion of the concept of social benefits it is possible to raise the question of whether we can ever hope to distinguish them from private benefits or individual utilities. Does the fact that social benefits accrue to all members of society (or that external economies in the form of lower costs and cost advantages can ultimately be internalized in the cost and price structure of private firms including perhaps the firm which originally contributed to the external economies) militate against the distinction between private and social benefits? No doubt, it may be difficult to disentangle social and private benefits. But "in practice" the whole process of dynamic socio-economic development may be said to consist in nothing else but a continuous incorporation of social or external benefits into private costs and private benefits. As a matter of fact, all benefits and utilities may be said to be experienced only by private individuals. It is their needs and requirements that are satisfied. Surely this common-sense realization does not make the distinction between private and social benefits useless or unsatisfactory. The fact that, in reality, everything can be shown to be interrelated cannot be held against the distinction as long as the latter points to significant and practically relevant characteristics by which phenomena can be classified and separated from one another. Social benefits are indivisible and hence elude him who produces them; they accrue automatically to everybody. Their systematic production calls for social action by specialized public agencies which are concerned with the formulation of social goals and public purposes. In short, since they will not be produced by private firms their creation presupposes a collective decision. We are thus led to the inevitable question of the objectivity with which social benefits (and social costs) can be defined.

The objective character of social costs and social benefits

Is it possible to identify and define social costs and social benefits objectively? Can these extra-market phenomena be defined only in terms of a given set of ultimate ethical postulates and ultimate values which are beyond the scope of any scientific treatment? Are we inevitably faced with a plurality of possible points of view and an infinite number of possible standards of value when we attempt to identify and define the social costs and social benefits which the market system tends to ignore or neglect? Or more specifically, do we abandon the realm of the objective, that is, of scientific validation and refutation, when we concern ourselves with social costs and social returns? Do we enter the realm of purely subjective and ideologically tinged judgments? Do we open the door to what Max Weber called the "ethics of conviction" with its unconditional and uncritical devotion to an absolute idea and fixed aim which leads man to do what he believes to be right without asking what the consequences are? Or do we stay firmly in the realm of the "ethics of' responsibility", in Max Weber terminology[8]—with its implicit demand for an objective evaluation of the situation as it really is and the insistence that our judgments remain subject to empirical validation and refutation? In short do we keep the door open for the possibility of disproving our evaluations? It is in this fundamental and pragmatic sense of susceptibility to revision in the light of experience and of the empirical test that we shall use the term "objectivity" in the following discussion.

As a first step it is important to recognize the purely formal objectivity of market values. It is true that market values are numerical and quantitative. As such, they can be added and compared in terms of operations which are simple and easily understood. But their numerical character, which enables us to compare and measure them unambiguously in the formal sense of all mathematical operations, conceals their substantively more or less arbitrary character. Both Max Weber and Veblen[9] (and of course many others since) recognized this clearly by referring to advertising and the effects of sales publicity on consumers' wants and commodity prices. Moreover, Max Weber, and again many others before him and since, has been explicit in showing that money prices are the outcome of market power, conflicts of interests and compromises. For this reason, market values, although expressed in numerical terms "without a wholly subjective valuation"[10] are substantively speaking far from being unambiguous and objective. Indeed, in a world of oligopolistic price-fixing they are as devoid of "objective" validity as many of the subjective value judgments which Weber considered to be in principle beyond the scope of scientific validation.

What do we mean by "formal" and "substantive" and what is the bearing of these terms on the objectivity of the definition of social costs and social benefits? Following Max Weber we shall use the term "formal" with reference to quantitative calculations or accounting in numerical terms. The prototype, but not the only kind of such calculation, is "capital accounting" (Kapitalrechnung) which establishes the numerical profitability of an investment. Substantive rationality, on the other hand, measures the extent to which a given group of persons is, or could be, adequately provided with goods by means of an economically oriented course of social action.[11] The identification of social benefits and social costs is not so much a problem of formal calculation as it is a matter of ascertaining actual human and social requirements or actual damages and harmful effects. When we try to determine the social benefits or social costs we are not concerned with a numerical profitability or a marginal importance attributed by an individual or a group of individuals to particular utilities or disutilities. Instead, we are aiming at an identification of substantive social needs and actual social damages and inefficiencies. Such identification calls for careful empirical research. What has been described as the starving of the public sector in modern affluent societies is not removed from objective analysis and the scientific test. For example, the recognition of the need for additional educational and housing facilities is not simply a matter of changing ultimate values based upon ambiguous ethical postulates. Such recognition is rather the outcome of a better understanding of growth correlations and the tendency toward social imbalance promoted by the traditional reliance on formal calculations in the allocation of resources. Similarly, the progressive congestion of traffic arteries to, and within, our expanding metropolitan areas, as well the heavy expenses incurred for urban renewal and redevelopment, are the outcome of a regional polarization which is characteristic of urban growth in the absence of zoning and regional planning.

Under such conditions, industrialization, migration, and natural increases of population combine to bring about the irrational overconcentration of the modern city.[12] That is to say the progressive deterioration of transportation systems, the continued shortages of adequate housing, education and hospital facilities even in the richest country of the world is the outcome of a refusal or an inability to draw up in time an inventory of substantive needs and foreseeable trends and to project these trends into the future with a view to determining the respective requirements as a basis of public planning and investment decisions. There is nothing mysterious about these growth correlations. They are the outcome of technical and economic interdependencies (complementarities) between an expanding population, the corresponding needs for housing, education, medical care, and transportation. What is required is a projection into the future of the role which private automobiles, railroads, buses, and trucks are going to play in meeting expanding transportation needs. Furthermore what is called for is a concentration of the authority to make decisions in the hands of a single agency rather than a number of departments and authorities each operating under different rules and controls.[13]

Growth correlations and technical interdependencies are also useful for the determination of social benefits and social requirements. The following illustrations may give a concrete idea of what we have in mind.

Underdeveloped economies are marked by regional imbalance and the lack of adequate overhead capital. Among the means to overcome this type of imbalance are regional development schemes, which may serve a variety of purposes such as the production of electric power, the storage and discharge of water in accordance with requirements of flood control, the development of inland water transportation—in short, the promotion and attainment of the transformation of the economy of the region. That is to say a multipurpose water utilization scheme produces joint products at joint costs. The economic success or failure of such a scheme depends upon the coordination of the various parts, which is, to a large extent, a technical problem. The ramifications of these technical interdependencies are so wide that it is possible to present here only a limited picture. The determination of the site for a dam and reservoir, for example, is a matter of physical comparisons in terms of technical criteria requiring detailed surveys of the catchment area (as to its annual run-off, the availability of fertile land and its suitability for farming in terms of its drainage conditions, and the number of people affected by the inundation behind the dam). The construction of the dam usually calls for the erection of new facilities for workers connected with the project. The production of electricity calls for the provision of a grid system to distribute power over a considerable area. The distribution of water for irrigation purposes makes no sense without the construction of distributaries, canals and irrigation ditches (and, in some instances pumping stations) through which the water can reach the fields. More than this, these distributaries must be constructed and maintained in such a fashion as to minimize seepage. Provision must be made for malaria control, as the increased supply of water may easily increase the incidence of the disease. Moreover, irrigation farming calls for greater use of fertilizers in order to be physically effective and economically efficient. In order to prevent premature sedimentation of the reservoir, proper erosion control schemes (e.g., anti-erosion benches throughout the catchment area) will be needed. If the water is made available free of charge, it may be wasted by the cultivator, with disastrous consequences in terms of water-logging, the seepage of soil-destructive salts to the surface and the promotion of water-carried diseases. If, on the other hand, water rates are too high, they may act as a disincentive for a farm population used to "gamble in rain." The result would be unused capacity of an expensive capital good just as delays or lack of coordination of the various technical phases of the water utilization scheme would imply underutilization of the stored water. These technical and economic interdependencies call for a physical coordination which in turn determines the objectives of rational social action. If these interdependencies are permitted to serve as a guide to action, utilization of capacity will be guaranteed which in this case means not only high benefits at low costs but a speedier readjustment and transformation of the regional economy.[14] In short, a regional development scheme is a physical and economic unit and must be treated by social science as a unit of investigation and planning. It calls for consideration of all physical and economic aspects simultaneously. If it is so treated and planned it is bound to attain its overall level of efficiency (substantively speaking) in the shortest possible time. The principle of substantive rationality calls, therefore, for a solution of the problem of socio-technical coordination since otherwise valuable capital investments would stand idle and be unable to make their full contribution to the development process.

Another basis for the determination of substantive needs is the elaboration of social minima. Admittedly, opinions may differ when it comes to the establishment of such social minima. And yet, in practice, the area of agreement may be much greater than we usually assume. Here again empirical research can provide us with the necessary data for the identification of, and a basis for the evaluation of, substantive needs and benefits. Once more an example from the under developed world may serve to illustrate our point. In India about two million people die every year of cholera, typhoid, dysentery, and other water-carried diseases and one seventh of the country's total population suffers ailments caused by an unprotected water supply. Public health experts estimate that 75 percent of the diseases would disappear if a protected water supply and sanitary facilities were provided.[15] While the mere identification of the situation does not eliminate the need to choose—for similar deficiencies may exist in education, hospital care, and other parts of the public sector—it cannot be denied that the exploration of social needs objectifies them.

Similarly, the identification of social costs is not a matter of subjective-ideological commitment to this or that program of social reform but a matter of empirical research. In fact, whether a particular loss or damage is a social cost depends at any given time on the state of our knowledge. As long as the causal relationship between specific productive activities and specific disutilities is not understood we do not know whether or not we are confronted with a case of actual social costs. For instance, there may be diseases whose occupational origin has not yet been recognized by our present medical knowledge. Only further advances in medical research will enable us to establish these causal links.[16] This possibility is not confined to the impairment of the human factor but applies also to other categories of social costs. We may speak of hidden or concealed social costs which are recognized only when scientific research identifies the relationship between a particular negative effect and specific productive processes or their products.[17] An advancing industrial technology is bound to expose its labor force to new materials, new processes and new products and thus is likely to widen the range of actual social costs. In short the identification of social costs and social benefits derives its objectivity from an orientation toward a substantive rationality which reflects the extent to which a given group of persons is or could be adequately provided with goods and services, or protected against unnecessary losses.

In contrast to Max Weber, we suggest that the substantive definition of social costs and social benefits is possible in terms of objective requirements which do not depend upon an infinite number of possible subjective standards (or an "infinite plurality of possible points of view")[18] but can be determined with a considerable degree of scientific objectivity. That is to say, the identification of social costs and social benefits calls for scientifically determined social minima and an awareness of economic and technical growth correlations which link private wants and public needs on the one hand and which trace the physical interdependencies between private productive activities and external diseconomies on the other. No doubt such a substantive orientation to economic life and economic action commits the economist to a new and broader perspective of the relationships between the economic and the noneconomic. What seems to be a perfectly reasonable distinction from the perspective of a purely formal orientation turns out to be misleading and untenable as soon as we deal with concrete situations in a substantive way. When we inquire into the actual state of want satisfaction, all levels of social existence must be viewed as intrinsically and reciprocally interrelated. The political, the socio-cultural, and the economic represent a unitary whole. Changes on one level affect all other levels of this interrelated structure. Indeed the conceptual distinction between the economic and noneconomic turns out to be a fictitious separation which may be useful for some scientific purposes but which is likely to serve some non-scientific objectives if the fictitious character is forgotten and becomes the basis for the normative conclusion that only private wants are "truly" economic, that social needs and requirements are meta-economic, and that the latter are beyond the scope of science.

Moreover, the substantive definition of economic action questions the validity of the tacit identification of an "infinite plurality of possible points of view" or "an infinite number of standards of value" (Max Weber) with a notion of a plurality of ends. In formal economics it may be legitimate to assume a plurality of competing ends, although even then it would seem to be problematical to identify the plurality of ends with the notion of "alternative uses."[19] In practice, however, and for all purposes of substantive analysis, the plurality of ends frequently disappears when intelligence is brought to bear upon the study of social needs and social costs. To be sure, the necessity of choice does not disappear but the number of alternative ends is considerably reduced. What is more, once we subject social needs to a deliberate analysis in the light of the concrete historical situation, including the available means, we increase the chances of harmonizing conflicts and establishing priorities by the constructive use of intelligence. This constructive use of intelligence differs radically from the purely "manipulative" use of reason which guides the procedures of business accounting and is the prototype of formal rationality. In fact, the "formal" comparison of numerical expenses and receipts in accordance with the canons of accountancy has only one aim: the maximization of net pecuniary gain. In contrast, the constructive use of intelligence is concerned with the realization of genuine opportunities and the exploration of new possibilities.[20] This requires the projection of repercussions of action or non-action under different circumstances. What will be the effects if we permit the social process to drift? What are the overall repercussions if social minima of public health were not enforced? What social losses are likely to arise? What are the consequences of maintaining or not maintaining certain growth correlations between different sectors of the economy? We have tried to answer some of these questions in our analysis of social costs.[21] Here we can indicate only briefly the possibility of defining minimum standards in various fields. Thus, in the field of air and water pollution it is possible to work out minimum standards of public health in the form of maximum permissible levels of concentration of pollutants. Social costs and social objectives can be identified in terms of existing deficiencies by comparing the actual state of pollution with the maximum permissible concentration of pollutants. Similarly, it is possible to work out safe social minima or maximum rates of depletion of renewable resources (e.g., wildlife and fisheries) as well as water and soil by the definition of a *critical zone*[22] beyond which any increase of depletion would give rise to an irreversible process of destruction of the resource. Minimum standards of requirements can be defined also in such fields as public health, medical care, education, housing, civilian defense, transportation, and recreation. Even the problem of unemployment, including technological unemployment, can be approached in terms of a minimum rate of growth required to absorb an increasing labor supply and the number of workers permanently displaced by machinery and automation.

With the elaboration of social minima it becomes possible, at least in principle, to demonstrate objectively the presence of social costs and social benefits. By projecting the consequences of private decisions and public action (or non-action) in a given field, the analysis of social costs and social benefits prepares the ground for the elaboration of social objectives, social priorities, and social choices. We shall discuss below some of the problems which we have to face in determining social priorities. It is true, the determination of social minima may not eliminate altogether the subjective ideological elements inherent in the attempt to quantify social costs and social benefits. However, such standards objectify these extra-market phenomena. As a result it is easier to reach compromises or even a consensus of opinion. For example, we no longer question the validity of our minimum standards of public health and no serious person will deny their objectivity.

Quantification and evaluation

The question of the quantification of social costs and social benefits is sometimes raised in the implicit belief that if a concept resists quantification and measurement in monetary terms it is necessarily vague, ambiguous, and outside the scope of economic science. To demonstrate that such quantification is difficult or impossible is then considered to be equivalent to having said practically the last word on the subject-matter: namely, to have ruled it out of existence as far as scientific inquiry is concerned. In economics this attitude is reinforced by an implicit identification of economic calculation with business calculation and of quantification with measurement in monetary terms.

No one will deny that quantification and measurement make for precision. Conclusions formulated in terms of quantitative concepts can be tested more easily than qualitative statements. Economics has adapted itself to the ideal of measurement and quantification. Everything connected with the conduct of business transactions—such as the production of goods and services, consumption and even goodwill—tends to be expressed in numerical terms and has been subjected to quantification in terms of money and prices. Indeed, money provides a common standard in terms of which all the typical operations of measurement can be carried out and repeated: addition, subtraction, multiplication. The application of statistics has lent further support to the belief that economics has been more successful than other social disciplines in the use of the quantitative method. Furthermore, many of our concepts seem to have assumed a quantitative connotation which supports the impression that the problem of quantification and measurement has found a solution in economics.

However, this widely accepted view tends to exaggerate the extent and actual success of quantification and measurement in economic analysis. Our concepts may be quantitative in form but the substantive measurability of the quantities under discussion is in no way established. We may speak of marginal productivity and opportunity costs but we tend to forget that these seemingly quantitative and precise terms refer to fictitious concepts. Indeed, how is one to calculate marginal costs under conditions of joint costs and multiple product production when overhead costs are large and fixed capital highly specialized and non-saleable? And how can elasticity and marginal returns in concrete market conditions, with varying degrees of oligopoly and countervailing power, be quantified and measured? It is one thing to use a quantitative term with reference to a theoretical category which has no counterpart in reality; it is altogether different to quantify and measure an actual social phenomenon. Any substantive quantification and measurement in a concrete situation encounters the greatest practical difficulties. Thus, what are believed to be clear-cut quantitative definitions and tools of analysis turn out, upon closer examination, to be pseudo-quantitative in content. Hence, actual quantification and measurement are not quite as successful in economic analysis as is commonly believed.

Before turning to the basic issues raised by attempts to quantify social costs, it is important to stress that there are several ways to express at least some of the social costs of business enterprise in quantitative and even monetary terms. Thus, the loss of wages and output due to occupational diseases and industrial accidents, and the costs of medical and hospital care due to partial and permanent disablement, can be calculated and compared with actual compensation payments available under Workmen's Compensation or Social Security Acts. Evidence of soil erosion and soil depletion can be measured in terms of reduced soil fertility and the commercial value of crops not produced. The commercial losses caused by soil erosion and floods can be ascertained with a reasonable degree of precision. We can even calculate the capital value of resources lost once we agree on the rate at which to discount a stream of income derived in the past which would have been available in the future had the competitive exploitation of given resources not led to their premature depletion. It is possible to indicate the extent of (technically) unnecessary wells in the competitive exploitation of an oil field and similar duplication of capital in mining and transportation: we can estimate the resulting higher costs of recovery and loss of unrecoverable underground resources; we can ascertain the social costs involved in the high bankruptcy rate of small retail trade; and we can calculate the costs of sales promotion as a percentage of national income.[23] An attempt has even been made to calculate the social costs of migration due to technological change.[24]

Another indirect approach to measure social costs, at least partially, would be to estimate the outlays required in order to remedy the damages caused by various private productive activities. For example, it is quite possible to arrive at quantitative estimates of the extra costs of cleaning buildings exposed to polluted air. Another method of quantifying social costs would be to calculate the costs of preventing their occurrence. For example, the costs involved in the installation of proper filters or waste treatment equipment might be used to measure at least some of the social costs of air and water pollution. This is a highly significant measure in so far as it would indicate the extent of the additional outlays which business enterprise would have to incur in order to eliminate social costs.

Just as social costs can be quantified in terms of the additional private costs involved in their prevention, so the social benefits of "public institutions and public works" can be given a quantitative expression (and even monetary expression) in terms of the public outlays required for their production. Such a quantification presupposes an estimation of the possible range of social and individual consequences if no steps were taken to secure these benefits. For instance, what individual and social losses are likely to arise as a result of inadequate facilities for education, transportation, research, public health or, for that matter, of the failure to insist on the installation of adequate water and smoke pollution abatement equipment. If it can be shown, for example, that an investment of $100,000 required for the installation of smoke filtration and pollution abatement equipment would have the effect of eliminating social losses to the extent of $200,000 we will have quantified social costs as well as social benefits.

The foregoing discussion points to genuine possibilities of quantifying social costs and social benefits if a serious intellectual effort were made to this end. However, it must be admitted that some real difficulties stand in the way of the quantification and measurement of social costs and benefits in monetary terms. First, there is the problem of joint causation. Air and water pollution are not only caused by private industries. Private consumers and public utilities are important contributing factors. Unemployment due to technological processes cannot be easily separated quantitatively from the unemployment caused by other factors. In the last analysis the general interdependence of all elements of the economy represents a serious obstacle to the precise measurement of the social costs of business enterprise.

A second and even more serious difficulty becomes evident if we consider the social costs resulting from the competitive exploitation and depletion of renewable and non-renewable resources. For clearly the magnitude of these social losses depends upon the value which these resources will have in the future. The discounted future value of these resources may be said to provide some measure of the present magnitude of the losses represented by their depletion. However, neither the discount rate nor their future value nor indeed the number of generations to be considered are objectively given. The future value cannot be ascertained since it depends largely upon the importance which the present generation attributes to the interests and values of its descendants. However, the fact that the social costs of depletion cannot be determined with a desirable degree of precision must not be taken to prove that no social costs arise from the depletion of resources. It would be hazardous to assume that the future will take care of itself and that technical progress and research will automatically provide us with alternative resources of energy as we deplete our present ones. On the other hand, it is problematical to subordinate the interest of the present generation to those of future generations, particularly if we consider that the future may depend upon a new and different technology and resource pattern. Somewhere between complete disregard and complete subordination of the present to the future lies the answer to a rational resource policy.

Finally we have to consider the heterogeneity of social benefits such as education, public health, and defense which are essentially incommensurable except in as far as they require scarce resources for their gratification. Interesting as it might be to supplement our national output and income accounting system of national book-keeping in terms of social benefits and social costs, the establishment of such a system of accounting would certainly raise more questions than can be answered here. What is needed is the promotion of empirical research designed to establish more precise measurements of the various categories of social losses and social benefits in monetary terms, as well as in terms of general social estimates of their importance, with a view to formulating the protective legislation that may be called for.

However, in the light of our distinction between formal and substantive rationality it would be unwarranted to confine the quantification of social costs and social benefits only to measurements in monetary terms or market values. As a matter of fact, as long as we look upon business accounting as the model of social evaluation and use the latter as a general yardstick of all quantification and measurement we effectively block any intellectual and practical progress in this field. As we have pointed out, business calculations deal with quantities such as receipts and expenses and net gains in monetary terms. Formal economic analysis which views all transactions in this light merely follows the pattern of business calculations. There is nothing wrong with this procedure as long as it is clearly understood that business decisions aim at a fixed objective which requires no further deliberation. Maximization of net profits (a numerical quantity) represents a single objective which neither admits nor requires any further reflection as to the kind and quality of purpose involved. However, as we have shown, such profit and loss calculations differ radically from the constructive use of intelligence and deliberation[25] about actual ends or actual damages and harmful effects. In the case of social benefits and social costs we are confronted with qualitatively different and heterogeneous benefits (or ends) and diseconomies which, even if they could be expressed fully in terms of market prices, would still call for deliberation before it would be possible to arrive at a valuation. Even if possible, a simple business calculation would not be enough. The question is not how "profitable" it would be to prevent the pollution of the natural environment but what importance we attach to clean air and clean water. In evaluating any of these objectives it is a prerequisite to know the consequences of polluted air and water on public health and other values. While it is doubtless helpful to inquire into the costs of pollution abatement, no refinement of our tools can finally help us to quantify the "value" of heterogeneous qualities in monetary terms.

Thus we reach once more the limits of our traditional approach to the appraisal of economic magnitudes in terms of market prices. Indeed, the problem of quantification of social costs and social benefits cannot find a completely satisfactory solution on the basis of exchange values. As extra-market phenomena their magnitude cannot be adequately expressed in numerical terms which serve the purely formal and much more simple business calculation. Nor is this surprising. For there is no reason to assume that it is tenable to transfer criteria of formal rationality to the sphere of social costs and social benefits, which can be properly evaluated only in terms of criteria of substantive rationality and dynamic analysis. The question of the adequacy and transferability of concepts raises issues which lie outside the domain of the present essay. And yet they cannot be entirely avoided. Suffice it to indicate here with dogmatic brevity what we regard as the essential implications of our general position.

We have made it clear that any concern with social costs and social benefits calls for a substantive approach to economic analysis. The evaluation of social costs and social benefits presupposes an emancipation from calculation in terms of formal market prices and a consideration of actual human wants and the ways and means by which resources can be mobilized for the enhancement of public welfare. This presupposes a deliberate concern for "the ultimate aims of man" as Alfred Marshall[26] put it. Substantive economics cannot refrain from taking account of individual wants and social requirements. That is to say we cannot avoid making distinctions between "essential" and "non-essential" needs.[27] Such a distinction can be based upon objectified social minima which could serve as a starting point for the identification of major social deficiencies. We must identify those sectors of the economy most likely to lag behind in economic and social development. This would enable us to determine social priorities in the light of available means and to decide upon the increase of resources in the light of established needs. To repeat, the criteria of social evaluation are not supported by the formal rationality principle (e.g., maximization of expected net monetary revenues) but are based upon the principle to maintain adequate levels of satisfaction of essential human wants at the lowest possible costs within the limits of available resources.[28]

This is not a problem of defining a formal general optimum but a pragmatic task of improving the actual state of individual and social welfare. Indeed, what matters most in this context is the determination of the general direction in which to move and less the attainment and calculation of equimarginal utilities from the last additional dollar spent in all lines of endeavor. In practice, the determination of social priorities, and hence the quantification problem, is considerably simpler than would appear in the light of the refinements of traditional formal value and price theory. While there are always a number of ends to consider (except perhaps in times of emergency) they are not as numerous as is sometimes believed. Indeed, if there were a multitude of ends, and if we permitted them to become unlimited in number and scope, we could not act at all. We must select and deliberate about our ends and, in this deliberation, we must be concerned less with the calculation of indeterminate and indeterminable future results, which escape our foresight and are always contingent on new developments, than with present deficiencies and short-term projections in the light of available means. The concrete situation, if properly surveyed and analyzed in the fight of available means, limits the possible number of goals and narrows our choice.[29]

In fact, objective and scientifically arrived at minimum standards tend to assume, for instance in the field of public health, the character of a norm of almost overruling importance in view of the fact that any violation of such standards endangers human health and survival. If this is granted, the maintenance of social minima once agreed upon becomes literally a technical question which, unlike an economic question, leaves little or no doubt as to the choice of the most appropriate means in accordance with the principle of achieving the result with the least expenditure of resources.[30] That is to say the maintenance of a safe social minimum, once defined and socially agreed upon, would call only for the traditional cost-consciousness and awareness of technical efficiency of the engineer. Needless to add, we are not suggesting that the establishment of social minima in some fields transforms all economic problems into technical questions. What we do suggest as undeniable is the fact that, as we extend the applicability of social minima, we "rationalize" and "objectify" the determination of social costs and social benefits and remove their evaluation increasingly from the realm of subjective or ideological self-deceptions and distortions.

This brings us finally to the problem of the social evaluation of social benefits and social costs which has remained the least explored problem of social theory, despite the fact that the issues have been raised from time to time. What has kept the discussion in a state of suspense is the subjectivist–utilitarian bias of our value theory and the Benthamite tendency to consider society (or the nation) as a theoretical fiction. Let us emphasize therefore, from the very outset, that far from being in conflict with individual wants, social needs and social benefits are actually the consequences of private decisions. The exploration of these interrelationships between private and social needs is the legitimate objective of government and the prerequisite of a civilized and democratic society. "A government that wants to meet the hopes and wishes of the citizen must take upon itself the consequences of the citizen's own planning."[31] The requirements of civilized life and the principle of substantive rationality demand that the tendency toward social imbalance of the price system be counteracted by the continuous objective determination of social needs and potential social benefits. Such determination must not be guided by market prices—not even competitive market prices because the market reflects only effective demand and, moreover, is directly responsible for the emergence of a social imbalance and social costs. That is to say, market demand reflects fully the inequalities of income, the time preference of the individual and, particularly in affluent societies, the effects of sales promotion. The determination of social needs and social benefits must reflect the substantive i.e., recognizable needs and desires of the average low-income consumer. In short, social evaluation must be more democratic (substantively speaking) than the evaluation which emerges in the interaction of supply and effective demand. If this consideration is relevant for advanced countries, it is even more so for the underdeveloped world which has long suffered from a neglect of social overhead investments and from even greater inequalities in incomes. In short, the theory of social value must be based upon a democratic theory of consumption.[32] There is no reason why, at least in principle, decisions as to social priorities could not be arrived at by a majority vote. The removal of India's deficiencies in sanitation, drinking water, or electricity, just as the elimination of air pollution in the United States, can be made the subject of a referendum.

We do not deny that the social evaluation of the relative importance of social benefits and social costs will always carry elements of a political decision as to social purposes and goals. In this connection it cannot be emphasized too strongly that the determination of social benefits and social costs does not take place in a vacuum but will always be at least in part derived from the concrete conditions and necessities of the socio-economic and political situation. Admittedly this relationship does not give rise to an unequivocal and self-evident determination of social goals and social values, but it limits the influence of arbitrary ideological factors and facilitates the formulation of aims and priorities which are accessible to scientific interpretation and the pragmatic test.[33]

There remains the important question of how the necessary consistency and interdependence of the various parts of the economic process can be established in harmony with social values and social development goals, particularly under dynamic conditions. With this question we cannot avoid reopening a discussion which has long been considered as closed and has all but disappeared from economic analysis: the problem of calculation in real terms. All experiences made during the last decades in connection with economic planning seem to support the conclusion of those who have argued that planning and the translation of social goals into an internally consistent development process call for a calculation in real terms rather than in terms of prices.

This is relevant for our discussion. For social costs and social benefits are, to a large extent, extra-market phenomena. Hence the price system cannot be relied upon to provide the criteria for their social evaluation. Social costs as well as social benefits are heterogeneous in character, they cannot be evaluated in terms of a single denominator. As far as social benefits are concerned, the criteria available are social minima based upon a substantive and democratic evaluation of social needs and requirements and their comparison in real (physical) terms with available resources. What makes it possible and necessary to reopen this problem afresh are recent advances in our techniques and our knowledge concerning the quantitative input-output relationships between different industries. These studies have opened up new possibilities to express in quantitative terms the real costs of different social goals. Input-output balances provide the basis for a rational approach to the important task of coordinating output targets and input requirements throughout the economy. They yield the necessary data for the calculation of interdependencies and growth correlations between different sectors of the economy. Finally, knowledge of the physical inter-industry relationships answers important questions related to planning the capacity of supplementary investments called for by any large-scale multipurpose project.

By informing us about the real costs in terms of resources or labor required for the achievement of particular goals or benefits, input-output studies would contribute to the quantification (in real terms) of social benefits. The problem of social choice, and the determination of social preferences, thereby becomes easier than is usually assumed. There is no reason why such choices and priorities cannot find expression in schedules of (controlled) relative prices expressed in monetary terms for accounting purposes. However, even if this is done, the criteria of substantive rationality and economic optimum will always have to be expressed in terms which permit the measurement of the attainment of higher levels of productivity or decreasing real costs. In practice this can only mean that conditions of economy-wide balances between total supply and social demand are maintained through the speedy removal of deficiencies, bottlenecks, and excess capacities. Indeed what often counts most in practical affairs is the making of decisions with a minimum of delay. This time dimension of decision-making is of the greatest importance in judging the substantive rationality of economic planning. For, due to the interdependence of the economic process, delays in decision-making often have more far-reaching effects than bad decisions made on time.[34] Admittedly we face here the question of how far measurements of dynamic technical efficiency can serve as an index of substantive socio-economic efficiency. To deal with this question would take us beyond the scope of the present essay.

As we have indicated above, calculations in real terms, as indeed any substantive approach to economics, has its own problems and sources of inefficiencies.[35] No one will deny that political factors and ethical value judgments are bound to influence the decisions to minimize social costs and to realize social benefits through social investments and public works. The economy is never completely free of such political and ethical influences. It is also true that conflicts of interest and elements of coercion will intrude into the political process and hence influence the evaluation of social benefits (and social costs) and the determination of social priorities. However, the fact that for many decades *silicosis* was not recognized as a social cost or that the same social costs may be treated differently in different societies may indicate differences in the distribution of political power but does not refute the objective character of social costs. Similarly, the fact that many underdeveloped countries do not provide an adequate system of education or sanitation cannot affect the objective character of the social benefits obtainable from "investments" in the human factor. Nor can the realization that different people may place a different (subjective) value on the benefits of education and health deny the objective character of the advantages which a literate and healthy population enjoys over an illiterate and disease-ridden one.

Social costs and social benefits: their implications for public policy and economic development

The foregoing analysis has left no doubt that the principles of formal rationality cannot define an optimum of social efficiency. On the contrary, by systematically neglecting the extra-market phenomena of social costs and social benefits, formal rationality is basically in conflict with and opposed to substantive rationality. While the former may be useful as a scientific fiction for explaining the behavior of the entrepreneurial unit engaged in business accounting—although even this usefulness has been questioned—it differs in content from substantive rationality and hence does not provide an adequate norm for the formulation of economic policies.

It is, therefore, pertinent to ask whether and how the presence of social costs and social benefits influences the formulation of practical policies in industrially advanced countries and what may be their significance for the underdeveloped world. We have already indicated that the recognition of social costs and social benefits is not simply a matter of empirical research but depends to some extent upon the distribution of power in society (both "original" and "countervailing" power in Galbraith's sense). The greater the spread of countervailing power the greater the likelihood that taxes and protective legislation will be used to translate

social costs into private costs and that provisions will be made for public investments for the creation of social benefits. Whether and which social costs and social
benefits will be taken into account depends therefore upon the political structure of
society.

There can be no doubt that the existence of social costs and social benefits
calls for planning and control of the competitive process. This planning which
has the purpose of protecting society against socially destructive processes is
designed to translate the "variable" (or shifted) social costs into fixed "social
overhead charges"[36] and by means of subsidies, public investments or public
enterprises, to encourage or enforce the production of social benefits. Such interference does not differ basically from the system of laws which regulates traffic
or declares certain activities as unlawful if they are directed against personal or
property rights of the individual. Whether these interferences with the competitive system have actually gone far enough or have gone beyond what is
necessary is a question which cannot be answered in general terms but requires
detailed case studies.

In any event, much of our contemporary labor and social legislation has the
purpose of internalizing the social costs of production into entrepreneurial cost
accounts. It has been suggested that not only the history of economic and social
legislation but of economic development in general could be written as the
history of the success or failure to internalize the social costs of production and
of the struggle to limit and resolve the conflict between individual and social
interests.[37] That is to say, economic history and economic policies have been
shaped by precisely those aspects of economic life which economic theory in its
preoccupation with formal rationality has either neglected or ignored altogether.

More significant, particularly in the context of the economics of growth, is
the question of the relevance of social costs and social returns for the acceleration of the development process. It can hardly be denied that the process of economic growth is bound up with substantial social costs such as the large-scale
disruption of traditional processes of production and of old ways of life. Indeed,
many of the classical cases of social costs such as the expulsion of farm workers
from the land, the impairment of the health of women, children and of adult laborers, the depletion and erosion of the soil, the pollution of air and water, the
obsolescence of old skills, the easy shift of the social overhead costs of labor in
periods of unemployment, and the development of city slums arose first in the
course of rapid economic advances in Western Europe during the Industrial
Revolution. Indeed, it may be argued that the institutional arrangements which
concealed the social costs of these early innovations and the absence of legislation which made it possible to shift these costs to third persons or to society-at-
large were largely responsible for the dynamic character of economic change
during the initial stages of the Industrial Revolution. Hence, any attempt by
social legislation to force entrepreneurs to bear at least part of these social costs
may have the effect of slowing down the process of economic development. In
the light of this doctrine,[38] it would appear that rapid economic development presupposes the systematic neglect of social costs, and that current attempts in many

underdeveloped countries to force their productive units to internalize some of the social costs of production will have the effect of slowing down the rate of economic growth. *Prima facie* this argument seems to be irrefutable. However, closer analysis particularly of the economic effects of social costs and social benefits on the process of economic development reveals its limitations. In the first place, while it is true that the systematic neglect of social costs may make it possible to invest in projects which could not be undertaken if the social costs had to be internalized, it is equally true that the social costs once shifted have important adverse and cumulative repercussions on economic and social welfare. Thus, if in their effort to minimize the cost of current production, farmers in the underdeveloped world increase the rate of soil depletion and erosion at a more rapid rate; if expansion of industrial production in the growing cities of Asia is associated with the uncontrolled growth of slums and the widespread pollution of air and water;[39] if the introduction of new industrial techniques is permitted to proceed without regard to the non-amortized value of older equipment in existing firms and the obsolescence of older skills; in short, if nothing is done to minimize these social costs of development, private costs are bound to rise before long if, indeed, the whole development process may not be brought to a halt by the exhaustion of the soil, the impairment of the human factor and the inevitable political polarization which such a policy of *laissez-faire* is bound to entail. In addition, and more specifically, it is an illusion to believe that social losses affect only future generations. Destructive farming practices and methods utilized in minimizing current costs of production in agriculture which deplete and erode the soil may raise the costs of next year's crops not only on those farms whose owners were responsible for the soil destruction, but on all farms in the region. Similarly, air and water pollution affect not only human health but raise the costs of production generally. The same point can be made in connection with all those practices which lead to the exhaustion of other renewable and non-renewable resources. In short, social costs are really not "unpaid"; if they are not avoided they have to be paid by somebody, and their cumulative effect may actually slow down the development process.

Finally, the thesis that protective legislation and the resulting internalization of social costs into private costs tends to retard the rate of economic growth also ignores the fact that the prevention of social costs may be considerably less costly for society than the damages caused by destructive productive practices or, for that matter, the attempt to repair the losses and damages once they have occurred. In other words, the (marginal) real costs involved in the prevention of air pollution are likely to be lower than the (marginal) real costs of repairs and additional medical care called for by the effects of air pollution.

The case for a more comprehensive system of social accounting and a determination of social priorities in underdeveloped countries is even stronger if we consider the case of social benefits and external economies. One of the characteristics of underdeveloped countries is their traditional neglect of social overhead capital. Investments in the human factor and in a variety of public institutions have been wholly inadequate or non-existent and have left a heritage of serious deficiencies in education, in road and transportation systems, and in public health, while available economic surpluses were used either for artistic or religious purposes, monumental constructions or for "leisure goods" in Veblen's sense of the word. The innovating entrepreneur in underdeveloped countries cannot hope to appropriate and internalize many of the external economies which are created by his investment decisions. In short, while profit and capital accounting may be formally correct, it is substantively speaking incorrect because it cannot consider the very real social and external benefits of investment. The practical implications of this divergence of private and social benefits for the development process may be summarized briefly as follows: Just as the social costs of production are not registered by the market test, the price mechanism fails to take account of social benefits and external economies. The neglect of these extra-market phenomena disqualifies the market calculus as an effective guide for investment decisions. An underdeveloped economy guided exclusively by the competitive calculus would destroy the fabric of society by the cumulative effects of a variety of social costs and the inevitable neglect of essential social overhead investments in such areas as education, sanitation, defense, administration, medical care, water supply, and a host of similar public services. Actually, no democratic society can and will tolerate this subordination of the social system to the dictates of formal rationality. The universal reaction of society to the neglect of social costs and social benefits has taken a variety of forms, all of which have had the effect of compelling the private producers to internalize as least a portion of the social costs and to assume partial responsibility in the form of higher taxes for public investments.

Notes

1 Paper presented at the Zweite Arbeitstagung der Gesellschaft für Wirtschafts-und Sozialwissenschaften, Bad Homburg, April, 1962 under the title "Social Costs and Social Benefits—A Contribution to Normative Economics." Reprinted with the permission of the Gesellschaft fuer Wirtschafts- und Sozialwissenschaften. Published 1963 in E. v. Beckerath & H. Giersch (Hrsg.), "Probleme der normativen Ökonomik und der wirtschaftspolitischen Beratung". Verein für Sozialpolitik Berlin: Duncker & Humblot, pp. 183–210; also in: Hindu Culture and Economic Development (1963) as "Social Costs and Social Benefits—Their Relevance for Public Policy and Economic Planning."
2 Adam Smith, *An Inquiry into the Nature and Causes of The Wealth of Nations*, New York: Modern Library, 1937, p. 681.
3 Henry Sidgwick, *The Principles of Political Economy*, Book III, London: Macmillan and Co. Ltd., 1901, p. 412.
4 J.B. Clark, The Philosophy of Wealth, Economic Principles Newly Formulated, Boston: Ginn and Company, 1885, p. 215.
5 However, it is at least doubtful whether Marshall's narrower concept of external economies which after all was developed only to refer to the favorable effects external to the firm but internal to the industry can be and should be made to denote also the much wider ramifications of social benefits which accrue to all members of society. Neither the theory of external economies nor modern welfare economics seem to be able to cope adequately with these broader socio economic benefits.

6 Only recently has the concept of external economies given rise to a body of literature which questions the validity of market criteria for the planning of investments in underdeveloped countries. See H. Leibenstein, *Economic Backwardness and Economic Growth.* New York: John Wiley, 1957; J.E. Meade, "External Economies and Diseconomies," *Economic Journal,* March 1952, pp. 54–67; and Tibor Scitowsky, "Two Concepts of External Economies," *Journal of Political Economy,* April, Vol. LXII 1954, pp. 143–151.

7 Fragment on Government. July 1, 1854. *The Collected Works of Abraham Lincoln,* R.P. Basler (ed.), vol. II, New Brunswick, NJ: Rutgers University Press, 1953, p. 221.

8 Max Weber, "Politik als Beruf," in *Gesammelte Politische Schriften,* Munich, 1921, pp. 441. On the potential conflict between the two "ethics" see F.H. Blum, "Max Weber: The Man of Politics and the Man Dedicated to Objectivity and Rationality," *Ethics,* LXX, No. 1, October 1959, pp. 6–9.

9 Whereas Max Weber speaks of the fact that to "a large degree the consumers' wants are 'awakened' and 'directed' by the entrepreneur," Veblen speaks of "the fabrication of customers" through the production of systematized illusions by experts and experimenters in applied psychology (and) creative psychiatry, who play on various infirmities such as human credulity in general and the fear of losing prestige and the anxiety engendered by mortal disease in particular. T. Veblen, *Absentee Ownership and Business Enterprise in Recent Times—The Case of America,* New York: The Viking Press, 1923, pp. 307–310. The reference to Max Weber is to *The Theory of Social and Economic Organization,* T. Parson (ed.), New York: Oxford University Press, 1947, p. 193.

10 Ibid., p. 203.

11 Ibid., p. 185. The important distinction between "formal" and "substantive" has been further developed by E. Egner, *Der Haushalt, Eine Darstellung seiner Volkswirtschaftlichen Gestalt,* Berlin: Duncker end Humblot, 1952; and K. Polanyi, "The Economy as Instituted Process", in K. Polanyi et. al (eds.), *Trade and Market in the Early Empires,* Glencoe, IL: The Free Press, 1957, pp. 243–270.

12 Lewis Mumford, *The City in History,* New York: Harcourt, Brace and World, 1961.

13 This is the case for example in New York City where eleven agencies are responsible for problems of transportation. See letter by Dr. Lyle Fitch, Former City Administrator, April 16, 1961, *New York Times,* April 17, 1961.

14 For a discussion of cases in which the neglect of the technical and economic coordination problem has led to serious underutilization of the reservoir see Rene Dumont, *Types of Rural Economy—Studies in World Agriculture,* New York: Praeger, 1957, p. 199.

15 See *The Economic Weekly,* Bombay, May 21, 1960, p. 758.

16 A case in point is the increasing suspicion that respiratory diseases including cancer of the lungs may be causally related not only to smoking but also to exposure to a polluted atmosphere—a suspicion which 10 years ago still seemed to be so questionable that I refrained from mentioning it in my analysis of the social losses of air pollution. Another illustration is provided by industrial noise. Current researches in the United States have shown that short-term exposure to industrial noise of high intensity can produce a hearing loss that may be transitory in nature but, if the exposure is sufficiently prolonged and severe, loss may become permanent. In other words a temporary short-term exposure repeated over a certain time may make a specific noise situation into a long-term hazard. See studies reported by H.J. Magnusson, Chief, US Public Health Service, *Scope Weekly,* September 2, 1959, p. 3.

17 The widespread and increasing use of toxic chemicals and pesticides (such as insecticides) in modern agriculture and the various preservatives, anti-oxidants, mold inhibitors, coatings, color additives and bleaches, substitutes, etc. in the food processing industries and various drugs have long been suspected of causing human diseases although these relationships are not yet fully understood.

18 M. Weber, *The Theory of Social and Economic Organization*, p. 185.

19 R.W. Souter, *"The Nature and Significance of Economic Science in Recent Discussions,"* Quarterly Journal of Economics, XLVII, May 1933, p. 380.

20 John Dewey, *Human Nature and Conduct*, New York: The Modem Library, 1930, p. 234.

21 K. William Kapp, *The Social Costs of Business Enterprise*, Bombay: Asia Publishing House, 1963.

22 S.V. Ciriacy-Wantrup, *Resource Conservation—Economics and Policies*, Berkeley: University of California Press, 1952, pp. 39, 256–259.

23 This is not to say that much reliable quantitative information is available on these elements of social costs or that any systematic effort has ever been made to collect statistical data concerning them. There is no time series indicating the extent and evolution of social costs.

24 J.G. Maddox, "The Private and Social Costs of the Movement of People out of Agriculture," *American Economic Review*, 1960, Vol. L, May 1960, pp. 392–402.

25 The distinction follows closely Dewey's distinction between deliberation and calculation. See *Human Nature and Conduct*, New York: The Modem Library, 1930, pp. 199–222.

26 Alfred Marshall, *Principles of Economics*, London: MacMillan and Co., 1938, 8th edn, p. 17.

27 See, for instance, Veblen's distinction between "productive consumption" and "conspicuous waste" and "superfluities", and Vershofen's equally dualistic classification of wants into those which serve the maintenance of human life and those which serve the desire for prestige and status (Geltung) in society. See T. Veblen, *The Engineers and the Price System*, New York: B.W. Huebsch, 1921, pp. 108–110; and Vershofen, *Wirtschaft als Schicksal und Aufgabe*, Leipzig: Kochler und Amelang, 1930, p. 265.

28 We thus support Gottl's insistence that the (substantive) notion of economy must include *ipso facto* the exploration and determination of actual needs and is concerned with the equalization and adjustment of needs to the "situation" and the "situation" to the needs. F. von Gottl, *Wirtschaft und Technik*, Grundriss der Sozialökonomik, vol. II, Tübingen: G.C.B. Mohr, 1924, p. 11.

29 While it would be "wilful folly", as Dewey put it (*Human Nature and Conduct*, p. 229) to fasten upon some single all-important end without regard to the consequences which such a neglect of other ends carries with it, it is nevertheless true that social goals must be set and deliberately selected and, as such, inevitably imply a subordination and perhaps neglect of other ends. This need not be a violation of the principle of substantive rationality provided we are proceeding in accordance with a social scale of essential and less essential needs.

30 M. Weber, *The Theory of Social and Economic Organization*, p. 161 and F. von Gottl, *Wirtschaft und Technik*.

31 Statement by Prime Minister Erlanger of Sweden in Washington, *The New York Times*, April 4, 1961.

32

> What kind of consumption should be planned? Should it take the consumption of the more highly developed countries as a model? Should it be guided by whatever market demand exists[…]? Or should production be tailored above all to serving as cheaply as possible the recognizable needs and desires of the average low-income consumers? If these questions are not faced deliberately they may be answered without thought. In particular there is danger that the consumption patterns of the more developed countries will be followed as a matter of course. The theory of consumption must, I think, be more democratic than this. […] Cheap bicycles are more important than cheap automobiles.
>
> J.K. Galbraith address at Bombay University, July 31, 1961. Quoted from official text, United States Information Service, New Delhi, p. 10

33 Max Weber did not deny that such aims and even political aims could be derived from a disciplined interpretation of the objective conditions of the historical situation. Certainly his great courage to stand alone and to say what he thought was often unpleasant for many and his insistent advocacy of clearly political aims and causes (cf. his concept of the lasting interest of the nation, his critical views on bureaucracy and socialism, his belief in the need for the entrepreneurial type despite his conviction of the nefarious political influence of the "gentlemen from heavy industry") can only reflect a basic conviction that it was possible to derive ends from a dispassionate analytical observation and comparison of events and social conditions ("Die Dinge aus sich selbst zu verstehen") and brings him almost close to John Dewey's position that ends are of the nature of hypotheses which can be established and worked out in the light of the concrete conditions available for their realization. See Dewey, op. cit., p. 254 and *Logic—The Theory of Inquiry*, New York: Holt, Rinehart and Winston, 1938, pp. 180, 497. On the whole problem see F.H. Blum, op. cit., and "The Meaning of Max Weber's Postulate of Freedom from Value Judgments", *American Journal of Sociology*, Vol. L., No. 1 July 1944, pp. 44–52. See also G. Weippert, "Zur Problematik der Zielbestimmung in wirtschaftspolitischen Konzeptionen," in H.J. Seraphim (ed.), *Zur Grundlegung wirtschaftspolitischer Konzeptionen*, Schriften des Vereins für Sozialpolitik, Neue Folge, Band 18, Berlin: Duncker and Humblot 1960, pp. 185–188. See, however, H. Giersch, "Das Problem der Objektivität des wirtschaftlichen Urteils und der Lösungsversuch der neueren Lehre vom wirtschaftlichen Wohlstand," *Zeitschrift für die gesamte Staatswissenschaft*, Ed. 107, 1951, pp. 247.

34 "A bad decision made on time will not usually be as costly as a good decision made too late. The bad decision can often be reversed at low costs. The time lost waiting for the good decision can never be retrieved." J.K. Galbraith, "Public Administration and the Public Corporation", Address, Indian Institute of Public Administration, August 25, 1961. Official Text, United States Information Service, New Delhi, p. 6.

35 Max Weber stressed the fact that the standards of substantive rationality may not command the necessary minimum of consensus in society; that the "administrators" may be swayed by their own personal sentiments which might differ from those of some social groups; that political pressures of important social groups might force them to adopt standards favorable to them; and, above all, that changes in technology and preferences would necessitate new calculations and a reallocation of the "input mix." Nevertheless, while Max Weber felt that Otto Neurath's plea for calculations in kind was open to criticism, he considered his suggestions as "penetrating" and "stimulating" and did not deny that calculation in kind could become a rational technique. In fact he expressly stated that as long as the maintenance of social minima objectively defined without discrimination of some sections of the population is the standard of calculation the substantive approach may actually satisfy the criteria of the formal optimum. Max Weber, *The Theory of Social and Economic Organization*, pp. 202–212.

36 Borrowing and extending the meaning of J.M. Clark's concept of overhead costs, Blum speaks of social overhead or constant costs with reference to all those elements of costs and benefits for which society has already chosen to assume responsibility and speaks of social variable costs with reference to those elements of costs and potential social benefits which society permits to be shifted or to go unrealized. See F.H. Blum, "Social and Economic Implications of the Fair Labor Standards Act", *Industrial Relations Research Association*, Proceedings, Cleveland, August 1956, pp. 167–183.

37 K.P. Hensel, "Über die wirtschaftliche und wirtschaftspolitische Willensbildung und Willensverwirklichung in verschiedenen Ordnungen," in H.J. Seraphim (ed.), *Probleme der Willensbildung und der wirtschaftspolitischen Führung*, Schriften des Vereins für Sozialpolitik, Neue Folge, Band 19, Berlin: Duncker und Humblot, 1959, p. 21.

38 For a recent elaboration of this thesis see A.O. Hirshman, *The Strategy of Economic Development*, New Haven: Yale University Press, 1958, pp. 58–59.

39 The average monthly fall of soot in Calcutta is currently estimated at 25 tons per square mile, *The Economic Weekly* (Bombay), 1–2–60. Needless to add that practically all domestic and industrial wastes in the underdeveloped countries are discharged without prior treatment into waterways.

8 Discussion between Professor Shibata and Professor Kapp by *The Economist*[1]

SHIBATA: First of all, let me say that we in Japan are deeply interested in your work, especially your book about social costs or public nuisances. It seems that American economists of the classical or Keynesian school are mainly concerned with private mechanism, private industry, or the *laissez-faire* system—a system that, as you have observed, is itself a kind of public nuisance or social cost. Japanese economists have found that point quite stimulating, because this is a very serious issue in Japan. So I would like to ask, first, how and why you became interested in this issue, since it seems to have caught the attention of only a small circle of American economists. But before putting the question to you, I would like to explain why we Japanese are so interested in this issue. Japan has experienced a rate of economic growth higher than that of almost any other country in the world, as high as and sometimes even higher than that of West Germany. Our economic expansion, however, has not been a balanced one; we have made this remarkable progress at the expense of living conditions, the environment, urban affairs, and public facilities, to name but a few. I would like to go into greater detail about some of the economic problems we are experiencing in Japan later, but first I would like you to explain why you started your work.

KAPP: Let me begin by saying that I am very pleased to be here, and that I am especially pleased to learn that my book has met with such a response in Japan. It is a great honor for an author to know that his ideas are gaining acceptance and influence, and that it has been found significant to the present state of Japanese economic development. This seems to me an indirect confirmation of the significance of social costs that are not accounted for in the competitive market mechanism.

When you ask me how my study of social costs came about, you are almost asking me to tell you the story of my life. But, ultimately, a question of that sort cannot be answered merely in autobiographical terms. I think I have to trace it back to my Ph.D. dissertation in Geneva, which dealt with economic planning and foreign trade. I wrote it in the thirties, and perhaps you are familiar with the great discussion that centered on the problem of economic calculation at that time. It was argued then, and still is in some circles, that as soon as a system of economic planning is established, the market mechanism is then of necessity eliminated. The result is that, at least as far as capital goods are concerned, you will be left without a free price mechanism, and will thus be unable to establish the rationality of your economic decisions. This was the great debate initiated by Ludwig von Mises and Max Weber. "Rationality" in economic life, as Weber said, has been greatly promoted by the introduction of money, the mechanism that allows us to count, quantify or calculate the pros and cons of a particular decision. It is not, in that sense, a typical rational procedure in which you compare what you put in (your costs) with what you get out (the returns). The prototype of this mechanism is found in the calculation of the private firm; that is, the market mechanism. That was the intellectual atmosphere in which the discussion of planning took place in the thirties, and even in the twenties for that matter. I came in at the tail end of that discussion. Interestingly, this thesis on economic planning and foreign trade was done in Geneva at the same time Mises was there. The concepts of social costs and social benefits were the outgrowth of my preoccupation with the problem of economic calculation. There is some treatment of these questions in my dissertation, but only in a very preliminary manner. But I would like to point out what I considered then, and still do today, the limitations of the market mechanism as a guide to economic decision-making.

In short, then, there was a backlog of unfinished business in my mind when I came to the United States. Then came my exposure to certain phenomena—I might even say historical data—primarily in American agriculture. These led me to believe that one should look into the social costs of land erosion and deterioration. I came to the US in the thirties, in the last stage of the New Deal, which was a remarkably stimulating period intellectually, with its many organizations, but I didn't want to hang the social costs on the New Deal. After all, I had just come to terms with historical economic development in America, and when you come to a new country you are pretty ignorant of the conditions that prevail there. Then you begin to acquire and assimilate these economic developments, and in the process you come across things that startle you to no end—deforestation, destruction of animal resources, and erosion, to name but a few, the extent of which you had no idea. (In Japan there seems to be no such evidence of erosion.) So I decided to do a study of the social costs of agriculture. I may not have called them "social costs" at that point, perhaps just "unaccounted-for costs," but before one gets very far, he is impressed by events in other fields—urban development, water and air pollution—and then there develops something like a general concept. One also begins to notice that this phenomenon of unaccounted-for costs is not just characteristic of agriculture, but is found in urban and industrial development in general, and the article on the social costs of agriculture never gets finished because one feels he has so much additional evidence in other areas. Thus, out of the preoccupation with historical economic development, and then with social costs in agriculture, there developed the whole notion of the social costs of private enterprise.

There had been a good deal of literature devoted to social costs here and there, but the concept had never been treated in any systematic fashion.

So, out of this work, that was partly theoretical and partly empirical, developed the conviction that social costs were phenomena associated with certain institutional arrangements which happened to exist in a particularly pure form in America—much purer than in Germany or other European countries, which had always had a background of regulations. In America the full force of free enterprise was felt much more strongly than in other countries, except perhaps during the New Deal, when the first governmental regulations were introduced. The New Deal economists, the National Resources Planning Board, and a variety of other organizations were bringing out data which all provided empirical evidence of what I called social costs. At the same time, America was the home of institutional economics, although I knew very little about them at that time. There was an undertone of institutional emphasis in some of the literature which I now feel I never fully assimilated, at least not in the first edition. It is much more developed in the second edition.

It is significant that you ask where the idea of social costs originated. In my particular case, it was the result of my contact with another culture, interposed against the background of my preoccupation with the problem of economic planning, the controversy about economic calculation, and my critical attitude, which was also expressed in institutional economics, towards a so-called free-enterprise economy.

SHIBATA: And then you discover many striking facts.

KAPP: And there I had a doctrine, so to speak. From then on, I was working empirically.

SHIBATA: And you deepened your study.

KAPP: Yes. Parenthetically, that is why my study took so much longer than I originally thought it would. I thought it would be a matter of half a year, but it took much longer.

SHIBATA: Sometimes the amount of material is ample, but it is not kept in any organized manner.

MRS. KAPP: My husband has always thought about two concepts, social costs and social benefits, and today these concepts have acquired a new significance in connection with the work on economic planning.

KAPP: As a matter of fact, I had originally wanted to call my study "Social Costs and Social Benefits," but I never wrote the second part of the book. I had drafted three chapters, but then I thought that if I pursued my studies of social benefits, it would take several more years before I could finish it.

SHIBATA: At first you thought of social costs *and* social benefits?

KAPP: Yes—those benefits that are not privately appropriated, that are not salable, that cannot be appropriated because they diffuse themselves to society as a whole, and play a very important role in the elimination of social costs. These are all social benefits. I am concerned that the market mechanism is neglectful and perhaps incapable of encompassing both social costs and social benefits.

SHIBATA: I understand you have been in India twice.

KAPP: Yes. One trip was devoted to research, mostly at the Gokhale Institute of Politics and Economics in Poona, near Bombay. I studied the social benefits and effects of the irrigation scheme; this was in some respects the second part of my book, the part that never got written in the forties. Water is a very crucial factor in India because of the shortage of food, and due to the insufficiency and unevenness of rainfall—monsoons alternate with droughts. Multipurpose projects are designed to collect water behind dams to provide a permanent supply of water, electricity, and flood control. Such projects have been prioritized in the first, and especially in the second, five-year plan of India, so that was my primary research subject during that first year in Poona. The second year I lectured at the University of Rajasthan in Jaipur on the problems of economic development and growth, and the history of economic analysis. During my stay in Jaipur, I also worked on problems associated with the Rajasthan Canal, which is a major irrigation canal to be constructed for bringing water from the Himalayan Mountains.

I will be going back to the City University of New York to teach the history of economic analysis, and economic development and growth.

SHIBATA: You said that in America there is a free-enterprise system, and that the issue of social costs is therefore particularly relevant.

KAPP: I was referring to the nineteenth century and the beginning of the twentieth, perhaps up to the advent of the New Deal, when we had the purest kind of free business enterprise. I now use the term "business enterprise economy" because the words "free" and "private" are rather ambiguous. Business enterprise is not as private as many people believe; there are at present an enormous number of regulations, in America and other countries, and I feel it is stretching the meaning of "free" too far to use it in this context. "Business enterprise" is more accurate. Veblen also used the term in his *Theory of Business Enterprise*.

SHIBATA: The Japanese situation at present is similar to that of nineteenth-century America. In Japan, great importance is attached to economic growth, and the government has encouraged such big industries as steel and shipbuilding, and also the military. And so we imported raw materials from the Chinese mainland or the United States, and the businessmen paid attention only to their own factories; they were in effect surrounded by barbed wire, with "No Trespassing" signs. The businessmen were only interested in their own factories and maintained a hands-off policy towards urban affairs, housing problems, and the like. As a result, there is still a great imbalance in Japanese economies, especially in Tokyo. The streets of Tokyo look much like those of New York, but, for example, only 20 percent of the city's sewage is processed by a sewage canal. For the other 80 percent, the conditions that obtain are much like that in the sixteenth century. Yesterday we were at the Public Housing Corporation, but only a very lucky person can get in there. The housing situation is very dire. Again, as a means of comparison, in New York a person can occupy a little more than a hundred square feet, but in Japan it is only about forty square feet. Public expenditures go mainly to encourage heavy industry, and only a very small amount is left for public improvements. The people have a very difficult time, but they are still not strong or organized enough to influence public policy. In the United States, however, I have found that the businessmen pay more attention to public affairs. It seems to me that they have some concept of social costs; if we go to Pittsburgh, for example, we find that Mellon himself is chairman of the city planning commission and pays special attention to such problems as pollution control. In Japan such a situation would be unimaginable. This change of attitude in the US seems to date from the thirties or forties. What caused it?

KAPP: I would like first of all to respond to your claim, which is, if I understand correctly, that American businessmen have by their own volition become more responsible and more concerned with social costs, and have even provided protective measures to avoid or mitigate them.

SHIBATA: In many places I have heard the term "social responsibility of businessmen." I would like to ask you whether you believe this to be genuine or false.

KAPP: I think that private businessmen are concerned primarily with making profits. We economists tend to think that they maximize their profits, and that they have an elaborate formal apparatus of marginal costs and returns by which they very carefully compare their options, to the point of equality of the marginal return. I don't want to say too much about that. But I do want to emphasize that business still is, and always was, concerned with making profits, and that I would not therefore put as much credence in the idea that business enterprise has recognized their need to reduce social costs of their own volition, without governmental aid, pressure, and enforcement. I think it has had more to do with a governmental apparatus that is responsive to the people, that has established protective legislation in a variety of areas, that has seen to it that these measures are enforced, and that has by doing so educated the population to recognize social costs. The political institutions of the United States have thus played a major role in the growing recognition of social costs and the protective legislation that is the expression of this recognition.

I also think that certain groups have gained in political power and consciousness, again as a result of institutional political arrangements, and have simply demanded that action be taken.

The proliferation of labor legislation, for example, has been the result of the increased strength of unions and their ability to work through the political process, by means of the established party system, in traditional American fashion, to punish their enemies and reward their friends. Those parties that did the necessary things from labor's point of view got re-elected. In that sense, I think we cannot separate the politics from the economics of social costs. And the New Deal is again a turning point in this connection, where formerly less-represented and weaker elements in a society found a very substantial support, and saw to it that legislation was enacted which helped them.

We are now at work on the serious problem of air and water pollution. This problem has been neglected even in America, although much has been done during the past ten years.

SHIBATA: It is said that the U.S. government, especially during the Eisenhower Administration, was controlled by businessmen. If this is so, it is difficult to imagine that they would countenance the passage of legislation which reduces their own profits.

KAPP: Although this is commonly believed, I don't think it true. I believe that even if General Motors is particularly well-represented in the Eisenhower Administration, it does not mean that opposing interest groups do not exist or have no power. Never underestimate the effect of a strong opposition party in putting checks on the power of the majority party. Besides, the Republican Party is not the party of businessmen only; any party in power must be cognizant of the wishes of the people if it wants their votes.

SHIBATA: So if water pollution hurts the citizens, they make a big noise about it.

KAPP: Well, again I would not exaggerate that influence either. There is a Department of Public Health. There are a variety of institutions that are entrusted with the maintenance of public health, and their function is to be watchful and to issue reports, and I think the Administration can act on these reports and say to the citizens, "Look at what we've done." And if they don't do enough, the opposition party can say, "You have not devoted enough money or attention to this problem." There is a constant give-and-take to the political process that pushes it forward on the road of legislation and social reform, but I don't think that the citizens themselves are constantly watchful. If there are dramatic events like the one in Pennsylvania where the air became so polluted that people were dying and gasping for breath, it gets into the news, but even there the number of people immediately affected represent only a small part of the population. It did, however, help put air pollution on the public agenda. Correcting such problems is always costly, and businessmen therefore hesitate to take the necessary steps. In that respect, the political process supports the agencies that are entrusted with the enforcement of protective legislation.

SHIBATA: It still seems difficult to understand how this kind of public nuisance can be so serious in Japan, and yet the businessmen pay so little attention to it. The situation seems much better in the United States. Many countries used to accuse Japan of dumping cheap products on foreign markets by keeping down labor costs, but if you examine it carefully, you see that while the labor costs are of course small, that is only one factor. The other is a neglect of social costs. For example, take the regulation of oil tanks. Regulations state that only one tank can be put within a certain distance of another, but usually this kind of regulation can easily be bypassed. And so, at the sacrifice of social welfare, Japan cuts costs in order to export goods at lower prices.

KAPP: I think that is a very interesting point, and one that deserves greater mention. But may I ask a question in return? I know very little about Japan, but I am under the impression that the country has always had a much greater degree of governmental regulation and control. That at least is the picture one gets from the literature on Japanese economic development, so it surprises me that the same government should have been neglectful or uninterested in the prevention of social costs. But perhaps it is the fact that the government concentrated on what it considered to be the most urgent priorities for Japan's economic development, and that in this process economic controls were established to guide investment, protect markets against excessive competition, establish monopolistic concessions, and achieve all the other goals that we know are consistent with the country's early economic history, and that have helped it catch up with more developed economies.

SHIBATA: I think you are correct. At any rate, the role of politics is very important. Could you expound a little on the air-pollution problem in the US?

KAPP: Modern industrial society is using increasing amounts of chemicals and toxicants in the production of new products and materials, the effects of which are not fully understood. I don't remember the exact data, but every year let us say 10,000 new products and 10,000 new materials are being introduced into rivers and other waterways. The most interesting new product, of course, is atomic energy, and it will be our most important source of air and water pollution. The disposal of radioactive waste product is a problem of such magnitude that we do not know where it will ultimately lead. Some of the waste is deactivated and put into the ocean or underground, but we do not really know enough about the ultimate effect this will have on the environment.

SHIBATA: In proportion to the technical innovation.

KAPP: Which is so rapid and pronounced that the legislation to control it seems always to lag behind, so that there is a continuous need for new research and new protective laws.

SHIBATA: That is fundamental.

KAPP: That is fundamental and general. If you call for empirical references, I will have to check. It is well known, however, that the chemical and steel industries are responsible for the most important waste products, and that they are disposing their wastes into the water more or less untreated. The problem is that treating the material before you dispose of it is expensive.

SHIBATA: And it often takes time before the effects are felt.

KAPP: I think another factor in this connection is that the harmful effects are distributed among a great number of people who are not very well organized, and it usually takes some dramatic incident to bring out a response.

SHIBATA: A rather diluted one.

KAPP: But not unimportant for that reason. Because the effects are distributed among so many people, that's not to say they are small, or diluted. All these effects are cumulative, year after year, and finally a dramatic event occurs.

SHIBATA: In that sense, it is a continuing problem.

KAPP: Yes, a continuous problem. At the same time, I don't want to appear overly pessimistic. Water pollution is on the research agenda in Germany, too, and in Russia. I think a responsible government should maintain technical-research organizations that study these problems, and I am a great believer that if knowledge can be made available to the population about the effects of pollution, then they will demand that their governments take necessary action.

SHIBATA: That kind of research will at least teach preventive methods.

KAPP: It will teach, first of all, the effects and their dangers; then, any good technician will probably be able to prevent or reduce them. In this sense, it is scientific research, which is a prerequisite.

SHIBATA: You have already answered my third question about scientific research.

KAPP: To do research, enact the conclusions into law, and enforce the legislation, control and monitor the process continuously, just as we do elsewhere.

SHIBATA: The regulations in Japan look very good on paper, but there are actually two bottlenecks. One is that big business says okay, we can understand the regulations, they say that in order to prevent air pollution, you must have such-and-such device in your chimney. And they say that it costs a lot, and if we spend so much money for the device, then we cannot compete with, let us say, Italian companies or German companies. We are in the market, we must compete against foreign countries, and to do so we must cut our costs, so we cannot afford such measures. In order to maintain our national economy, we cannot follow them.

The second problem is that the government is bureaucratic and there is terrible sectionalism. The different departments—agriculture, construction, etc.—each claim their own territory, and public nuisance falls within the jurisdiction of all the departments. So the Ministry of Health is concerned with the health issue, the Ministry of Industry is concerned with the chimney, but as far as the device itself is concerned, each ministry says that this is my responsibility and I will take care of it. Sometimes it takes six years to reach a final decision. Do these bottlenecks occur in America?

KAPP: No. I was going to answer you in a more facetious way and say that maybe you need a Department of Social Costs that deals across the board with the problems of various sectors of the economy. But I think you are making too much of the stasis of ministerial departments in the central government. I understand that a bureau or department of public health must be concerned with the fundamental research into water and air pollution, for example. But I believe you can leave the legislation and enforcement to responsible *local* governments. In America at least, the problem of air pollution is not Washington's responsibility, but rather that of the Commissioner of Air Pollution (or whatever his title) in the City of New York, or in other affected cities.

MRS. KAPP: They have not only a Department of Public Health, but also several other commissions.

KAPP: But that raises a question. Suppose there is a small city that has no Commission of Air Pollution. There the problem can continue to exist—but we also have a system, as you know, of public grants to local governments. Once the problem has become acute in one area, has been studied scientifically by the central government's Department of Public Health, let us say, it is then possible to suggest to smaller industrial areas that they will have the same problem very soon if they don't monitor it, and the central government is sometimes ready to provide subsidies to help get filters and other controls installed. But while I believe that local governments are important in this connection, central government cannot abdicate its responsibilities. The problem is of such magnitude in many respects that local governments cannot cope with it alone. I would, therefore, reject the idea that we can leave the responsibility to local governments alone. I would say that central government should do the fundamental research and formulate the laws, then suggest to local governments that they be fully enacted and enforced. I wouldn't worry about delays of only six years; I think in fact that the delays are much longer. Sometimes it is a matter of fifty years. I feel that institutions and legislation are very often fifty years behind their time.

SHIBATA: Going back to the economic theory: you mentioned the importance of social costs and benefits. The classical school of economics is mainly based on price mechanism. Everything should be counted in terms of dollars or currency—but how do you make it measurable in terms of social costs? How can we put the social-cost issue into terms of economic theory? That is my last point. In the last chapter of your book, you suggest that a new political economy can be established. Could you paraphrase a little?

KAPP: I think you are quite right that the measurement of social cost is a problem; in fact, it is the central problem.

SHIBATA: Is it not true that we cannot solve this problem as long as we stay in a neo-classical model?

KAPP: That is a good point, and it leads me to the conclusion that the more we deal with social costs, the more we get outside the traditional boundaries of classical and neo-classical economics. I think that even modern welfare economics is much too narrow to handle this particular issue. I think, as I have indicated in the last chapter, that ways and means of measuring costs and benefits can still be constructed, and that the result will be a theory of social value to society. Perhaps this requires a political evaluation, and I think we are in the midst of just such a process. I think you have made a political-social evaluation, for example, in Japan. You have come to the conclusion that it is important for Tokyo to host no new industries, and that residential areas are located outside the city to avoid the social costs of the type of sprawling metropolises that are getting more and more out of hand all over the world. But I am not satisfied with these generalities.

I think that a fundamental element of such a theory of value, in the quasi-political sense of the word, must be based on what I call objective technical standards of, let us say, social efficiency. Let me put it this way: Scientific research should tell us that if air pollution exceeds a certain level, it will be harmful. It is possible to find minimum safety standards of water and air pollution, and possible to say that if these standards are exceeded, they will cause illnesses and epidemics. After the water and air in Tokyo reach these levels, it becomes a matter of life and death, literally, for a large portion of the population. So when the technical and scientific standards are established, public decisions can be based on them, and we can say that once the air in Tokyo is polluted to a certain degree, we cannot tolerate any more pollution. We must then perhaps even think of decentralizing existing industries in the interest of maintaining pure air.

This finally leads me to the point which we have never gotten around to, and which you have raised at least three times. It is a significant question. It is argued that these measures are too costly. I would like to make a counter-proposal of the consideration of the cost of public measures, since these measures have been made necessary by neglect over a period of many years. Tokyo, and any other city, is today paying the social cost that has been caused by the industrial processes of the past. If the necessary measures had been taken earlier, if the government had avoided these social costs to begin with, we could run our governments more cheaply. Our taxes would not need to be as high, because we would not be paying to correct the problems that incurred social costs in the past. In other words, I would answer the critics of the costs of prevention by referring them to the public measures, such as urban development and slum clearance, with which the present generation has been burdened by the previous generations. Perhaps the time frame of those saying they cannot compete is too short. It may be true that their competitive situation is made worse in the short term, but in the long run, the effects of dealing with these problems are clearly beneficial to society.

Note

1 The handwritten note on the manuscript indicates that this interview was conducted on August 2, 1962.

9 Towards a normative approach to developmental and environmental planning and decision-making[1]

In this brief paper, I will address some key issues of long-term development planning. The term "development" is understood to be used here in its broadest sense; it may be regional, national, or global, and includes the protection and possible improvement of the human environment. The term "human environment" is in turn not confined to the physical and ecological foundations of human life, but includes social and working conditions as well. Both development and environment, then, are not only broad, but also interrelated, categories. Their multi-dimensional character calls for a consideration of multiple objectives which are usually regarded as heterogeneous and incommensurable; hence the application of such formal methods and analytical techniques as cost-benefit analysis; operations research; and planning, programming and budgeting systems to public choice and decision-making in developmental and environmental planning is problematical and even dangerous.[2] Thus, planning of development and of the human environment cannot proceed in an isolated, compartmentalized fashion, but must instead take an integrated and unified approach. Such an approach raises methodological, theoretical, and practical policy issues of considerable complexity which cannot be solved in a satisfactory manner within the present scope and framework of social or economic analysis (and particularly not the latter). This is true for the following reasons:

1 Conventional analysis has viewed social and economic systems as being largely closed ones, while in reality they are open in a double sense: first, the economy is intimately connected to the social and political systems, and dependent on its power for important organizing and disorganizing impulses; second, the economy is inevitably dependent upon physical and ecological systems of various sorts. In fact, the economic processes of production and consumption cannot go on without a continuous interaction with the physical environment. They depend upon the physical input of energy and matter, and they emit residual waste into the environment. In the course of this interaction and exchange between the economy and nature, economically and physically accessible resources are reduced and pollution of the biosphere is increased. This interaction in turn affects the economic process, due to the simple fact that inputs of accessible energy and matter

are not inexhaustible, and also because the volume of wastes and other pollutants cannot be indefinitely increased without reaching limits critical to human health, survival, and the maintenance of the prerequisites of long-term reproduction. Any sort of planning which fails to consider the critical time range of the long-term schedule of available inputs and their exhaustion, and the effects of pollution, is socially irresponsible; it is equivalent to ignoring the interests of future generations.

2   By confining itself to the analysis of fictitiously closed economic models not connected with the ecosphere, conventional neo-classical economics is ill-adapted to the analysis of either short- or long-term development or its environmental effects, which can at best be introduced *ex post facto* as so-called externalities. As such, their substantive character, their causes and complex effects, and above all their circular interdependencies and cumulative character remain largely unanalyzed and inadequately understood. Although it is admitted, rather reluctantly and belatedly, that market prices are "distorted" and reflect neither the relative scarcity and importance of inputs nor the relative social importance of environmental and developmental goals, they are nevertheless used for the determination of the question of which policies, policy instruments, investments, and priorities are warranted. This approach suffers from serious shortcomings and contradictions, not the least of which are that it hopes to achieve developmental and environmental goals without explicitly specifying their substantive content, and that it relies on the very market mechanism and principle of profit maximization that created the disregard of the social costs of production in the first place. Environmentally, the approach is usually an attempt to make the polluters pay by concentrating on penalties (taxes, effluent charges, the enactment of prohibitions and restrictions) and rewards (subsidies, the establishment of property rights). In reality, however, the effectiveness of indirect measures is uncertain. Their information and transaction costs are high, the adoption of the necessary legislation is slow, and administrative and control agencies are not immune to the influence of groups which have a vested interest in the status quo. Additionally, the costs of such measures may fall disproportionately on the weaker segments of society, including the very persons most injured by environmental deterioration. This entire approach, then, suffers from the defects of all attempts to come to terms with social problems without defining, specifying, and evaluating what is desirable, essential, and possible. This is not to say that indirect measures and policy instruments are altogether ineffectual, however; they may in fact lead to incremental improvements. But they offer no guarantee of an optimal solution, and may in some cases become an obstacle to the systematic search for workable alternatives. Such alternatives will call for fundamental changes in technology, location policies, and institutional arrangements in general. It is in order to avoid such fundamental changes that the indirect approach is so frequently preferred, particularly in market economies.

In conclusion, environmental and developmental policies guided by the idea of "internalizing" social costs in accordance with the polluter-pays principle (PPP) may in effect and practice turn out to be largely a delusion. The promotion of development and the protection and possible improvement of the human environment—whether on a regional, national, or global level—will not be achieved as long as we deal with environmental deterioration only with *ex post facto* controls, such as penalties and rewards guided by the doctrine of the internalization of social costs, and the corresponding delusive polluter-pays principle. The advocacy of such measures is based upon a faulty understanding of the substantive and interrelated character of the problems of pollution and development, and their actual causes and synergetic effects. Instead of the futile attempt to internalize social costs and induce polluters to pay, it will be essential to reverse the approach by defining and specifying long-term developmental and environmental goals and objectives, and elaborating the appropriate policies in a continuous adaptation of ends to means, and vice versa. Thus we are confronted with theoretical and practical policy issues which cannot be solved adequately without altering considerably the scope and nature of socio-economic analysis itself.

While the objectives of business enterprise may be said to be quantifiable and therefore unproblematic, in that they can be expressed in terms of one common denominator—the maximization of profits—such is not the case with the objectives of developmental and environmental planning. Here there is no common denominator. The market does not provide the criteria for their evaluation and measurement, nor does it record societal preferences and priorities with regard to environmental and developmental goals. It provides no hint as to what would be desirable, possible, and necessary; on the contrary, the market mechanism and the goal of maximizing profits encourage the neglect of environmental costs, and of societal goals and benefits. Environmental and developmental objectives, then, are not given but problematical, and must be discovered and defined in a continuous interaction of factual research and the formulation of goals and priorities. The same applies to the choice of means, that is, the courses of action by which the objectives, once defined and chosen, may be attained. Both ends and means are themselves open questions, under continuous discussion and explored and defined only in the process of an action- or policy-oriented process of research.

Increasing threats to the human environment have finally led to the realization that the economic processes of production and consumption are not closed but fundamentally open systems, dependent on continuous interaction and exchange between the economy and nature, with the consequences I have noted in the first part of this paper. This will make it increasingly necessary to coordinate developmental and environmental decisions, and to base them on specific societal goals and explicitly formulated solutions. Such goals and solutions must be based upon both ecological-environmental and socio-economic requirements, in the narrower sense of economic growth, and the objectives of both will need to be reconciled. As has been noted, this can be achieved only with a multidisciplinary, unified approach, taking into account the open character of economic processes and their circular interdependencies with, and effects on, ecological systems. More concretely, the protection and improvement of the human environment must be viewed as one of the key societal objectives to be included in all economic policy decisions concerning production, investment, and consumption, and in both highly developed and underdeveloped countries. What is needed, then, is nothing less than a new and modified concept of economic growth and alternative development patterns, including new styles of living and consumption, new technologies, and new location patterns. New procedures for the formulation and new criteria for the evaluation of societal objectives must be developed which account for, and indeed start from, a systematic inventory of existing ecological conditions—the present state of environmental deterioration on the local, regional, and global scale; present and prospective pressures on the human environment; and resource constraints which must be considered in all decision-making and public planning. Most important, the full range of possible desirable solutions must be explored beforehand, as a prerequisite to all rational planning. The choice of technologies, including the development of alternative technologies with a low ecological impact and those adapted to local conditions and available local resources, and the use of alternative patterns of location for production and human settlement at the national and regional levels, must be elaborated on the basis of precise and sound knowledge open to revision as new information becomes available.

Finally, appropriate and effective instruments of implementing chosen goals and planning decisions must be explored and decided upon at all decision-making levels. In short, the entire process of decision-making and developmental planning must incorporate the environmental dimension. Economic development planning thus conceived includes environmental planning and management that takes into account existing ecological conditions, the state of deterioration of the environment, its carrying or assimilating capacity, present and estimated future resources and energy constraints, and the available labor force (that is, the demand and need for work). In this sense it is indeed appropriate to consider the process of development as being ecological *and* socio-economic in nature—a process of normative decision-making which necessarily includes the environmental dimension among its policy objectives and its means of action (or choice of inputs). These will ideally include alternative technologies with a low ecological impact and locations in close adaptations to environmental conditions and basic human needs, in a regional, national, and even global context.

Notes

1 This article was most likely written around 1973.
2 "It is impossible to quantify and compare the overall costs and benefits of the programme because the values attached to each policy objective cannot, usually, be measured in terms that allow one to be directly compared with others. Conceptually this kind of problem can be handled in terms of multi-dimensional social welfare functions.

In practice, however, there is no possibility of determining, in the abstract, multi-dimensional trade of functions amongst different, usually incommensurate, values. [...] We simply cannot determine in the abstract our ends or values and the intensity with which we hold them. We discover our objectives and the intensity which we assign to them only in the process of considering particular programmes or policies. We articulate 'ends' as we evaluate 'means.'" Charles L. Schultze, *The Politics and Economics of Public Spending*, Washington: The Brookings Institution, 1968; cited from Claude Maestre, *Analytical Methods in Government Science Policy: An Evaluation*, Paris: OECD, 1972, p. 13. For a systematic appraisal of the shortcomings and dangers of formal methods and analytical techniques, see in addition to Maestre Paul Streeten, *The Political Economy of the Environment: Problems of Method*, Symposium, Maison des Sciences de L'Homme and École Pratique des Hautes Études.

10 Should the development process itself be seen as representing a kind of economic system in newly developing economies today?[1]

My initial reaction was to regard this as a leading question to which there could be only one answer: Of course the development process is a system and should be viewed as such; any other approach to the development process of newly developing countries is bound to lead us astray, both in our analysis and our formulation of policy.

Having said this, a question of interpretation arises as to the meaning of the term "economic system." If the term is to be interpreted in the conventional sense of an "isolated" system, my answer would be negative: The development process is not and should not be seen simply as an economic process. If we do so, we neglect some of the most important factors and relationships which influence the process of development and underdevelopment in actual situations. But then, one may say that what is really referred to above is "a kind of" economic system, and wonder whether this definition does not allow for precisely the kind of interpretation of the question that will serve our purposes—or should I say *my* purposes?

I propose to interpret the question, then, in such a way as to give it a meaning which allows me to respond to it constructively. By "constructive," I mean I will attempt an answer which permits me to elucidate certain aspects of the increasingly important concept of socio-economic systems. Let me explain first why it seems possible, and indeed necessary, to view the development process as a socio-economic system. The reason is partly a matter of empirical observation and partly the result of theoretical reflection. If we study some of the most successful development processes, as well as some of the failures of economic development, we will probably agree that their successes or failures cannot be explained simply in terms of such aggregate economic factors as the rate of savings and investment or the output-capital ratio, but must include a complex of social, political, and economic factors which transcend the relatively narrow scope of economic analysis.

As an illustration, let me cite the case of Israel. Its exceptional economic development seems particularly instructive for our discussion. Its natural and external political environment can hardly be said to be favorable to development, and yet "nowhere else in the Middle East and nowhere among the presently underdeveloped nations can there be found a combination of cultural values, institutions, and linkages so conducive to rapid economic growth."[2] In Israel, the cultural values have included such important attitudes as

(1) *nationalism*, based not only upon a burning sense of historical wrongs that have been suffered, but also upon the biblical vision of a return to a "Holy Land." [...] (2) *instrumental activism*, i.e., the attitude that people can change the world instead of having to accept a predestined order; and (3) *collectivism*, in the sense of orientation toward group action and organization rather than purely individual activity. The institutional structure of the Jewish community in Israel, even before the new State was established, has included a remarkable set of powerful trade unions, political parties, pressure groups, and economic enterprises. [...] Finally, the country has enjoyed organized support from a large number of Jews in other countries—support that has evidenced itself not only in direct assistance but also in favorable action by the governments of these countries.[3]

A similar intersection of cultural values, institutions, and economic features, although not necessarily of the same character and content, can be found in Japan[4] and the Soviet Union, as well as in other Soviet-type economies. Conversely, the much slower rate of economic growth in some of the Arab countries, and in India, Indonesia, and many others, is due to traditional institutional value orientations and social arrangements which either insufficiently support the development effort or actually delay and obstruct it.

These conditions lead us to conclude that, instead of viewing the development process as an economic system in the conventional-model sense of the term, it would be more fruitful to regard it as a social system from the very outset, particularly in traditional societies. I reach this conclusion not in any doctrinaire spirit of methodological contentiousness, but rather from the conviction that any real progress in the explication of economic development depends today more on our ability to see the process as a socio-economic system than on the further refinement of some of our current analytical tools.

Some of the questions which must be answered in this context include: What is a system? What is a social system? What are its component parts and characteristics? What are the analytical tasks which follow from this way of viewing social processes in general and the development process in particular? I am sure you will concede that adequate and properly qualified answers to questions of this nature require much more time than I have here. Therefore, I trust you will make the proper allowances for the somewhat dogmatic brevity with which I must proceed.

Let me first advance a working definition of the term "system." I propose to use this term in reference to "any complex of components in mutual interaction,"[5] or, if you prefer a definition more directly related to social systems, a system can be defined as a complex of components with more or less regularized relationships between institutionalized behavior patterns, organizations, groups, and individuals. The components referred to may be systems themselves (or subsystems). The term may refer either to concrete, empirical units or abstract ones designed to provide a conceptual representation of empirical entities.[6]

Systems or networks of components in mutual interaction are in process; that is, they move—they exhibit internal changes, as we will see. The term "system" may therefore also refer to these processes of change. Thus, the term may imply more than one connotation: it may refer to an empirical entity with definable component parts in mutual interaction; it may designate the process of interaction between these parts; or it may refer to the abstract conceptual representation of components in mutual interaction, or the process of interaction itself. It is important to keep these connotations in mind when using the term.

Is it possible to regard the process of development as "a kind of economic system"—or, as I would suggest, a kind of *socio-economic* system? I would claim the affirmative, provided we use the term "system" in its dynamic-institutional sense, that is, with reference to the actual course of interaction taking place between the various components or subsystems.

The first question, then, is: Which components of the socio-economic system do we regard as the development process? In addition to the *economic system* (i.e., the system of production and distribution as a mechanism of allocation), I would list the following subsystems:

1   the *system of ideas* by which man interprets the world and his role in it (his world outlook);
2   the *system of values*, motives, and attitudes;
3   the *system of socially shared knowledge and technology;*
4   the *power system* through which individuals and groups influence economic and social progress in accordance with their own aims;
5   the *kinship and family system.*

I do not claim that these categories exhaust all the conceivable possibilities of subsystems relevant to the development process, or for that matter that they constitute the best way of classifying them. Nor do I believe that we yet understand all the interrelationships that connect the various subsystems. After all, most of our social sciences are highly specialized, and as such have shown little interest in elucidating these interrelationships. Economists interested primarily in the explication of developed economies have steered clear of these problems by confining their studies to the economic system, and to the small number of so-called economic variables, while regarding all of the other elements and influences the economy may receive from society as constants, or parameters. Despite this lamentable lack of interest, considerably more is known about the process of circular interaction than is usually realized by the specialists. Therefore I think it possible, and indeed fruitful, to view the development process within the framework of a social-system analysis, with various components in mutual or circular interaction. Most of those who have had first-hand experience with traditional societies have been impressed not only by the fundamental differences between their social systems and those of advanced industrial societies, but also by the relative consistency and internal coherence of their respective patterns of ideas, values, and institutional arrangements. Their patterns of motivation, their attitudes and knowledge, their technology, their power and kinship systems *are* more or less organized entities—a characteristic which, as we shall see, is not contradicted by the coexistence of traditional and modern sectors, such as urban centers in proximity to the vast agricultural hinterland.

Let me be specific: Pre-scientific and fatalistic or even animistic world views support a disbelief in improvements; they co-exist with a system of knowledge and a relatively backward technology resulting in low levels of productivity of labor and capital goods, thereby making it necessary to employ a high percentage of the population in agricultural production merely to supply adequate amounts of food. This, in turn, perpetuates a power system in which the prevailing tenancy regulations and the growing number of landless laborers are the most important symptoms. This power system also affects the distribution of the national product, and causes relatively weak incentives for modernization, as well as limiting internal purchasing power while at the same time restricting the domestic market for manufactured products. Additionally, systems of traditional values and patterns of motivation persist which continue to attach considerable importance and expenditure on ostentatious ceremonies of national prestige. These factors all lead to an inadequate domestic rate of savings and investment, and an inefficient use of the nation's potential surplus. A relatively high death rate, the peasant character[7] of the operation of the agricultural sector, and other factors related to traditional patterns of values and attitudes, also put a premium on the maintenance of an extended family system which favors high fertility.[8]

If this sounds like just another case of the vicious circle, it is precisely that. However, it also illustrates how the process of underdevelopment and development fit our definition of a social system, how circular causation affects economic development, and suggests a framework of analysis which does not single out one or two factors as the primary causes of the process. I agree with Myrdal that

> the ideal solution would be to formulate the functional relationships between the various parts in the form of an interconnected set of equations describing the movement—and the internal changes—of the system studied under the various influences which are at work on it.[9]

I doubt, though (as Myrdal also does), that we will ever be able to acquire the complete and quantitative information required to formulate an interconnected set of equations describing the movement and internal changes of the relationships within a social system. But even without complete and precise knowledge of such relationships, a good deal can be achieved by analyzing and planning a process of development viewed as a social system. Even qualitative knowledge, or "explanation on principle," of the general nature of the relationships and the possible direction of the changes can be of considerable importance. Therefore I feel that, rather than rushing into a mathematical formalization of a theory of social systems, it would be more efficacious to seek a better understanding of the characteristics of specific social systems. Of course, social systems do attain conditions of relative constancy, in which the system as a whole does not change its character, but this constancy may be a state of stagnation in which the sustaining impulses (such as foreign aid, in the case of development) are absorbed and counteracted by the inhibitory effects of institutions, cultural values, attitudes, power systems, and other elements. In contrast to conventional, stable equilibria, such steady states of social systems seem to be marked by a measure of liability.

Despite their inertia and stagnation, however, social systems are in process, they have a dynamic,[10] they move, they exhibit internal changes. Marginal and incremental changes may accumulate combined effects that yield qualitative and structural changes; conflicts may arise between different components of the system which undermine and change its character; extreme forms of conflict may destroy a system altogether. Some conflicts, however, may set in motion the essential dialectical process through which an adaptation of the system to new conditions takes place. At any rate, social systems which do not possess this adaptability to new conditions and to the requirements of the survival of their human elements cannot cope with the challenge. This is why one of the tasks of the analysis of the development process, viewed as a social system, is to identify those internal contradictions and tensions which may force traditional societies to adapt to the survival needs of its members. Let me add, however, that this is not the simple three-step dialectic of thesis, antithesis, and synthesis envisioned by Hegel and Marx, but a much more complex dialectical process with no determinate, and probably more than one conceivable, outcome.

Viewing the process of development as a social system emphasizes its interdependence, with several subsystems in mutual and circular interaction; thus any search for a primary cause of development is necessarily futile, indeed as futile as the conventional concentration on the rate of investment as the determining factor of development. Instead, what is needed, and all one can hope for, is to be able to identify the factors which can more easily influence the others, and are themselves capable of changing the pattern of interaction in the direction of economic development. My own hunch is that improvements in technology, land use, and tenancy regulations; techniques to control the birth rate; and improvements in education and public administration offer the best possibilities for positive change, and as such constitute strategic factors. There may be others which can be identified through empirical studies of specific social systems.

It seems to me, then, that an attempt to view the development process as a social system with several components in circular interaction provides an alternative to the conventional approach to the study of economic development. Not only does it offer an explanation for the failures of many development projects, it can also yield pragmatic indicators for a more successful planning of such projects, and of development effects in general. An illustration may serve to make this last point clear. Pre-industrial societies with traditional forms of agriculture, land tenancy systems, and rates of population growth between 3 and 4 percent face formidable problems, the full complexity of which can be grasped only with a social-system approach. For all indications point to the conclusion that, given their levels of knowledge and technology (as reflected in the available capital goods such as plant and animal varieties and their agricultural techniques), their climatic and soil conditions, their inherited land-tenancy problems, their credit and marketing organizations, and their rates of increase in the number of persons seeking employment, these traditional economies have effectively exhausted the range of their economically profitable agricultural investment opportunities. Therefore, neither a reliance on private profit incentives, nor the improvement of present marketing (or market) structures, nor the provision of a better infrastructure (irrigation systems, roads, etc.), nor institutional reform, nor even the simple transfer of the highly sophisticated Western agricultural methods and technology can be expected to be sufficient or effective—at least not when taken separately. Economic development, when viewed as a socio-economic system, points to the conclusion that only a combination of measures can hope to cope adequately with the modernization of the traditional agricultural society.

What may offer a way out of this dilemma is the development of agricultural technologies—the creation of new varieties of plants and animal stock which, under the climatic and natural conditions of specific regions, are capable of raising the currently stagnant yields per acre; the diffusion of the technical knowledge required to produce and protect these new capital goods; the choice (as far as possible) of labor-intensive methods of cultivation; comprehensive measures of land reform; the creation of strategic infrastructure, including the provision of a dependable water supply and transport and distribution facilities; and a reformed tax system. I will mention the necessary industrialization of the economy only in passing, despite its obvious importance as a means of reducing the reliance on imports and providing opportunities for useful work for the growing army of the unemployed. By stressing the mutual interaction of a complex of components, then, the social-system approach to economic development not only induces us to stay closer to the factual conditions of underdeveloped countries (including their institutional and technological conditions), but can also help us develop workable indicators for a more adequate strategy of development planning than any conventional theory formulated only in terms of so-called economic variables.

Kapp replies to the points raised in regard to the identification of process and system:

While systems are in process, it is of course true that not all processes are systems. All systems, particularly such open systems as biological and social ones, are in movement; they receive impulses (inputs) from the outside and produce outcomes (outputs) which may be steady states or even conditions of stagnation. Nevertheless, since such systems are in process, they can and should be viewed as such. Our difficulties in viewing systems as processes and processes as systems stem from the fact that we have in the past been concerned almost exclusively with mechanical systems. If systems are in movement, it should not be difficult in principle to regard processes as systems.

The development process is one of interaction between the various components of a social system. The problem is to properly categorize these components and explore their interaction, with the goal of discovering the most appropriate points where necessary action may be taken, in the form of policy decisions, to influence the processes in the desired direction.

True, different social and political power groups will take different positions on development policies; in fact, they may even block the development process altogether. However, this is not a refutation of the thesis that development processes must be interpreted in the context of the interdependencies within a socio-economic system. In fact, development planning without the appropriate interdisciplinary approach—namely one adapted to the plan or project under consideration—must remain futile, and is bound to lead to wasteful investment, delay, and ultimate failure.

As an illustration, Kapp refers to the development of new capital goods (e.g., new varieties of rice plants offering higher yields per acre) in Southeast Asia:

The International Rice Institute in Los Banos, Philippines developed these new plants within a period of only three years; however, the new varieties call for a new, highly-sophisticated and industrialized form of agricultural cultivation, involving insect control and the proper mix of fertilizer, water, and soil, which the traditional peasant is neither inclined by habit nor equipped by training to use. Hence arises the problem of diffusing the knowledge required to use the new capital goods profitably to the actual cultivators—a task well beyond the traditional scope of agricultural extension services. The social-system approach recognizes these difficulties, and points to the need for new research methods and practical tactics—only one example of the potentially fruitful effects of such an approach.

The question of whether the institutional changes or the economic investment should come first seems to be wrongly posed. Similarly, the traditional belief in an "automatic" or long-run adaptation of an institution to prior economic changes, while plausible as a *post hoc* explanation, may have the effect of concentrating on so-called economic changes, which are then inadequately supported by the socio-institutional matrix of society. What is called for is a sufficiently comprehensive project plan, with various inputs that support each other's effects, to guarantee that the contemplated policies yield the anticipated results.

Notes

1 Paper read at the International Conference of the Association for Comparative Economics, Villa Serbelloni, Bellagio, September 3–9, 1967.
2 B. M. Gross, "Planning as Crisis Management." Preface to Benjamin Akzim and Yehezkel, *DROR Israel-High-Pressure Planning*, Syracuse, 1966, also reprinted in *Mitteilungen der List Gesellschaft*, Fasc. 6, No. 1, 1967, p. 18.
3 Ibid., p. 18.
4 Takekazu Ogura (ed.), *Agricultural Development in Modern Japan*, Tokyo: Fuji Publishing, 1963; and S. Tobata (ed.), *The Modernization of Japan*, vol. 1, Tokyo: The Institute of Asian Economic Affairs, 1966.
5 Ludwig van Bertalanffy, "General Systems Theory of Psychiatry," to be published in S. Arietic (ed.), *American Handbook of Psychiatry* (mimeographed 1967), p. 3.

Several alternative definitions of systems may be mentioned, for instance "a network of interrelated organization groups, individuals" (B.M. Gross); a totality consisting of elements connected according to certain rules or regularities; organized complexities (Weaver); stabilized or regularized relationships [citation cut off here].

6 Theoretical systems may be models—a term which I would reserve for conceptual systems in which the relationships between the various elements or components are expressed in terms of the relationship between numbers or algebraic functions. Cf. Peter Caws, *Science and System, On the Utility and Diversity of Scientific Theory* (mimeographed 1966), p. 3.

7 In Chayanov's sense of the term. Cf. A. V. Chayanov, *The Theory of Peasant Economy,* New York, 1966.

8 Kingsley Davis, "Institutional Patterns Favoring High Fertility in Underdeveloped Areas," *Eugenics Quarterly* 2 (1), March 1955, pp. 33–9; reprinted in Lyle W. Shanon (ed.), *Underdeveloped Areas,* New York: Harper and Brothers, 1957, pp. 88–95.

9 Gunnar Myrdal, *Economic Theory and Under-Developed Regions,* London: Gerald Duckworth & Co., 1957, p. 19.

10 On the dynamics of social systems, see the pertinent observations of B. M. Gross, *The State of the Nation—Social Systems Accounting,* London: Social Science Paperbacks, 1966, pp. 30–35.

11 Environmental control and the market mechanism[1]

Thus far, our main concerns have been the market mechanism as a causal factor of the environmental problem, and the substantive character of the problem itself. In this context, it may not be so obvious that conventional economic theory and analysis is destined to play a major role in the formulation of the methods, instruments, and policies of environmental control and protection. While economists have dealt with the allocation of inputs, including the choice of techniques and location, and have synthesized their conclusions into a general theory of choice and economic decision-making, they have done so based on narrowly circumscribed micro-economic models which regard economic processes as taking place in essentially closed systems. The "exchange" between the economy and nature has not been considered. (To economists, exchanges are bilateral, reciprocal, voluntary, two-party relationships, which are viewed as taking place in competitive or, more recently, oligopolistic markets, with the aid of partial or total equilibrium models.) The problem of decision-making is analyzed based on such specific assumptions about human behavior as the maximization rule, which also includes implicit and explicit rules of optimization (marginal valuation and equalization of marginal costs and returns), which in turn introduce tendencies of self-equilibration in accordance with the analogies of classical mechanics.

Similar assumptions also underlie the analysis of economic growth. Macro-economic growth models are just as useless as micro-economics in considering the environmental effects of increasing outputs and inputs, or the increasing discharge of wastes into the environment. The effects of increasing savings and investment, of higher or lower interest rates, and of public spending and investment in income and growth (as measured in GNP) are analyzed, and policy arguments are made, without considering higher or lower rates of waste, their effects on the environment, and the resulting disruption and social costs. Conventional economic theory favors increased production (output), in keeping with market principles, but this increased output also increases pollution. Thus it appears that conventional economic analysis has little, if anything, to contribute to the problem of environmental control.[2] However, many economists have expressed a contrary view, and have not hesitated to use their models of optimal allocation and decision-making as a basis for suggestions and general principles for environmental policies which have won some theoretical and practical acceptance.

Perhaps the best-known guiding principle is that of "internalizing" the unaccounted "external" costs into entrepreneurial cost accounting, to correct the distortion of the price and cost structure resulting from the failure to account for the social costs inflicted by pollution. This principle, also known as the "polluter pays" principle (PPP), is inferred from the fact that environmental disruption and social costs shift part of the costs of production to third parties and to society as a whole, and are thus not accounted for in the price or market mechanism. The PPP, in turn, is used to justify a wide spectrum of environmental policy measures: effluent charges, utilization fees, taxes, strengthening of liability and compensation laws, establishing private and public property rights to common property resources, and even the sale of permits to discharge waste into rivers, watersheds, or lakes. The widespread appeal of the PPP derives from the reassuring impression it creates that resolving the environmental problem will not require fundamental changes to the market system, and indeed can be solved (or at least minimized) by indirect controls that rely on the very market mechanism responsible for incurring the social costs. Indeed, it creates the impression that pollution can be controlled by using a decentralized system of decision-making and allocation, and by balancing the costs of environmental control and environmental damage—hence the term and concept of environmental "management."

The merit of the PPP is that it recognizes the argument that the market mechanism, operating under traditional institutional arrangements, is causally related to a misallocation of scarce environmental resources, since economic units cover only part of the costs of production and consumption. I consider it an additional merit of the PPP that it insists, at least in principle, on the need to account for the actual unpaid environmental costs when making private or public investment and production decisions. In reality, however, the principle's meaning is much more restricted; it does not imply that all of the social costs resulting from pollution should be charged to the polluter, but only those that are created by preventive measures introduced by government. In addition to this shortcoming, the feasibility and practical effectiveness of the PPP are open to many questions and doubts.

It is interesting that the guiding principles adopted by the Environmental Committee of OECD define the main objective of the PPP in only a narrow and partial sense, for example to consider as costs only those involved in executing the

> public measures [...] necessary to reduce pollution and to reach a better
> allocation of resources by ensuring that prices of goods depending on the
> quality and quantity of environmental resources reflect more closely their
> relative scarcity and that economic agents concerned react accordingly. [...]
> This [PPP] principle means that the polluter should bear the expenses of car-
> rying out the above-mentioned measures decided by public authorities to
> ensure that the environment is in an acceptable state. In other words, the

costs of these measures should be reflected in the costs of goods and services which cause pollution in production and/or consumption. Such measures should not be accompanied by subsidies that would create significant
distortion in international trade and investment.[3]

It should perhaps be added that the Environmental Committee considers it essential to apply the PPP in concert with the establishment of tolerable levels of pollution, and to stringent but flexible and (as far as possible) non-discriminatory
emission standards. The PPP envisioned by the OECD, then, would avoid conflicting policies both within and between member states, is clearly linked to
explicit quantitative standards, and is meant to be mainly preventive.

Let us now examine the question of the feasibility, probable effectiveness,
and practical application of various aspects of the PPP.

Effluent charges, taxes, and penalties

Determining the level of charges and estimating the response of the polluter are
the two biggest difficulties in this aspect. The rate of effluent charges and taxes
must be related to an estimate of the damages and/or the cost of measures of
public control, such as the construction of treatment facilities and their effectiveness. This, of course, presents the problem of determining a fixed level of
charges in relation to two uncertain variables. Any agency administering a
system of charges would need a data-gathering department to conduct studies of
the ongoing costs of these variables, and the cost of gathering this information
would introduce a third variable to the equation. In this respect, there would be
no advantage in this method over alternative, and more direct, approaches to
environmental control.

The response of the polluter would also influence the effectiveness of this
method. Much would depend on market structure, including the elasticity of
demand, and whether or not the charges would be allowed as tax-deductible
business costs. If the latter were the case, the economic disincentive created by
such charges would be reduced. The more monopolistic and oligopolistic the
market structure and the more inelastic the demands, the less effective taxes and
effluent charges would be. In fact, if such charges were not high enough, they
could be absorbed, and pollution would continue, even as the increase in governmental revenues would allow the building of public treatment plants. Alternatively, the charges could be shifted to the consumer, resulting in the elimination
of any incentive on the part of the producer to stop or lessen polluting.

Is the true purpose of the PPP, then, to prevent or reduce pollution, or merely
to shift its costs to the polluter or the consumer? If the former, how much will
taxes and effluent charges really contribute to changes in inputs and techniques,
or changes of location to less congested areas? These issues are, in reality, influenced much more heavily by fiscal and monetary growth policies affecting
aggregate spending, interest rates, and the marginal propensity to save and
invest. Thus, while it is conceivable that the public agency in charge of levying

taxes and penalties may induce the manufacturer to reduce pollution, the agency in charge of growth and employment policies may well induce the opposite effect. Also, if effluent charges for waterborne waste become effective enough in reducing those emissions, they may act as an incentive for increasing airborne wastes, or vice versa.

> Relatively high water quality standards or effluent charges will undoubtedly induce shifts in production processes toward greater pollutant load to the atmosphere via burning or industrial sludge, or toward creating waste disposal problems, unless the air and land resources are also protected by standards or effluent charges.[4]

Nor is there any assurance that relying on taxes and penalties as a means to decentralized decision-making and individual optimal allocation will actually lead to a social optimum and not the partial suboptimization characteristic of the causal process of environmental disruption. An additional problem endemic to regulatory agencies is that their decisions may be influenced by liberally financed interest and pressure groups, which may engage in selective research and release of information, counter-information, denials, and counter-denials which render the search for correct and impartial decisions difficult or impossible.[5]

None of the foregoing should be taken to mean that penalties, charges, and taxes have no role to play as important instruments of environmental control, only that their effectiveness as integral parts of a system based on the PPP is problematical.

Liability laws and property rights

A related approach to a resolution of environmental problems based on the PPP relies on strengthening liability or compensation laws, and establishing private or public property rights with respect to common property resources.

Traditional liability laws governing compensation for damages and nuisances incurred by third parties remain inadequate for securing proper compensation for the losses caused by environmental disruption. This is because of the substantive nature of the problem, particularly the complexities of the process of causation, the difficulty in identifying polluters, and the full range of the damages incurred. Liability laws which were designed for different and simpler cases of damages than those caused by environmental disruption rightly place the burden of proof of damages and the identification of the party responsible for those damages on the injured person, or claimant. In the case of environmental damages, this burden to prove damage and identify the polluter is usually an insurmountable one for the injured person. The high cost of legal transactions also renders liability laws an unsuitable and ineffective way to redress damages through compensation to the injured person.

A number of suggestions have recently been made to strengthen liability laws and make them more effective in obtaining compensation from polluters, which would then allow the damages caused by pollution to be incorporated into entrepreneurial cost accounting. Among these suggestions are proposals that would enable groups of damaged persons to bring a common suit against the polluter, or to allow interested parties with a legitimate interest in the prevention of environmental losses to establish themselves as claimants, with the right to demand legal redress or preventive court action. Alternatively, it has been suggested to put the burden of proof on the decision makers proposing to introduce technological innovations, such as the use of new inputs, techniques, production designs, and new production sites. The latter suggestion is closely related to the concept of technology assessment and technology-impact statements. Such an approach to the problem of compensation (and prevention) would constitute a radical departure from established legal procedures. Its ultimate effectiveness would depend on a host of legal and procedural provisions which are beyond the scope of this essay. Suffice it to say, however, that such a change in the socio-legal structure, while far-reaching in its possible repercussions on decision-making and allocation, is likely to be strongly opposed by organized producers, whose right to choose inputs, techniques, and locations would be severely restricted by the new responsibilities placed on them.[6]

Further suggestions for the internalization of social costs relate to the establishment of private property rights to such common resources as air and water. It is argued that actual and potential polluters would have to enter into negotiations with private owners, who could then be induced through compensation (or bribes) to permit the use of "their" property for the discharge of waste, without fixing any public standards or upper limits of allowable pollution. We mention this proposal only to illustrate the general direction in which the logic of the bilateral or market approach to the resolution of the environmental problem leads. A similar approach is found in proposals to establish explicit private or public property rights to environmental media, and make arrangements for the sale of licenses or permits to discharge pollutants into rivers, lakes, etc. for a limited time and to a limited degree. Such permits, it is suggested, could be freely bought and sold in special markets and auctions, and would be negotiable or transferable at market prices. It has even been suggested that those interested in environmental protection could purchase permits or licenses to pollute and withhold them from use or transfer, so that pollution is reduced below the fixed upper limit.

While these and similar market approaches to social costs create the illusion of recognizing the environmental problem, their solutions do not seem to be based on a full understanding of the substantive character of the problem. They interpret it as the result of imperfect or nonexistent markets, or lack of information and transparency resulting from "market failures" or "market malfunctioning." Thus, while it is acknowledged that environmental disruption is the expression of a (possibly serious) misallocation of resources, their solution is to make the problem assimilable into the analytical matrix of conventional neoclassical and welfare partial and total equilibrium theory. And it is within this matrix that remedial action and general policies of control are constructed—

policies intended to restore conditions of optimal allocation, optimal emission of pollutants, and presumably the choice of optimal technologies and locations. This is to be achieved by providing economic decision-makers with more adequate and appropriate price and cost signals, in the hope that there will again be room for balancing the marginal returns and costs of the polluter, after the internalization of social costs, as a royal road to optimization.[7] What is needed, then (so the argument goes), is to establish new markets or correct the market mechanism, in order to correct the behavior of decision-makers through a system of incentives, disincentives, penalties, and rewards, including the strengthening of the liability laws. By increasing the opportunities for bilateral bargaining between polluters and damaged parties, optimal private management of output and resource use (including the use of the assimilative capacity of the common property) can be maintained without, or with only a minimum of, interference with decentralized decision-making in a more perfect market economy.

The limitations of such an approach should be evident. It possesses all the defects of the basic postulates of the neo-classical and welfare-equilibrium approach. It treats the problem of environmental disruption as if it were a bilateral one, ignoring its regional and global scope. The cumulative nature of environmental degradation is also disregarded. Self-interested behavior and maximizing rules are relied upon as if they were unambiguous and unproblematic. Individual willingness to compensate or even bribe is regarded as an appropriate monetary expression of the importance of environmental "goods" and values, as if such willingness is not dependent on ability to pay, and hence on the distribution of income. As in similar traditional-welfare economic considerations, then, optimization is abstracted from the distribution of income according to the motto "Try to be efficient at the current distribution level; if you dislike the latter, change it, provided no one is worse off than before."[8] Changes in the rules of the game and the establishment of new socio-legal structures are advocated as if these alone are sufficient, without considering what *should* be done, or as if what *needs* to be done is not possible or feasible. The entire approach stays within the boundaries of an analytical system which considers economics only in the context of individual decision-making and preferences.[9] Policy measures based on the theoretical framework of neo-classical welfare economics fail to account for the composite and complex character of the process that causes environmental disruption, and neglect to consider the intrinsic interconnection of the various types of pollution, or its cumulative or synergistic effects. It is a piecemeal approach that deals with phenomena in isolation. Problems and consequences of critical limits of pollution, and the disproportionate effects of exceeding those limits, are outside the scope of this approach, as are such problems as congestion and over-concentration. Energy and entropy problems are similarly disregarded.

The neo-classical welfare and market approach, and the policy proposals that stem from it, maintain full confidence in the steering mechanism of the market and market prices, although it stands to reason that the absence of markets for common property resources or their assimilative capacity is not the only cause of price distortion. The establishment of a market for such resources and the internalization of social costs will not eliminate the distortion of prices that results from such factors as inflation, unemployment, control and manipulation of the banking system (and hence of the cost and quantity of money), or the fact that consumers' tastes and preferences are not independently determined but are subjected to the influence of those who have a commercial interest in consumer demand. The market approach also fails to account for the fact that the rate of non-renewable resource consumption and the production of environmental waste cannot be indefinitely increased without reaching critical limits affecting future generations. Given the fact that the market approach derives its policy norms and objectives from purely pecuniary standards of efficiency, rather than a substantive concept of rationality related to the satisfaction of actual human needs, it is evident that this approach must lead to an impasse; it cannot supply a satisfactory or adequate solution to the problems caused by the disruption and destruction of the human environment by economic processes. An adequate approach to environmental policies and planning, as in all types of social planning, "requires first a clear conception of what is desirable and what is essential."[10] The market mechanism provides neither information nor adequate criteria for this purpose. It cannot call our attention to what is essential or possible. While the utilitarian bias of neo-classicism and marginalism may be a guide to maximizing utility, it does not help us in the more important task of minimizing human suffering; to accomplish this, we must concentrate on the satisfaction of essential human needs, and on the minimum requirements for human life and survival. Nor does the market and the neo-classical approach emphasize the possible and the desirable—to identify, for example, which alternative technologies, inputs, and locations will reduce pollution and lessen inputs and waste; which investments are needed to increase the assimilative capacities of specific environmental media; how the recovery and re-use of materials can be increased; which patterns of growth and development can reduce both the consumption of scarce input resources and the production of environmental waste; or which lifestyle consumption patterns are most compatible with such growth patterns. These elements will necessarily form the building blocks of any alternative approach.

Notes

1 The handwritten note attached to this article reads "orginal draft for Kyoto partly used in keynote address [...] this has not been read out in Kyoto 1975." This reference is most likely to the meeting of the Social Science Council, which Kapp attended along with other notable economists focusing on the interactions of socio-economic and ecological systems, such as Ignacy Sachs and Allen Kneese.
2 At least one courageous economist has concluded, therefore, that conventional economics is hopelessly unsuited to deal with problems of environmental disruption and control, and that the greatest service economists could render to posterity would be to shut up. Alan Coddington [citation missing].
3 OECD, 12 May 1972, p. 5.

4 Ralph C. de'Arge, "Essay on Economic Growth and Environmental Quality," *Swedish Journal of Economics* 73, 1971 (1), p. 27.

5 For a particularly persuasive, though amusing and hypothetical, account of the counterproductiveness of such influences, see Ralph C. de'Arge and James E. Wilson, "Governmental Control of Externalities or the Prey Eats its Predator," *Journal of Economic Issues* VIII (2), June 1974, pp. 360–365.

6 Such changes in the socio-legal structure would be impossible were such modification of the status quo made dependent on unanimous support, and/or compensation of those adversely affected by the proposed changes. For a fuller discussion of the ambiguities and hidden value judgments of the unanimity-consensus-compensation rule as a means of preserving existing power relations and their advantages, see Victor P. Goldberg, "Public Choice: Property Rights," *Journal of Economic Issues* VIII (3), September 1974, pp. 555–579.

7 A social optimum of pollution would be reached if the relation between the marginal costs of pollution control and the marginal costs of production of all goods and services equals the relations of their marginal benefits.

8 Goldberg, "Public Choice: Property Rights," p. 564.

9 "When non-individualistic norms are introduced, economics, *as I define the discipline,* is abandoned." J. Buchanan, "Congestion on the Common: A Case for Governmental Intervention," *Il Politico* 33, 1968, pp. 778–786; quoted from Goldberg.

10 G.V. Price, "Experimentation in Social Planning," *Social Science* 11 (3), 1936, p. 236.

12 Energy and environment
Inadequacy of present science and technology policies[1]

Before discussing the main problem, let me state that a rational energy strategy must address two objectives simultaneously: to conserve energy and to develop alternative sources of supply. The former entails such economizing measures as the more efficient recovery and conversion of primary energy sources, curtailed consumption, anti-waste measures that apply to consumers *and* industries, and the like. Most of these measures will require alternative solutions to technical problems, and hence also systematic research into these problems. The development of non-fossil fuels requires alternative technologies, some of which seem technically feasible and commercially viable, provided we disregard their socio-ecological costs. Nuclear-energy reactors belong in this category, although this technology is still fraught with many uncertainties and potential hazards. Other non-fossil sources include everything from geothermal power, solar energy combined with hydroelectricity,[2] the harnessing of wind and sea currents, and perhaps also the use of such unconventional hydrocarbons as tar sands and oil shale. Their technical and commercial feasibility is still in question, at least on a large scale, and will require substantial long-term research. Their ultimate commercial viability depends on future developments in the price of conventional energy sources, and the chances are good that rising oil prices will hasten both innovation and profitability. Other constraints may arise, however, such as negative environmental impact, and the ratio of the amount of energy required to install new facilities compared to the amount produced, which may make it many years before a net energy surplus is achieved.[3]

The massive increase in oil prices, and the inflation that has resulted, dominates our current economic and political discussion. The so-called energy crisis has created a new interest in alternative energy sources and technologies which is likely to determine our science and technology policies for years to come. Modern industrial production, including modern agriculture, has become highly dependent on fossil fuels; as a result, these non-renewable resources have been depleted at unprecedented rates which are closely correlated to the uncontrolled economic growth rates of the last two decades. Very little attention, however, has been paid to the depletion and exhaustibility of these vital socio-capital resources. The price system has been of no help; on the contrary, the low price of oil has induced countries in Europe and elsewhere to become dependent on foreign sources of energy to an unprecedented extent.

I wish to raise the following questions: What are we doing to cope with this new situation? Are existing science and research organizations adequate to solve the urgent problem of finding alternative energy sources and technologies? What approaches to science and technology policy are needed to prevent the possible breakdown of the system of production and social reproduction? What is necessary to create a breakthrough in energy and environmental policies better adapted to individual and socio-ecological needs? (Let me make it clear that I do not intend to appraise alternative technologies; as the title of the paper indicates, I am concerned with the problem of science and research policies.)

Reactive planning vs. normative planning

How are we coping with the energy and environmental crisis? We do the same as we have always done: we react. We did not anticipate the problem, and now it threatens to overwhelm us. Having assumed, despite repeated warnings, that the supply of energy was limitless, we now project the future demand for energy in a one-dimensional, linear fashion; that is, we extrapolate future demand on the basis of past rates of economic growth and conversion of primary energy, i.e., rates of increase between 5 and 10 percent per annum. We confuse demand with need, and thus see no other way but to expand energy output. We engage in the same problem-solving exercises as ever, only this time the problem to be solved is the *supply* of energy. More immediately, we seek to solve the balance of payment deficits by recycling the financial surpluses of the oil-producing countries—that is, by solving the so-called liquidity crisis. The moribund international monetary "system" is relied on to do the trick, if not in the long term then at least in the short run.

In the long run, many believe that we can solve the energy shortage by building hundreds of nuclear power stations (or with fast breeders or fusion). The techniques used to produce nuclear energy are feasible and apparently commercially viable, or at least look so at present, so it is suggested that we put them into practice on a large scale. As in the past, feasibility controls the future, whether or not it is socially desirable, and environmental problems are pushed into the background. What *can* be done *will* be done; or, as Ozbekhan said, "can" becomes "ought," regardless of the uncertainties and potential environmental hazards. If citizen groups and responsible scientists protest and call for delays, further study, impact appraisals, or moratoria, they are labeled idealists, obstructionists, or worse.

The AEC asks for careful cost-benefit analyses of nuclear power stations and even issues their own impact analyses on the safety of nuclear reactors and related facilities; however, the response of one distinguished and responsible expert, Allen V. Knesse, to an AEC request for a statement on the relevance of cost-benefit studies to the nuclear-reactor program is worth quoting:

> I am submitting this statement as a long-time student and practitioner of benefit-cost analysis, not as a specialist in nuclear energy. It is my belief

that benefit-cost analysis cannot answer the most important policy questions associated with the desirability of developing a large-scale, fission-based economy. To expect it to do so is to ask it to bear a burden it cannot sustain. This is so because these questions are of a deep ethical character. Benefit-cost analyses certainly cannot solve such questions and may well obscure them.[4]

As Knesse's response makes clear, a nuclear energy program is a Faustian bargain, and cost-benefit calculations fail to address the ethical questions such programs engender. The uncertainties and long-term hazards, the magnitude of possible disasters, the effects on the life and safety of future generations, the fact that the safe use of fission technology would require the storage of radioactive waste for tens of thousands of years (if not longer), all make nuclear-reactor programs a pact with the devil:

> Our society confronts a moral problem of a great profundity; in my opinion, it is one of the most consequential that has ever faced mankind. In a democratic society the legitimate means for making such a choice is through the mechanism of representative government.[5]

Scientists, technicians, and science-policy planners may be qualified to help us make choices about the technical problems involved, but they have no authority, moral or political, to make decisions that may affect future generations, or even the ultimate survival of the planet.

Just as Knesse's refusal to participate in cost-benefit calculations underlines the fact that they are ethically and cognitively irresponsible as an aid to planning and decision-making, it is also clear that the same considerations apply, *pari passu*, to all science and technology planning regarding alternative energy sources. Such planning is not merely normative; whether we like it or not, it shapes the conditions and quality of life for future generations.

Depletion by Pentagon research

Since the advent of World War II, science and technology policies have been shaped increasingly by government decisions. In the United States, their objectives have been, to a large extent, military: nuclear weapons research; intercontinental missiles; and space research. In Europe, government expenditures on science and technology have served both military and civilian purposes, at least since the middle sixties: the improvement of the economy's competitive position and the acceleration of economic growth, in an attempt to close the "technology gap" between Europe and America by supporting governmental and industrial research and encouraging technical innovation. Total public expenditures for research and development in Western Europe, however, are still only one-third to one-half of those in the US. Technology and technical change, then, have long since ceased to be the outcome of an autonomous and self-regulating process, but have become the result of an organized mobilization and allocation of public funds for specific purposes. Public promotion of science and research, paired with generous financial support of applied and basic research, have guided innovational activities, technological change, and even (albeit indirectly) the diffusion of new techniques.

It should perhaps be emphasized in regard to military and space research that the goals of such projects are clearly defined, even when kept secret (as in the case of chemical warfare). They are high-priority projects of considerable national prestige, and participation in them is considered a privilege; thus, highly-qualified and creative scientists and engineers are attracted to them. Since their tasks and objectives are new, their challenges are clearly defined, and their value is apparently beyond doubt, the emphasis has been on finding technical solutions; working conditions have thus been favorable, and the chances of success quite good.[6] I stress these factors for two reasons: one, they describe the preconditions of successful technological research; if these conditions are not fulfilled, if the technological goals are in doubt or subject to constraints by vested interests (as for instance in most endeavors connected with alternative technologies and related to environmental and/or energy issues), financial support by government will by itself probably be insufficient to effect the desired results. Two, attracting gifted scientists and engineers to these projects has had, in addition to certain positive "spill-over" effects on physics, chemistry, and biology, far-reaching negative consequences for industrial and university research establishments, and thus indirectly on the quality of society itself. I refer here to what has come to be known as *the depletion by Pentagon research.*

There has, in fact, been a marked concentration of industrial engineers within government-financed military and space research in the United States since 1950. Thus,

by 1970 more than 20 percent of all engineers served military industry (aeronautical engineers, 59 percent; electrical engineers, 22 percent; mechanical and metallurgical engineers, 19 percent). In the vital research and development sphere, more than half of the nation's relevant manpower served the military-space operations.[7]

This concentration has had a profound effect on engineering education, and has created a shortage of industrial engineers trained for civilian purposes.

A preponderance of new engineers were directed to the new military-space agencies, firms and laboratories. The training for and experience in this work created a population of engineers with a special characteristic: a trained incapacity for the traditional civilian work of engineering.[8]

The long-term commitment of large sums to large-scale military projects also makes it difficult to shift resources to civilian purposes as priorities change to such subjects as alternative technologies (including energy sources) with a less destructive environmental impact. In fact, it may logically be concluded that the priority currently given to nuclear reactors as a substitute for conventional energy sources is because this technology is readily available, and because scientists and engineers have worked in this field for years. Conversely, it may not be unreasonable to argue that the general hostility to science and technology, particularly among the young, is because it has been used to develop highly destructive and inhumane instruments of chemical and environmental warfare, and has given us the hazards of nuclear power.

The limitations of the present research system

In raising the fundamental issue of how to change and promote technologies with a less disruptive environmental impact, we also raise the question of the adequacy of the present research system. Although the system has undergone some important changes in the last twenty-five years, its formal tripartite divisions into university, industrial, and government research have largely been maintained. As we have seen, the biggest change has been in the increased role of government. Governments finance their own military and civilian projects, they subcontract and award subsidies for research and development to industry, and they offer research grants to universities. The financial, and hence also the decision-making and priority-setting, role of public and semi-autonomous agencies has increased in almost every industrialized country. In this, as in many other respects, European countries have followed the American example.

While the emphasis on military research has reinforced the elements of secrecy and non-participatory decision-making by government commissions, industrial research has continued to be marked by decentralized and mostly secret applied research, guided by the market calculus. Industrial research concentrates on the development of technologies which help create new products that promise to be profitable (including, of course, government contracts on a cost-plus basis). Considerations of competition and profit make it difficult, if not impossible, to coordinate the research laboratories of different companies, and there is thus little exchange of information about the problems under investigation or the practical results achieved. Consequently, there is no way to avoid duplication of effort, and the same problems are likely to be investigated in the laboratories of different firms.[9] Additionally, a considerable part of industrial research is devoted to the development of differentiated commodities rather than new technologies. As a result, industrial research and development commits large sums of money and research talent to creating products, with no appraisal of their social usefulness in comparison with similar or identical goods already on the market.[10]

Government and university research suffer from their own inadequacies:

> Government agencies traditionally work in extravagant isolation, in systematically watertight compartments. Parallel research work on the same question is frequently carried on in the laboratories of different branches (in

itself an excellent idea), but the branches (and this is by no means excellent) ignore each other almost completely. Research workers of the Army exhaust themselves on problems already solved by the Navy or the Air Force. Technicians of the Army and those of the Navy arrive at different solutions of the same problem and proceed to apply their results without ever subjecting them to comparative tests so that both branches might avail themselves of the best apparatus or methods.

Research work in universities is characterized by a fair degree of anarchy resulting from the tradition of total freedom, of unbridled individualism, which prevails in the university laboratories. [...] The truth is that scientists all too often incline to total anarchy as a doctrine. The stories of how Archimedes discovered his immortal principle while getting out of his bath, and how Newton discovered the law of gravitation when a falling apple chanced to strike the tip of his nose, have played havoc in the minds of scientists. They have given seductive but fallacious arguments to those who proclaim that discovery is the child of imagination alone, that research rebels against all organization, and that all endeavor to give a rational form to scientific work is a bureaucratic effort serving only to hinder a scientist's freedom of mind and consequently the process of discovery itself. This disastrous doctrine is not yet through with its mischief [...] scientific research in the universities has until now completely escaped all the efficacious compulsions of organized freedom.[11]

Although this evaluation was made by a distinguished French scientist at the beginning of the mobilization of science and research for World War II, it is still relevant today.

Our science and research policies, then, suffer from a lack of overall coordination and a fragmentation of decision-making. A multiplicity of financing and planning authorities and bureaucracies in government and industry determine the allocation of considerable sums devoted to science, research, and the development of new techniques. Of course, this is the result of the way in which the research system has expanded in response to the emergence of new political and economic problems of considerable complexity, and involving great risks. It is also the product of such traditional premises as the importance of free scientific inquiry, the impossibility of planning basic research, and the imperative that government must not interfere (too much) with competitive industrial research. Whatever justification these notions of *laisser-rechercher* and *laisser-innover* may have had in the past, they must now be seriously questioned, because of the major role they have played in developing the technologies that have contributed to the disruption of the environment, and because they have been found totally inadequate in solving the new economic and environmental problems. What is now needed is a science and research policy which can promptly and efficiently develop alternative energy resources and alternative technologies more compatible with the requirements of "ecodevelopment,"[12] and in harmony with basic human needs and the maintenance of the environmental conditions, both physical and social, which are the prerequisites of social reproduction.

Toward a more adequate organization of science and technology

As I have indicated, science and technology policies are, whether we are aware of it or not, necessarily future-oriented. The planning of today will determine the quality of the environment and of society in the future, just as the technologies developed over the past century, and especially the last thirty years, have shaped the quality of our present environment. Today, science and research for new technologies are financed and developed, often with government support, by a number of industries and universities, by various divisions within government, and by semi-autonomous grant-giving organizations. Most of these bodies work with consulting and advisory committees comprising technical experts, specialists from specific academic disciplines and industrial research laboratories, and government representatives. These nominally advisory committees prepare the recommendations which form the basis for the selection of the projects to be undertaken, and hence for the allocation of research funds. While there is a certain division of labor in accordance with the traditional tripartite organization of science and research, there is very little, if any, coordination.

In Western Europe, there seems to be a lack of scientific planning in such large-scale, international scientific research and technology projects as CERN, EURATOM, ELDO, and ESRO.[13] A similar lack of planning seems to characterize R & D activities within the countries of Europe. Of course, as has been noted, some long-range policy-making is taking place in government agencies and private firms. Investigations into energy problems and desirable technologies are being conducted, but there is no goal-seeking institution and no coordination or organization, resulting in duplication, rivalry, lack of efficiency, and the waste of scarce resources. What I am questioning, then, is the present organization and coordination of science and technical research, particularly with respect to the development of alternative energy resources and technologies with a less destructive impact on the environment. These alternative technologies derive their importance from social goals which must be defined in regard to the individual and social needs under consideration. The market does not provide the criteria for such determination and evaluation.

The fact that neither air and water pollution nor radiation respects any national boundaries; the social nature of environmental goals; the size, complexity, uncertainty, and costs of the necessary projects; and the existence of conflicting goals all point to the need for a new approach to planning and coordinating science and research policies. The manner in which they are organized today is inadequate to deal effectively and democratically with the new tasks which the environmental and energy crises have made necessary. To solve these new problems, we must look beyond the limitations of the present institutions currently engaged in formulating science and technology policies and programs. A new form of institutionalized organization and a coordination between science policies and environmental and energy programs is needed, one which would direct and synchronize the innovative process: the investigative and diagnostic activities; the goal-seeking and program-determining decisions; and the choice of agencies to implement the chosen programs, monitor the work in progress, and evaluate the possible social impact of the results.

Although the creation of a Ministry of Science and Technology, or an Office of Technology Assessment, are the first steps that come to mind, I fear that such measures will turn out to be ineffective and insufficient, particularly if they fail to account for the cultural lag that has resulted from our policies being outdistanced by the urgency of the environmental and energy problems which confront both modern, industrialized countries and less-developed ones. The most fundamental obstacles to effective science and technology planning, then, are institutional in nature, in the broad sense in which Veblen used the term—i.e., customary behavior patterns, including attitudes and value orientations, all strongly influenced by conflicting vested interests. Our institutions have become divorced from reality, and are ill-adapted and unable to cope with the problems at hand. Under these new circumstances, determining general goals for science and technology research must be increasingly a matter of future-oriented decision-making under democratic conditions which presuppose a high degree of political consensus and participation.

I believe that the proposal for the establishment of an innovative branch of government, as advanced by Francois Hetman, deserves serious consideration. This fourth branch of government (in addition to the executive, legislative, and judiciary branches) would have

> the particularly responsible task of assessing the overall state of society and proposing alternative blueprints for its future. It would take the initiative of elaborating proposals for alternative future actions and submitting them to the executive branch, the legislative branch, and the public at large. It would take continuously into account new social demands and new problem areas emerging both in the executive branch and the legislative branch.
>
> It would be "independent" in studying desirable social futures and in framing possible futures and feasible variants of political action. Its main duty, consistent with its main task, would be to make available to all institutions and the public at large the results of its investigations and proposals in such a form that they be fully understood and that a deep public discussion of future issues could be engaged in all relevant parts of the social body.[14]

It is not within the scope of this paper to discuss this proposal in detail. Suffice it to state that, while it would by itself not solve all the problems of the necessary coordination of science and technology research, it would at least prepare the ground for such coordination. In conclusion, I offer an organizational scheme of government that includes an innovative branch, as offered by Hetman.

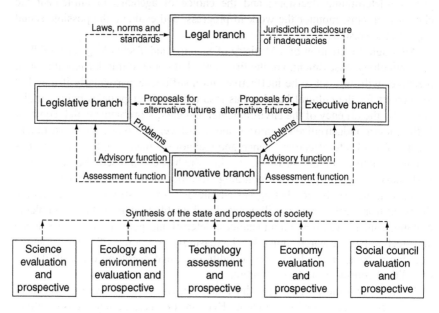

Figure 1 The innovative branch of government (source: François Hetman, *Society and the Assessment of Technology*, Paris: OECD, 1973, p. 348).

Notes

1 Symposium on Energy, Environment and Society, Maison des Sciences de l'Homme, St. Breau Sans Nappe, November 12–15, 1974.

2 In Switzerland, it is estimated that reflector projects extending over an area of ten times ten kilometers high in the Alps would supply all the energy needed to lift water from lower to higher reservoirs, thereby increasing the present installed hydroelectric capacity several times (estimate by Battelle Institute, reported in *Nationalzeitung*, November 1, 1974).

3 It is estimated that nuclear reactors may require an expenditure of energy for their construction equal to 17 years' worth of full-capacity production of the reactor itself. Klaus Michael Meyer-Abich, "Wertsetzung bei beschränkten Ressourcen," in Jörg Wolff (Hrsg.), *Wirtschaftspolitik in der Umweltkrise- Strategie der Wachstumsbegrenzung und Wachstumslenkung*, Stuttgart: Deutsche Verlagsanstalt, 1974, S. [rest of note cut off].

4 Allen V. Knesse, "Benefit-Cost Analysis and Unscheduled Events in the Nuclear Fuel Cycle," reprinted under the title "The Faustian Bargain," RfF, *Resources*, September 1973, p. 1.

5 Ibid., p. 2.

6 This is not to say, by any means, that military and space projects have proceeded without failure, misallocations, or technical blunders. In fact, in the US "there were 65 major defense projects cancelled from 1953 to 1968 on which 210.5 billion dollars had been wasted. Since then, there have been further billion-dollar fiascos of which the F-111 fighter aircraft and the C-5A transport plane are prime examples, both having been cut back after huge overruns and bad performance." J.E. Ullmann and Seymour Melman, "The New Engineer," in R. Gross and O. Ostermann (eds.), *The New Professionals*, New York: Simon & Schuster, 1972, p. 245.

7 Ibid., p. 241.
8 Ibid.
9 K. William Kapp, *The Social Costs of Private Enterprise,* Cambridge: Harvard University Press, 1950, p. 212 (reissued by Schocken Books, New York, 1972).
10 Rolf Berger, "Forschungsplanung als Kommunikations—und Inhaltsplanung," *Wirtschaft und Wissenschaft,* 1974, No. 1, S. 22.
11 H. Laugier, "How Science Can Win the War," *Free World* I (1941), No. 1, p. 59.
12 I am appropriating here a term and concept put forth by Maurice F. Strong. Cf. *Ecodevelopment—Note pour un Projet de Recherche,* Centre International de Recherche sur l'Environment et le Development, Paris: Ecole Pratique des Hautes Etudes, 1974.
13 J. Gueron, "The Lack of Scientific Planning in Europe," *Bulletin of Atomic Scientists,* Vol. XXV, No. 8, 1969, pp. 10–14, 25 (this article deals exclusively with the European transnational research organizations, such as The European Organization for Nuclear Research, The European Energy Community, The European Launching Development Organization, and the European Space Research Organization).
14 François Hetman, *Society and the Assessment of Technology,* Paris: OECD, 1973, p. 349.

13 The future of economics[1]

The question of the probable impact of the environmental crisis on the future of economics is being answered today in very different ways. There are those who argue that economics has little if anything to contribute to the explication and solution of the environmental dilemma. In other words, ecologists, natural scientists and chemical experts hold the key to the problems and economists would be well advised to keep out of the field which they have neglected (ignored) for decades. Another line of reasoning takes the position that problems raised by the environmental issue are not so very new and that economics has simply to apply its traditional modes of reasoning and adapt its general principles which can be brought to bear upon the theoretical analysis and the formulation of practical criteria for the solution of environmental problems.

We shall take the position that both these attitudes can advance significant arguments in favor of their respective views. However, the impact of the environmental crisis raises much more fundamental issues than either of the two schools of thought seems to anticipate. While the ultimate outcome is a matter of conjecture, the general direction of the impact of the environmental crisis on economics is in the direction of a radical reversal of past trends and procedure in our view. Of course, statements of this sort are necessarily conjectural and contingent upon a number of factors including certain (pre-)conceptions concerning the nature of the problems raised by the environmental crisis.

Those who argue that economics has little or nothing to contribute and would do well to withdraw from the field can point to the fact that economics has dealt with problems of production, allocation, distribution within closed or semi-closed systems and that its conceptual and theoretical apparatus (tools) and its basic paradigms are ill adapted to take account of the fact that economic systems are radically open systems in continual interaction with and dependent upon environmental systems as far as their inputs and the disposal of their residual waste products which threaten and destroy the stability of the former in addition to exhausting strategic non-renewable resources (are concerned). Furthermore, it can be argued, not without justification, that the evaluation by economic theory of goods and services in terms of market values, which moreover are distorted by various 'imperfections' provide no adequate basis and are not adapted to the general and extra market character of environmental goods and damages, particularly as far as their social effects (e.g., on human health and survival) are concerned. Finally, it could be argued, and it is being argued, that we are reaching the limits of the carrying capacity of the environment (of the planet) both as far as the capacity to provide necessary inputs and the capacity of absorbing pollutants is concerned (given modern technologies). Even if we are extremely skeptical with regards to the validity of a global approach to relating total world population (including total output, consumption, pollution etc.) and its "necessarily" exponential growth to world resources considering the "world" as a whole and regard it as more relevant to be concerned with the impact of man on the environment in specific situations and regions, it cannot be denied that human health and survival are indeed threatened in specific situations. To the extent that these environmental threats to human health and survival in highly industrial countries as well as less developed countries (also for other reasons) are becoming more generally recognized (under the influence of the effects of greater publicity of environmental catastrophes and scandals), the economic—i.e., the valuational—comparison of total costs and social benefits may indeed be pushed into the background and the environmental problem assumes increasingly the character of specific emergency situations which need to be approached as such. However, this emergency stage and/or its perception as such has not been reached generally and until then (until this is the case) it will be important to approach the environmental issue not simply as a technical problem but as an economic issue by the search for and definition of economical and efficient solutions in the light of a comparison of the overall advantages and disadvantages of alternative approaches and policies, i.e., in terms of valued inputs and outputs in the broader sense of the term. In this sense, economics has still a role to play and has certainly not yet lost its function. The question, however, is what kind of economics is required to cope with the new tasks which confront us under the impact of the environmental crisis and whether conventional neo-classical economic theory is on the way of "solving" the new problems and requirements of human survival.

Under the pressure of public opinion stimulated by the publicity about major cases of environmental disruption, neo-classical economic analysis has begun to assimilate the "new" phenomena of social costs and environmental disruption to the main body of its thought and its textbooks although individual economists had called attention to these phenomena and their significance long before Pigou. But the integration of these disturbing phenomena into the dominant traditional analytical apparatus has been highly (and somewhat) selective. Perhaps the crudest and most problematical approach is that of subtracting from the conventional calculation of G.N.P. those "disamenities" and "externalities" which have been accruing as social costs and to add social benefits which G.N.P. has simply omitted or ignored such as expanded leisure, housewives' services and presumably next the "amenities" resulting from improvements of the environment resulting from more effective environmental controls in the future. The result, it is hoped, will give us some measure of net economic well-being (or welfare?) (N.E.W.). Another and earlier approach was to introduce into the formal apparatus of supply and demand analysis some supplementary social costs (and benefit) curves said to reflect additional social costs and benefits. Older still are, of course, all those attempts to appropriate (illegitimately we believe) A. Marshall's concept of externalities for the assimilation of all those omitted extra-market facts of environmental disruption which have long been known to exist but have been conveniently defined away or placed in parenthesis in our micro-economic models. The concept of externalities also serves as the theoretical tool and justi-fication for most attempts to find positive solutions on the basis of and "internali-zation" of social costs mostly by means of indirect methods such as all sorts of taxes or charges on effluents or subsidies (including accelerated depreciation allowances) for the installment of filters or other remedial action. At a less real-istic level, the traditional theory provides the ideological basis for all sorts of proposals for the establishment of private or public property rights with respect to rivers and lakes (the sale of rights to pollute or even for bilateral negotiations between polluters and those who are damaged by pollution).

It would be interesting to subject this incorporation of the environmental crisis (phenomena) into the theoretical apparatus of neo-classical micro-economics to a critical analysis, particularly with respect to the question as to which considerations could lead an established body to such a response to new and highly disturbing facts and phenomena. Which factors, one may ask, induce a body of thought to assimilate new and evidently important phenomena in such a fashion that in the end the new facts are incorporated "without pain" (without tears) and into an established frame work of analysis without upsetting appar-ently the traditional normative conclusions in favor of solutions via the market or in conformity with the principle of the market-economy.[2] Could it be that it is the age-old social philosophy in defense of the market and the political reassur-ing belief in the automatism and optimal solutions by market equilibria and sub-jective decision-making that is once more at work in this theoretical (and "Practical") response to the environmental crisis which the market behavior has brought about in the first place through the choice of technologies and location without regard to its social cost and environmental consequences? One is reminded of Thorstein Veblen's view according to which new ideas and new conclusions in an age of business enterprise will impose themselves upon the imagination of a wider audience of economists and practical men of affairs only if they are drawn up in terms of business finance and the market test.[3] Veblen felt that ingrained habits of thought reflecting the predominant climate of opinion characteristic of a system of business enterprise have a tendency of being trans-mitted from one generation of economists to the next as they did in the past: institutions of "higher learning" (colleges and graduate schools) would expose each subsequent generation to the traditional habits of thought and this would take place precisely during the third decade of adult life when there is still suffi-cient intellectual flexibility to absorb the "wisdom of the past". Once this period draws to a close both flexibility and ability to think in non-conventional terms i.e., our receptivity to new paradigms, as we call them today, is waning. The stage is set. In short, Veblen regarded the prospects for a reconstruction of economics as dim. Of course, Veblen knew what he was talking about; he wrote at the end of his long and productive career as a critic and an analyst of the system of Business Enterprise and "Absentee Ownership". In effect, he spoke out of his own experience of the response (or lack of it) to his writings (critique) of the preconceptions of classical and neo-classical economics and those of the historical school and certain teleological elements of classical Marxism. While Veblen left some reasons for hope mainly due to increasing social inefficiency of the system of business enterprise which he had analyzed and perhaps also due to the existence of alternative forms of economic organization and their potentialities he was basically correct in his pessimistic appraisal of the prospects of economic theory in the "calculable future".

Since Veblen explored the subject of economics in the calculable future about 50 years ago we have witnessed how the economics of J.M. Keynes in a process of natural selection has undergone a process of "purification" very much similar to that hinted at by Veblen. This process of selection has tended to play down whatever "radical" ideas and novel policy implications directed against the prevailing neo-classical economic and fiscal orthodoxy Keynes suggested (advanced) in favor of deficit financing and public works planning and the related redistribution of income and the "euthanasia of the rentier". While it is true that Keynes was not "radical" in the sense that his normative policy implications would have involved an interference with private market decisions and private allocation of resources along the lines of the test of business enterprise deficit expenditures, rational public works planning and perhaps long-run socialization of investment, it could have led to and required an analysis and evaluation of public and private investment and of socially useful expenditures vs. military, space and lunar expenditures. Little if any of this sort has actually happened or survived in so far as it was indeed attempted and instead we have witnessed the gradual absorption of the Keynesian "revolution" into what has been aptly called "the neo-classical resurgence" where the positive analytical synthesis blends into the "monetarist counterrevolution".[4]

There are indeed many grounds to believe, as we have shown, that a similar process of defusing the explosive issues of social costs and of the degradation of the human environment (both physical and social) is under way and in process of being absorbed into the traditional neo-classical framework of analysis under the selective influence of ideology and power structures which are opposed to the normative policy implications of the theory of social costs. And yet, Veblen's earlier glimmer of hope for a reconstruction of economics should not be dismissed out of hand, at least not by those who share the conviction that the degradation of the environment constitutes a more fundamental challenge to the scope and method of traditional economics than anything that has happened before. Unemployment may be remedied by military and other expenditures even though the current inability to curb the inflationary influence of public deficits and the transaction by transnational corporations by indirect methods of control is still an open and unsolved if not unsolvable question (problem). Unemployment may be curbed by an expansion of production; the degradation of the environment rather increases with greater output unless alternative goals and criteria of determining inputs and location can be developed.

The environmental crisis forces economics to reconsider the scope and indeed the whole framework of its analysis. It raises the fundamental question of the adequacy of dealing with economic problems in closed or semi-closed systems and of relying upon exchange-values and measurements derived from such values for the evaluation of costs and benefits. In short, what is required are not minor or even major adjustments which can be added to the great body of old knowledge. In other words, it calls for new, fundamental paradigms which are adapted to the dynamic interaction between systems of production and ecological systems in the broader physical and social sense of the term. That is, what is needed are new ways of looking upon the interdependencies or new analytical frame of analysis which would make it possible to formulate more adequate concepts and theories. Upon such new "paradigms" which entail the disturbance and ultimate disintegration of the old knowledge depends the evolution (creation) of new knowledge. Such new paradigms are not to be expected to be forthcoming from the wisdom of the past; such "destructive" innovations can be expected to be forthcoming, if at all, only from the outside of the discipline—from men and ideas who possess a wider range of reference and possible range of application.[5] The environmental crisis (and other unsolved problems such as the problem of the underdeveloped world) has the characteristics which call for and may stimulate such innovating new approaches.

Notes

1 This article was written around 1974.
2 Jan Dessau, "L'écologie est intégrée sans douleur par la theorie neo-classique et la nature devient un secteur économique susceptible d'être compatibiliser dans les shémas rassurants de l'equilibre," *Modèles dualistes de l'Environment et Choix de Techniques.* Paper mimio, Grenoble Conference, 1972, p. 8.
3 "Loosely speaking, no argument on economic matters will get a reasonably wide hearing until it is set out as a 'business proposition' in terms drawn from the conduct of business administration, business finance, national trade, salesmanship and publicity." Thorstein Veblen, "Economic Theory in the Calculable Future," *A.E.R.* vol. XV, No 1 (supplement) March, 1925, p. 53.
4 Warren S. Graham, "Natural Selection in Econonic Thought," *Journal of Economic Issues* VII No 1, March 1973, p. 16. "The counterrevolution, the process of selection and emphasis that evolved into post-Keynesian aggregative economics, essentially involves the normative dimension, or the elimination of the radical elements and implications of Keynes' ideas. The selection process stemming from the influence of ideology and power structures works like a sieve to screen out undesirable thoughts. This process must be sharply distinguished from that of development and refinement, whereby the errors, ambiguities, or heuristic elements of an analytic system are respectively eliminated, clarified, or refined. The latter is scientific progress; the ideologically based sieve is retrogression." Ibid., p. 10.
5 In this respect we follow John Dewey's interpretation of C.D. Darlington's "The Conflict of Society and Science," London, 1948 in *Reconstruction of Philosophy* (1950), pp. 14–15, and Kuhn, *The Structure of Scientific Revolution.*

Index

Bellagio Center 11, 19n5, 140n1
Bertalanffy, Ludwig 11, 140
Buchanan, James 12, 149n9
business enterprise 6, 14, 15, 42, 43, 94, 105, 106, 115n9, 122, 123, 131, 162–3

causation, circular 137; cumulative xii, 8, 11, 13, 17
Chayanov, A.V. 25, 33n12, 141n7; *see also* Tschajanow
China xii, 11
Churchill, Winston 93n11
Clark, John Bates 69, 97
Clark, John Maurice 5–7, 38–40, 79, 117
Coase, Ronald 1–3, 12, 14–16, 18
Coddington, Alan 148
control 90, 100, 112, 127, 130, 131, 146; environmental 142, 143, 144, 145, 148n2, 161; flood 75–84; government 56, 125; indirect 143; insect 140; method of 161; pollution 123; public 37, 80n3, 144; social 6, 17, 18, 51

Dewey, John 10, 116n20, 117n33, 164

externalities 2, 12, 14, 15, 130, 149n5, 161, 162

Galbraith, John Kenneth xiii, 111, 116, 117

Hamilton, Alexander 59, 65, 66, 80n13
Hayek, Friedrich 4, 5, 35
hedonism 10
Hobson, John 39

ideal type 27
institutions 45, 63, 80n8, 81n26, 82n56, 84, 94, 97, 105, 113, 123, 124, 127, 133n2, 135, 138, 140, 156, 157, 162; dynamic-institutional sense 136; institutional analysis 96; and institutional approach 39, 94; institutional arrangement 96, 97, 112, 121, 123, 130, 136, 143; institutional change 140; institutional condition 96, 139; institutional economics 80n2, 121; institutional emphasis 121; institutional patterns 143; institutional reform 96, 139; institutional structure 135; institutional theory 80n1; institutional value orientation 135; institutionalized behavior patterns 135; institutionalized organization 156; socio-institutional matrix 140
interaction, circular 136, 138
interdependencies, circular 130, 132

Keynes, John Maynard 119, 163, 164n4
Kneese, Allen 3, 12, 148n1

Lederer, Emil 5, 26
legal failure 15, 18
List, Friedrich 2, 4, 8, 33, 39, 59, 60, 61, 62, 65, 97

market failure 15, 146; external benefits 98, 114; external costs 14, 143; external diseconomies 95, 102; and external economies 95, 97, 98, 113, 114, 114n5, 115n6; external effects 14; external losses 95
Marshall, Alfred 97, 108, 114n5, 162
Marx, Karl 2, 3, 6, 7, 16, 33n12, 44n3, 138, 163
Maslow, Abraham 10
Max-Neef, Manfred xii
Menger, Carl 4, 10, 15, 28

For Product Safety Concerns and Information please contact our
EU representative GPSR@taylorandfrancis.com Taylor & Francis
Verlag GmbH, Kaufingerstraße 24, 80331 München, Germany